The emblem of the City of Frankfurt.
Woodcut by Eugen Sporer, 1409.

A History
of the
Frankfurt Book Fair

by Peter Weidhaas

Translated and edited by
C.M. Gossage and W.A. Wright

This work was first published in German. © Suhrkamp Verlag Frankfurt am Main 2003

Designer: Erin Mallory
Copyeditor: Jennifer Gallant
Printer: Tri-Graphic Printing, Ltd.

Library and Archives Canada Cataloguing in Publication

Weidhaas, Peter
    A history of the Frankfurt Book Fair / by Peter Weidhaas ;
    translated by C.M. Gossage and W.A. Wright.

Translation of: Zur Geschichte der Frankfurter Buchmesse.
Includes bibliographical references and index.

ISBN 978-1-55002-744-0

1. Frankfurter Buchmesse--History. 2. Book industries and trade--
Germany--Frankfurt am Main--Exhibitions--History. I. Gossage, Carolyn, 1933-
II. Wright, Wendy, 1933- III. Title.

Z320.6.F7W4413 2007   070.50943'4164   C2007-903542-6

1 2 3 4 5   11 10 09 08 07

**Conseil des Arts
du Canada**

**Canada Council
for the Arts**

**ONTARIO ARTS COUNCIL
CONSEIL DES ARTS DE L'ONTARIO**
an Ontario Government Agency | un organisme du gouvernement de l'Ontario

Canada

We acknowledge the support of the **Canada Council for the Arts** and the **Ontario Arts Council** for our publishing program. We also acknowledge the financial support of the **Government of Canada** through the **Book Publishing Industry Development Program** and **The Association for the Export of Canadian Books**, and the **Government of Ontario** through the **Ontario Book Publishers Tax Credit program** and the **Ontario Media Development Corporation**.

> The translation and publication of this work was supported by a grant from the **Goethe-Institut**.

Care has been taken to trace the ownership of copyright material used in this book. The author and the publisher welcome any information enabling them to rectify any references or credits in subsequent editions.

J. Kirk Howard, President

Printed and bound in Canada
www.dundurn.com

Dundurn Press	Gazelle Book Services Limited	Dundurn Press
3 Church Street, Suite 500	White Cross Mills	2250 Military Road
Toronto, Ontario, Canada	High Town, Lancaster, England	Tonawanda, NY
M5E 1M2	LA1 4XS	U.S.A. 14150

A segment from a 1770 map of the City of Frankfurt
by Matthias Merian.

Table of Contents

Acknowledgements

$\mathcal{I}$nitially, the translators wish to express their gratitude to Peter Weidhaas, the author of this book and a man of many talents. Without his dedicated efforts to present a detailed documentation of the Frankfurt Book Fair's history in German, the possibility of an English translation simply would not exist. We are indebted, as well, to the Goethe Institute for its generosity in contributing financially to the translation of this work.

To our friend and ever-gracious provider in Wiesbaden, Severina Coppo-Metzdorf, we extend our heartfelt thanks. Closer to home, what would we have done without the invaluable assistance of Karen Heath and Rodolpho Fiallos of the University of Toronto's DEEDS project who so expertly scanned the images provided to us by the author? Nor should the meticulous work of our eagle-eyed copyeditor, Jennifer Gallant of the Dundurn Group, go unrecognized. A raised glass, also, in the direction of our publisher, Kirk Howard, for his faith in our ability to accomplish this occasionally daunting task.

Carolyn Gossage wishes to pay tribute to the memory of the late Joanne Kellock (1931–2003), friend, literary agent, and intrepid veteran of countless book fairs. She will long be remembered as a woman with a consuming passion for life, for books, and for good red wine. In addition, Wendy Wright would like to thank Ila Bossons, her friend, neighbour, and "native informant" on problems of dialect, as well as Anna Porter, noted and quoted author, former publisher, and continuing frequenter of the Frankfurt Book Fair.

Carolyn Gossage and Wendy Wright
Toronto, 2007

For many years I bore the primary responsibility for the direction of the Frankfurt Book Fair, and during that time I gained extensive knowledge of the innermost workings and dynamics of this modern marketing medium. Based on this experience, I have decided to record the history of what is widely regarded as the world's oldest and most important book fair. Ultimately it is an annual event that, in essence, has been innovative from the outset and, in fact, remains so to the present day.

In terms of the Fair's history, there is a distinct possibility that Gutenberg himself, who was alive at the time, may well have attended the Frankfurt Book Fair of 1454 in person. In any event, in that same year, he would undoubtedly have witnessed lively business activity related to the occasion. This is not to suggest, however, that the marketing of books in Frankfurt actually originated in Gutenberg's time. We know, for example, of the existence of a "book fair" that took place there in 1370, when the renowned cleric from the Netherlands, Geert Groote, purchased books at the Frankfurt Fair for the Brethren of the Common Life monastery that he had founded. Moreover, there had been handwritten copies of books for sale at Frankfurt Fairs since the twelfth century, and the same was true of Leipzig just a century later.

The town situated at the ford across the Main gained a place in history when Emperor Charlemagne convened an imperial synod at the "Franconian Ford" in 794. Here, in this relatively unknown location, the emperor spent almost three-quarters of a year and made Frankfurt the site of a great many decisions that would affect the entire sphere of medieval Europe.

The next imperial visit to Frankfurt took place twenty years later in 815 with the arrival of Charlemagne's son, Ludwig, who had fallen heir to the Frankish Empire after his father's death the previous year. Immediately work was begun on the construction of an imperial palace — the delineation of which is still visible today in front of the city's historic cathedral — the Frankfurter Dom.

By the ninth century Frankfurt was regarded as the main seat of the East Frankish Empire, and it was here that men of influence from the various principalities within the empire converged to meet and consult with their monarch. As was customary at the time, each of these court visitors travelled with a considerable retinue who, in turn, would have had to provide for their own needs. Given these circumstances, it appears a virtual certainty that a marketplace was already in existence in Frankfurt even at that time.

Towards the end of the first millennium, in spite of the fact that the influence and power of the Frankfurt palace had diminished during the time of Otto the Great and his successors, the settlement's favourable location at the only crossing of the Main for miles around afforded it ever-increasing importance as a business and marketing centre.

The first written record attesting to a relatively sizeable marketplace in Frankfurt stems from 1074, when the city was specifically mentioned in a document in which Emperor Henry IV absolved the businessmen of Worms from the payment of levies at the imperial customs stations. In 1147, under the reigning Hohenstaufen, or Swabian, dynasty, the prosperous city of Frankfurt was finally designated as the official coronation centre for Germany's present and future kings.

The 1745 coronation of Emperor Franz I in Frankfurt's Römerplatz.
Copper engraving by J.G. Funk.

In his Talmud commentary of 1150, Elieser ben Nathan of Mainz, one of the foremost rabbis of his time, made reference to Jews "who come to the Fair of non-Jews." As an example, he cited the fair that was held in Frankfurt. Here, for the first time, we encounter documentation of the word "fair" in reference to Frankfurt. An actual fair in Frankfurt! This was further confirmed in 1227 when the Frankfurt Fair was specifically mentioned in a royal proclamation. Then, almost fifty years later, Emperor Frederick II proclaimed the famed Freedom of the Fair, granting all potential visitors the assurance of his royal protection.

From approximately 1470 to 1764 Frankfurt acquired widespread renown as the leading trade centre for books printed using Gutenberg technology — a literary mecca not only within Germany but for the intelligentsia of Europe as a whole. From Antwerp, Basel, Paris, Venice, Amsterdam, Cracow, and London, as well as from within Germany itself, printers arrived in droves. In addition, the authors of the books being traded there, such as

Reuchlin, Melanchthon, and Giordano, were also drawn to this increasingly popular book fair.

As for the role of Leipzig? As far as can be ascertained from what are admittedly incomplete records, fairs have been held in the city on the River Pleisse since 1268. Dealings specifically related to the Leipzig Book Fair have been documented dating from 1478, although, not unexpectedly, times of increased activity were followed by periods of decline and then regeneration.

By the mid-eighteenth century, as the Leipzig Book Fair was distinctly flourishing, the prospects for Frankfurt were bleak. The year 1764 brought a serious blow to Frankfurt, when the noted bookseller Philipp Erasmus Reich transferred his allegiance from Frankfurt publisher Franz von Varrentrapp to Weidmann's of Leipzig. On returning home from the Frankfurt Book Fair, Reich is said to have exclaimed, "At the last Book Fair, along with various other friends from Frankfurt-am-Main, I took my final leave and more or less personally wrote off the Book Dealers' Fair located there."

The following 150 years saw the development in Leipzig not only of a highly successful system of book trading but also of a booksellers' organization that sought out various contacts and counterparts throughout the world. It is, in fact, a system that is still functioning today, and it remains the blueprint for the modern-day book fairs held in both Frankfurt and Leipzig.

In the last decade of the nineteenth century the Leipzig Book Fair, which had been taking place cyclically, ended quietly and without fanfare. It appears to have been rendered superfluous, perhaps due in part to the emergence of agents. These agents represented almost all German publishers, as well as many foreign presses, who participated in the Leipzig Book Fair at the time.

For its part, the Frankfurt Book Fair, once so highly regarded, deteriorated in the second half of the eighteenth century, for the most part because of the influx of unscrupulous printers. Ultimately it became an event of regional character and, as the nineteenth century ran its course, it slowly but surely sank into oblivion.

With the dawn of the twentieth century both cities made concerted efforts to revive their book fair traditions. As an aftermath of the First World War, Leipzig attempted to resuscitate its dormant book market with an innovative culture and economics exhibition aimed at attracting the graphic arts professions — known as the BUGRAs. Frankfurt, for its part, concentrated on introducing an international fair featuring an integrated cultural exhibition and book fair. For political as well as economic reasons, the period between the two world wars was scarcely a propitious one for such ambitious ventures and, in fact, it would have been most surprising had either of these initiatives proved successful.

After the Second World War, like the phoenix, a spirit of resurgence arose from the ruins, despite the fact that, once again, the times seemed far from favourable. Germany's economy was in tatters and international trade and commerce a distant dream. As for culture and the state of the nation's morale, only time would tell.

Moreover, the two fairgrounds were controlled by conflicting social systems and reconstruction plans. In 1946 Leipzig instituted a Peace Book Fair. Then in 1949 two Frankfurt booksellers set their sights on launching a reconstituted book fair in the time-honoured tradition of the historic Frankfurt and Leipzig models.

The Frankfurt success story that emerged from this early initiative gradually led to its evolution into an acclaimed international event — a model in terms of organizational principles that was emulated by emerging book fairs in such far-flung centres as London, Beijing, Moscow, and Cairo. In conclusion, however, there must also be due recognition of the fact that the history of the Frankfurt Book Fair is inextricably linked with the marked impact of the Leipzig Book Fair, which so decisively changed the future of the marketing of books for all time.

Peter Weidhaas
2007

Part One

〜〜〜

The Original Frankfurt Book Fairs (1454-1764)
from the Middle Ages to the Reformation
and the Age of Reason

Frankfurt cityscape as viewed from a bridge.
Watercolour by Thomas Jacob Bauer, circa 1830.

Chapter 1

~~~

A Man Hurries through Frankfurt – October 1454

As he makes his way across Frankfurt's Römerplatz, a man — who is neither tall nor otherwise remarkable in any particular way — strides purposefully forward with a distinct spring to his step. Over his high-buttoned linen shirt, he is wearing a short fur-trimmed overcoat — perhaps to help ward off the autumn chill. From time to time he snatches at his beret as unexpected gusts of wind threaten to dislodge it. Then, from out of nowhere, a wagon drawn by four horses and laden with a dozen heavy wooden casks crosses his path and turns into Mentzer Street, forcing him to an abrupt halt.

Almost everyone who is out and about at this early hour, whether on foot, on horseback, or travelling by cart or carriage, is laden with packages, stacks of books, and rolls of paper. Carpenters have set up booths stretching from the Römerplatz all the way down to the city gate and to the banks of the Main. In front of most of the prosperous-looking houses on one of the narrow streets — later destined to be known as Buchgasse, or Book Lane — barrels, crates, and packages are being unloaded from wagons and brought through an arched entrance. Those on horseback or in carriages cast their eyes about in search of an inn.

As for our subject, he continues making his way through the narrow gabled Holt Gate to the banks of the Main, where one of two wooden cranes is unloading casks from the ships that are moored at the quay. Here he pauses briefly to question one of the drivers waiting there. The driver, busy calming his horses, which have become skittish because of the screeching of the crane, points a short distance downstream to the Leonhard Gate, where another crane is in the process of unloading freight from a larger vessel — the market ship from Mainz. The man raises his hand in a fleeting gesture of thanks and the driver nods respectfully in acknowledgement before turning back to his horses.

A present-day observer familiar with the period would immediately recognize that our man on a mission has the bearing and demeanour of a gentleman, yet his worn clothing suggests that he has fallen on hard times. There are, however, no instant answers to our questions about what brings him here or precisely what he might have been expecting on the ship from Mainz. It could merely have been a message, but it might just as easily have been page proofs from a typesetter, paper, parchment, or even money sent expressly to Frankfurt by his friend and lawyer, Conrad Humery. What we do know is that this man, observed hurrying through the rain on the eve of the opening bell of the Frankfurt Fair, was none other than Johannes Gensfleisch of Mainz, also answering to the name of Gutenberg after the print shop bearing this name.

It is entirely possible that Herr Gutenberg may not have conformed exactly to our imaginary description since there are no contemporary pictures or descriptions of him. Several centuries later, Eduard Schmidt von der Launitz, the favourite pupil of the great neo-classical Danish sculptor Bertel Thorwaldsen, created the image of a tall, erect man with a classic profile — a figure that was used as the model for the imposing stone and bronze monument erected on the occasion of the Gutenberg celebration held in 1837 in Frankfurt. Remarkably, the same commemorative bronze statue is still standing today in Frankfurt's famed Goetheplatz and is still the object of admiring glances. The fact remains, however, that today's statue is as much a figment of its creator's imagination as our own scenario on the banks of the Main in 1454.

Intensive historical research on Gutenberg's life began in the nineteenth century at a time when there was a perceived longing for national heroes. Once created, time enshrined this popular representation of Gutenberg as a significant icon until ultimately its authenticity became regarded as sacrosanct — a specific mythology destined to become imprinted in the minds of future generations. It should be noted, however, that Gutenberg's legendary status bears little resemblance to reality. He was purely and simply a man of the times: "Gutenberg can only be understood as a man of his time [...]. His personality is a combination of a faithful representation of the old order, submissive to fate, and the new order of inventors pursuing ever more knowledge in the new and burgeoning society of the early bourgeois economic relationship between goods and money."[1]

Whether or not Gutenberg actually walked through Frankfurt that October of 1454 is certainly open to question. It is not even established whether he was staying in Frankfurt at the time. Scholarly opinion on the subject varies considerably. The Gutenberg scholar Gustav Mori maintains, for example, that Gutenberg was indeed in Frankfurt at that time and was living at the house of Else Vitzthum, the daughter of his sister who had been married since 1428 to Henne Humbracht, a gentleman of stature. Evidently Gutenberg had also set up a new workshop there during the previous summer — just a year before he declared bankruptcy because of a lawsuit initiated by Mainz businessman Johannes Fust. Gutenberg had fashioned simplified type characters and had also had new typesetting letters cast. With these, he would finally be able to print in substantial quantity copies of three pamphlets — one heralding the thirty-one-line indulgences issued by the current pope, a second featuring the rhymed chronicle of the next Crusade, and finally a German translation of the papal bull, or edict, issued by Pope Calixtus III.

> Calixtus III called upon the whole Western world to rise against the Turks. In order to finance the Crusade, he published in three successive years, 1453, 1454, and 1455, a comprehensive dispensation which many of the faithful acquired by purchasing letters

of indulgence. The Crusaders were scheduled to set off on May 1, 1456. Papal emissaries were recruiting in all major cities for the holy undertaking.

In the late autumn of 1454 Emperor Frederick II (1415–1493) convened an imperial Diet in Frankfurt, the main purpose of which was to advise on the Crusade. On October 15 the Diet met in the imperial Roman Auditorium. A conference of cities was to follow in December. Enea Silvio (Piccolomini), the papal chancellor, personally solicited princes, bishops, and mayors — but, alas, in vain. The call to arms for the Crusade met with little response. The strong devotion of the Middle Ages had given way among the upper classes to self-serving scepticism. Only people of lesser means were inclined to purchase the letters of indulgence with any enthusiasm. In the end, the Crusade failed to take place; a lot of effort had been expended for nothing, Gutenberg's included.[2]

On the other hand, Gutenberg biographer Albert Kapr maintains that Gutenberg had no print shop of his own in Frankfurt. In his opinion, the letters of dispensation were printed in the little shop Gutenberg still retained in the Gutenberg Courtyard in Mainz. Enea Silvio Piccolomini, who was later to become Pope Pius II, in a letter from Vienna dated March 12, 1455, to his friend Cardinal Juan de Carvajal in Rome, writes that he has met a wonderful man (*vir mirabilis*) named Gutenberg, who presented the layout for five pages of a Latin bible. These pages were "so very clearly and correctly printed" that one could read them "without glasses." The fact that Enea Silvio had been staying in Frankfurt from the fifth to the thirty-first of October 1454 lends considerable weight to the theory that Gutenberg was also there at that time.

To his subsequent sorrow, Gutenberg had borrowed from a wealthy Mainz businessman, Johannes Fust, the considerable sum — compounded with interest — of 2,026 florins, scarcely a paltry amount since, at the time, it would have been enough money to purchase four houses. According to official documents, Fust called in his loan to Gutenberg alleging that the latter had paid him no interest, and further that Gutenberg had used the money for purposes other than those stipulated in their agreement. In 1455, the case came before the court, and the ensuing judgement required Gutenberg to pay back the money lent to him by Fust. Since Gutenberg was unable to come up with the necessary funds, Fust, together with his son-in-law Peter Schöffer, took over Gutenberg's printing establishment in Mainz's Umbrecht Courtyard as compensation for the unpaid debt.

It is also documented that around 1450 Gutenberg had already begun printing his famous bible with forty-two lines per page. Each volume contained 1,280 pages, and he printed 180 copies, 40 on parchment and 140 on paper. For one page — typeset and print-ready — three thousand type-characters were required. To accomplish this, approximately six typesetters, twelve printers, and various helpers were kept busy in the shop for a year, yet none had been paid in full. As a result of the elevated number of church-ordained holy days, they had only two hundred working days in the year to accomplish their task. The paper alone, brought in from Italy, came to six hundred florins. The high costs must have stretched Gutenberg's finances to the point where he could not continue without finding additional funding, although a single edition of this bible — probably about 180 copies — could have been sold out before it was off the press. Sadly, Gutenberg was only a few months short of being able to pay off his debt to Fust when the court ruling forced his hand.

We began this first chapter of our history of the Book Fair with evidence — real or imaginary — of Gutenberg's presence in Frankfurt. There is no question, however, that without this man's inventive genius, the book trade could never have developed so quickly, nor could the future of the Frankfurt and Leipzig book fairs have been determined with any certainty.

Long before Gutenberg, the Frankfurt Book Market had been operating as a part of the larger and well-known Frankfurt Fair.

Early evidence of an extensive market in Frankfurt, as noted earlier, dates to the year 1074. Less than two hundred years later, on July 11, 1240, while in the midst of the siege of Ascoli, Emperor Frederick II proclaimed the famed "Freedom of the Fair":

> We, Frederick, Holy Roman Emperor by the Grace of God, and King of Jerusalem and Sicily, wish to make known to the world that we extend to each and every person travelling to the Fair in Frankfurt our personal protection and that of our Empire. We command that no one shall harm or hinder them in any way whether they be on their way to or from the Fair in Frankfurt. Whoever shall then dare to do so shall have to deal with the wrath of our Majesty. We have had this proclamation produced in order to emphasize this command and have ratified it by affixing our imperial seal hereunto. Delivered in the field camp at the siege of Ascoli on July 11th 1240.

The sale of handwritten books had been conducted at this Fair from the outset. In 1422, it is certainly feasible that Johannes Fust, who later took over Gutenberg's printing operation, was already dealing in handwritten books. He offered old manuscripts for sale at the Frankfurt Fair, and as a dealer in handwritten books, he travelled around to the university cities. By 1449 he most probably had established a casual business relationship with Gutenberg, since Gutenberg's workshop in Mainz needed a dealer to market its wares.

Now Gutenberg was obliged, being unable to repay Fust's loan, to surrender not only his Mainz printing establishment with its valuable masters and type-forms, but also the 180 forty-two-line bibles he had just finished printing. Fust exhibited the printed copies at the Frankfurt Fair. Gutenberg's gifted former journeyman-apprentice, Peter Schöffer, took over as technical foreman of the printing operation, while Johannes Fust worked as a contract printer.

Because of growing political turmoil in Mainz, Fust and Schöffer decided to move to Frankfurt in 1462 in order to facilitate selling their wares at the Frankfurt Fair. Two years later Fust died, and his widow, Grede Fust, married Konrad Henkis of Gudensberg, bringing as her dowry the Gutenberg print shop. Peter Schöffer and Konrad Henkis thus became the first printer and publisher to offer their printed books at the Frankfurt Fair. More than five hundred years later, the Fust-Schöffer trademark still embellished all official correspondence from the Frankfurt Exchange until 1987.

In conclusion, it should be emphasized that no official founding date for the Frankfurt Book Fair actually exists; it can be established, however, that at the very latest it had definitely developed into a printers' and publishers' fair by the year 1462.

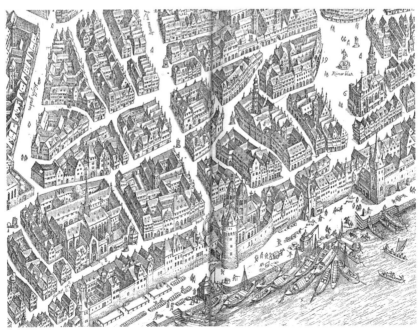

A bird's-eye view of Frankfurt reproduced from a copper engraving by Matthias Merian printed in 1770.

Chapter 2
~~~
A Book Fair Is Created

With good reason, Gutenberg had made every attempt to keep his invention secret. The applied technology of reproducing lengthy texts quickly and accurately with pre-poured and moveable individual letters was superior to the practice of his predecessors and competitors. Above all, his strategy was to increase the numbers of copies that could be printed:

> He wanted to secure his place in the market with a technically enhanced increase in production. Printing books and trading in them allowed for the possibility of rapid business expansion and of potential profit, just as was the case with the cloth trade and mining. Book production had increased rapidly since 1470. In the last decade of the fifteenth century, there were approximately as many titles published as in the three preceding decades combined.[3]

In 1462 the city of Mainz was subjected to a power struggle of warlike intensity between various factions. However, the popularity of the art of printing everywhere increased by leaps and bounds and spread rapidly. Workshops sprang up in Italy, the Netherlands, Hungary, France, and Spain.

Without question, the new-found possibility of printing books was a giant step forward, but without paper, it benefited only those who could afford to buy a book printed on parchment. For their carefully made copies, the monks of the Middle Ages had used a parchment made of prepared sheep- or calfskin.

The art of making paper from linen rags had been invented as early as the second century A.D. in China, and in the tenth century the Arabs became aware of the process. By the thirteenth century, the need for books for the universities of Europe had become critical, and, as a result, the product of the ingenious Eastern invention was increasingly sought after. In southern Europe, mills for the manufacture of paper sprang up. And before long the use of paper had spread northward. With the invention in 1450 of a technology incorporating the use of a printing press with moveable letters, paper was being produced in such quantity that, in this respect as well, the growing demands of the book market could be met.

The Market

The question now arises, precisely what was on offer in that first year of the emerging book market? What specific subject matter was sought after, and what kinds of books were being sold?

The intellectual appeal of humanism, which had its beginnings in Italy, peaked in the decades after 1400, and by the early sixteenth century its influence had spread increasingly throughout Europe. Humanism was originally based on the concept of emulating ancient classical literature in both form and content. It gave inspiration to a whole new generation of scholars in search of a new model more suited to the times and based on the classical view of man. This, in turn, gave rise to widespread debate involving all the great minds of Europe.

By the middle of the fourteenth century the great Tuscan poet and scholar Francesco Petrarca — better known today as Petrarch (1304–1374) — following the example of Virgil's *Aeneid*, had written part of his Latin epic poem *Africa* to celebrate the life of the great Roman General Scipio Africanus. Although it was never finished, Petrarch's intention was to document the story of the Roman conquest of Carthage. With his enthusiasm for Cicero, Seneca, and Virgil and his search for lost and forgotten works of classical Latin literature, Petrarch led the way into the age of humanism. Since that time, the main interest of scholars everywhere has been the investigation of primary sources.

Erasmus of Rotterdam (circa 1466–1536) became one of the foremost proponents of the humanist movement. A contemporary of Luther and a capable Greek and Latin scholar, at age thirty he turned his attention to the study of the sources of Christianity. Basing his studies on the original Greek version of the New Testament, Erasmus devoted himself to a critical examination and translation of the Bible. His work on the original sources exposed to criticism St. Jerome's fourth-century Latin Vulgate version of the biblical text, which had been used by the Church throughout the Middle Ages. His insightful editing, as well as his translation of the original Greek sources, provided a reliable foundation for Luther's translation of the Bible into German.

Without the discovery of the printing press, the extensive interchange of scholars from one European country to another would scarcely have been possible. It is certain that the spread of the Renaissance from Italy to all of Europe was thereby substantially enhanced. In this regard a few printers, who themselves espoused humanist ideals, played an important role in its proliferation. It seems clear that even at that early phase of the art of printing, profit was not the only motivating force. People were motivated by a conviction that superseded business concerns. It would become a claim made by subsequent generations of publishers, as well.

> A decisive role in the revival of the classics was played by a group of accomplished printers, particularly in Italy, the Netherlands, and Switzerland, who functioned as middlemen between the humanist scholars and the educated reading public. The high esteem that Erasmus enjoyed even during his lifetime

would have been unthinkable without the existence of the printing press and the support of like-minded printers such as the Venetian Aldus Manutius and Basel's Amerbach and Froben. Aldus Manutius had himself studied humanism in Ferrara, and his elegant editions of classical Greek texts give eloquent testimony to his personal enthusiasm for the classics.[4]

What the humanists needed more than anything else was an ample supply of copies of printed works for their readers and fellow scholars. This kind of scholarly literature proved to be highly marketable and immediately took over the expanding book market.

Not unexpectedly, in this initial phase of the rapidly growing industry, other works appeared that had no specific connection with humanism. Primarily these were works engendered by debate between opposing schools of thought at the universities, where respect for tradition was deeply entrenched. Here the proponents of scholasticism were pitted against the theologians, and philosophers took issue with those who favoured the scientific approach.

The use of Latin — the language not only of the humanists but also of all other scholarly literature — significantly limited readership. In addition, the format of the books also came into play. Many were still published as unwieldy leather-bound folios, printed on expensive parchment: books designed for preservation in monasteries and university libraries, but scarcely for individual study. The considerable expense involved in their production was also a significant factor in the quantity of books available.

One consequence of the humanists' focus on ancient literature was the publication of new editions of many Roman and Greek classics (the latter often in Latin translation). Venetian printers were often in the forefront when it came to the publication of these editions from original sources. As for Germany, the printers of note were situated in Mainz, Cologne, Augsburg, Nuremberg, and Ulm.

The first "classical" work printed in Germany was an edition of Cicero produced by Fust and Schöffer — the partnership that evolved partly as the result of the court order that had left

Gutenberg insolvent. By 1500 Fust and Schöffer had published more than one hundred editions of various works in the same category. Around the same time, close to seventy editions of Virgil's works had appeared, the first being produced in 1469 by Sweynheim in Rome.

By the end of the fifteenth century, large numbers of legal pamphlets were also being produced. By virtue of their clear format and the commentaries that accompanied them, a broader knowledge of Roman law was facilitated. This, too, was the result of the widespread interest in the humanist school of thought, which extended gradually into all areas of popular endeavour. The fundamental work of this type, *Institutiones juris Justiniani*, was first printed by Peter Schöffer in 1468.

In the realm of philosophy, demand for the writings of Aristotle topped the list. Originally they had been translated into Latin from Syrian or Arabic handwritten manuscripts. The first complete Latin edition was produced by Andreas de Asola in Venice in 1473. Then, roughly twenty years later, Aldus Manutius in Venice printed the first Greek edition between 1495 and 1498 in five volumes.

At that point, the number of publications relating to the sciences was relatively insignificant. Only a few texts by Roman, Greek, and Arab physicians had made their way into the marketplace. Among these were the writings of Avicenna, otherwise known as the "prince of physicians," which became bestsellers in the field of medicine, with more than twenty-five editions of his works in print before 1500.

According to printers' reports, travel-related publications were even more in vogue. Accounts of great voyages of discovery, such as those undertaken by Christopher Columbus, Amerigo Vespucci, Vasco da Gama, and Alfonso de Albuquerque, enjoyed great popularity. In particular, the published description of the Venetian Marco Polo's travels and lengthy stay in China at the court of Kublai Khan attracted the interest of a great many readers. Translated from Latin, it was first published in 1477 in German, while the Italian edition did not appear until 1496.

The Printers

By 1498, a total of 118 publishers had already been established in Europe. The most important centres for the production of books included Nuremberg, Lyons, Venice, and Paris, and there were also printing houses based in Strasbourg, Rome, Milan, Cologne, Florence, Leipzig, Bologna, Basel, Augsburg, Naples, and Antwerp. At the time, Mainz was considered a secondary source of book production, and even Frankfurt-am-Main lacked any great significance. Among the 12,887 titles produced during this era (over 90 percent in Latin-based languages), 6,736 were the product of Italian printers, whereas 3,979 titles were produced in Germany. Clearly, when it came to the production of books, Italy was in the forefront. According to German historian, Mathias Tank:

> The first printers, publishers, and book dealers worked very closely together at the outset. For them, the printing of books meant assuming total production costs as well as taking on the additional burden of selling the product. As a result, the so-called printer-publishers were forced to undertake long and difficult journeys to university cities and noble estates, as well as attending fairs and yearly markets, in order to personally sell their books and other printed material.
>
> It should come as no surprise that almost immediately these same printer-publishers availed themselves of the services of one or more "promoters" who undertook at least a portion of these time-consuming sales trips to various destinations. Another new development among the printer-publishers was the establishment of sales outlets in important centres both domestically and abroad, using reputable local booksellers to conduct business on their behalf.

It was not long, however, before these same booksellers realized the advantages of independence and they soon began selling the products of other printers and publishers in their business premises and storehouses.[5]

A 1543 copper engraving of Nurnberg book dealer
H. Kepner packing books into a barrel.

Book Fairs

In various European printing and publishing centres, such as Lyons, Strasbourg, Basel, and Leipzig, market areas were set up in due course, which eventually evolved into fairs. Frankfurt-am-Main became one of the most important book markets, even though the city did not boast a university, nor was it among the foremost printing centres.

The first well-known printer-publishers, whose visits to the Frankfurt Book Fair in 1480 have been documented, were Johann Amerbach and Michael Wenssler from Basel. They were followed, in turn, by Johann Petri, Thomas Platter, and Christoph Froschauer from Zurich, and Johann Froben from Basel. Froben had made a name for himself as the publisher of the works of Erasmus of Rotterdam. Johann Mentelin and Nikolaus Kessler came from Strasbourg. Amerbach enjoyed close business ties with the biggest and most important printer-publisher of the era, Anton Koberger from Nuremberg, who at that time had more than twenty-four printing presses and more than one hundred printers at his disposal. Moreover, he had sixteen book marketing outlets within Germany and outside the country. On April 13, 1506, Koberger wrote to Johann Petri in Basel that he, in partnership with Johann Amerbach and Johann Froben, had contracted for the purchase of sixteen hundred copies of the works of St. Augustine, plus an equal number of copies of a concordance, or comprehensive index, of the Bible, and the *Magerita poetica* for seven thousand florins. For Anton Koberger, the Frankfurt Book Fair was an irreplaceable necessity that ensured the expansion of the business dealings of his very large commercial enterprise. Quoted is an excerpt from his letters to his business partners: "As God has helped us to reach Frankfurt, so we must deal honestly with one another, and I will pay you there all that I justly owe."[6]

In 1483 Peter Schöffer was taken to court based on a duly sworn statement from the plaintiff for having failed to deliver on time a promised four hundred missals for which Wilhelm Ruscher of Nuremberg had paid a sizeable advance. We know also from the court documents that Frankfurt had become a transshipment centre where people could buy large numbers of books at favourable prices and also exchange or order them for the next fair.

Among the regulations of that era governing the running of a library were the following stipulations: "The librarian shall ensure that book dealers find, present, and offer new books from the Frankfurt and Strasbourg Fairs. He must himself go once annually in the Spring or in the Fall to Frankfurt and seek out not only new but also old materials."[7]

Of course, the Frankfurt Book Fair was still first and foremost simply a part of the general fair scene in Europe. However, the volume of business generated by the book trade showed a substantial gain over other areas in the transfer of goods. The account books of the Frankfurt City Council showed, for example, in 1488, that printer-publishers of books had contributed one-twelfth of all market and show stall fees collected at the Lenten Fair of that year. The pace of the expansion of the new medium was nothing short of remarkable.

In the year 1501, more than 1,100 printing establishments were operating in 254 European cities and produced almost 30,000 works for a total of more than 12 million copies. Of these early printing centres, at least one was located in Croatia, Austria, Poland, Turkey, and Hungary; at least three were located in Denmark, Sweden, and Bohemia; four in England; five in Portugal; seven in Belgium; nine in Switzerland; fourteen in Holland; twenty-seven in Spain; forty-three in France; fifty-two in Germany; and those based in Italy numbered an impressive eighty.

From virtually all of these cities, printer-publishers thronged to Frankfurt; among these were Justus de Albano (Venice), Petro Antonio Sesso (Milan), and Aldus Manutius (Venice), who was, among other things, the inventor of the cursive script typeface, which had been in use since 1501. In the Frankfurt chronicles of Canon Johann Rohrbach, the ecclesiastic scholar recorded that he had purchased books from Venetian publishers at the so-called Lenten, or Easter, Fair in 1497: "In decorative presentation and beauty of smaller typeface, the Venetian printers stand out above all others of that time. In any case, the Frankfurt Fair's ties with Italy are clearly indisputable."[8]

Although the Frankfurt Fairs first developed primarily in the area of direct sales from the printers to individual consumers, from 1500 onwards exchange deals increasingly gained the upper hand. The word for "publisher" in German (*Verlag*) derives from the word meaning "moneyman," literally the man who laid out the necessary sum to finance the printing.

Clearly, a book market had been created and had already developed its rudimentary commercial structures. Social life of the era, strongly imprinted by Church influence, had its centres in the cloisters and cities of southern Europe and concentrated its business in Frankfurt. The place was favourably situated, both strategically and geographically. Moreover, it functioned as the coronation site of the German Catholic emperors. The city at the crossroads of the two most important trade routes — the one leading from the south through Basel and Strasbourg into the north to Cologne and on to Belgium and Holland; the other coming from the west out of Paris and leading into the east towards Magdeburg and Leipzig — possessed the oldest German fair tradition. As well, the transport of goods could be quickly and economically expedited by ship along the Rhine or the Main.

There is no question that its proximity to Mainz, the birthplace of the printing press and the cradle of printing with moveable letters, played a role in enabling Frankfurt to develop more dramatically than any other city as a centre of commerce — including the sale of books. If Mainz had had a similar tradition to that of Frankfurt, it would most certainly have become central to the book trade. But Gutenberg, Fust, and Schöffer had chosen to go to Frankfurt to sell their products. Many printers who followed their example first learned their trade in Mainz. And so, twice a year, off they went along the Main to Frankfurt, to the Lenten Fair, held two weeks before Easter, and to the Fall Fair, ready to market their latest editions.

The transport of books to and from the Frankfurt Book Fair was an arduous and expensive undertaking for commercial travellers. Court documents about a dispute over the cost of transporting books between Lyons and Frankfurt reveal that: "the weight of the two book crates was composed of 10 centners [one centner equals a fifty-kilogram weight]; the driver received 1.5 florins per centner for the approximately 700-kilometre trip, making a total of fifteen florins."[9] In today's terms, this amounted to between two and three hundred euros (or between three and four hundred dollars) in freight charges. Inefficient packing inevitably produced complaints that rainwater had penetrated the shipping crates or casks and soaked the books. "In the sixteenth century books were mostly shipped unbound. The binding of books at the point of sale was cheaper than the freight charges calculated by weight for bound books. It must be remembered that the covers for the thick, valuable folios were often made of solid, heavy wood."[10]

In the business of selling books, there were also other costly hazards to be considered. Even a royal guarantee of safety did not always provide the necessary protection, as is shown in Koberger's letter of December 20, 1504: "… several of my crates were hacked to pieces while under the protection of the local noble, only two miles from this city, when I had thought they were quite safe."[11]

Chapter 3

~~~

A Thriving Centre

Yet it was not only the transport of books that was a problem. Travellers to the Fair frequently experienced great difficulty finding suitable accommodation. A well-established network of inns and hostelries along the way remained a distant dream. If a conveniently located monastery was not available to provide a place to sleep, then, all too often, the traveller's only alternative was to settle for whatever dubious type of accommodations the vicinity had to offer.

In Germany, roadside accommodations had acquired a particularly bad reputation. Erasmus of Rotterdam, who had a personal affinity for the Frankfurt Book Fair, where many of his books had been presented for the first time to the European intelligentsia, offers an evocative description of the prevailing hospitality found in German inns of the day:

> On arrival no one greets you lest it seem they are actually seeking out paying guests, the latter being something they consider demeaning since it reflects badly on German sensibilities. After you have stood in front of the building for quite some time announcing your presence in a loud voice, a head finally appears, turtle-like, at a tiny window. It is then incumbent upon you to ask this person whether or not they have

any lodging available. If he doesn't refuse, you may conclude that they have room for you....

The question of a stall for your horse is answered with a hand gesture. You are then left to tend to your horse on your own because no servant is forthcoming. Once the horse is taken care of, you enter the sitting room, standing just as you are, with boots, baggage, dust, and dirt. This heated room is for the use of all guests. Individual rooms for changing, washing, getting warm and resting are not on offer. And so it can happen that eighty or ninety guests are crammed together in the same room: foot travellers, businessmen, farmers, boys, women, the healthy and the sick. Here someone is combing his hair; there someone is wiping the sweat from his brow; still another is wiping off his shoes and travel boots. It is the mark of good German innkeeping that all guests are dripping with perspiration. If anyone, unused to such clouds of fetid steam, should dare to open a window so much as a crack, there is an immediate clamour to close it at once.

Finally the wine, generally of inferior quality, is served to the weary travellers. If it should occur to a guest to ask for a superior quality of wine, the innkeeper seems not to hear his request at first, but directs a murderous glance at the presumptuous fellow. If the person should repeat his request, the response comes back: "Many dukes and lords have frequented this inn and none has complained about the wine. If you don't like it, then go and find another inn," for the Germans consider only the titled nobility of their own country as people worthy of service and respect....

Soon, with great fanfare, the dishes are brought forth. The first course is almost always pieces of bread with a meat broth, followed by some kind of warmed-up meat, pickled meat or salted fish. Only then is a better wine set out.

It is surprising what an unholy racket arises when heads are heated by drink. Differences of opinion quickly come to the fore. Often jokesters and rogues mix into the tumult much to the delight of the Germans, who appear to revel in the ensuing hullaballoo. With the room so full of prattle and shouting, scuffles and brawls, it seems that it threatens to cave in on itself.

If a guest, exhausted from his journey, wants to go to bed immediately after the meal, he is told that he must wait until the others decide to call a halt and turn in. Then each is shown his bed; for nothing other than a hard bed is available to lie on. As for the bed linens, these were washed perhaps six months ago.[12]

In spite of all these difficulties along the way, those bound for the Fair continued to travel to their chosen destination at Frankfurt-am-Main. From Holland and Belgium, from France and Switzerland, from Italy and Poland, and even from England, they made their way in ever-increasing numbers. Of course, German and German-speaking cities were also represented, including Strasbourg, Cologne, Leipzig, Wittenberg, Nuremberg, Augsburg, and Salzburg, among others. For all those who dealt in books, the Frankfurt Book Fair had become a firmly fixed annual engagement.

Even then, however, the manufacture of books was under severe time constraints. As a result, in 1505 the proofreader for the Strasbourg publisher Johann Pruss entreated readers of the newly published work *Epitome rerum Germanicarum* to forgive any printing errors they might encounter. Because of the looming Frankfurt Book Fair, it was necessary to produce the book in the shortest possible time. The publisher Christoph Froschauer in Zurich explained to the city council in 1522 that he was obliged to breach the Lenten fasting regulations because it was the only way he could finish printing the work *Episteln Pauli* in time for the Frankfurt

Book Fair. Evidently Ulrich Zwingli, the Reformer, was sympathetic to Froschauer's excuse. And even Erasmus of Rotterdam wrote in 1530 from Basel that he was always swamped with work before the Frankfurt Fair. His publisher, Froben, employed six printing presses operating virtually non-stop in the months and weeks leading up to the Fair, in order to be able to produce the new works on time.

As soon as the imperial flag had been raised on the gates or on a tower, and the bells of the city of Frankfurt had tolled for the opening of the Fair, active business dealings began among the publishers and the book-buying dealers. On the doors and windows of the storage and sales areas, publishers' catalogues in poster format and title pages of books were posted so that those passing by could see at a glance what was being offered for sale in each outlet.

The moment the flag was lowered and the closing bells had sounded, all dealings at the fair ceased. Unsold books had to be packed into crates and locked up in a rented storage area until the next fair. Publishers did not usually demand immediate payment but rather sold on credit until the next fair. Between fairs, the book dealers were able to sell these books for cash, which proved an advantageous arrangement for all concerned. Those book dealers who exchanged books with one another so that each had a selection for sale from foreign publishers in their local retail shops also had no cause to worry and were able to use their inventories to pay off their outstanding balances by the next fair.

The book business was profitable despite all the difficulties it entailed. In any case, book prices continued to rise as a result of an expanding number of readers. An example of the relative costs to a potential buyer was the price demanded for a copy of Martin Luther's *September Testament* of 1522. The German translation of Luther's New Testament cost 1.5 florins when purchased from Melchior Lotter, a book printer in Leipzig. At that time, for the price of a bible, it was possible to acquire 2 calves, 6 sheep, 15 geese, 220 herring, 1,200 bricks, or 1,300 eggs. The same amount would pay the yearly wages of a housemaid.

From one year to the next the numbers of printers, publishers, and book dealers coming to Frankfurt increased by leaps and bounds.

Among them were important names such as publishers Thomas
Anselm from Tubingen and Franz Birckmann from Cologne,
as well as book dealers Nikel Nerlich from Leipzig and Samuel
Selfisch from Wittenberg. Other well-known participants included
Nikolaus Beckermünze (Mainz), Georg Willer (Augsburg), and
Friedrich Peypus (Nuremberg). Then, too, Nikolaus Kessler and
Johann Mentelin from Strasbourg; Johann Petri, Thomas Platter,
and Christoph Froschauer from Zurich; and Johann Froben and
Johann Amerbach from Basel had their permanent sales and
storage areas at the Frankfurt Book Fair. From France, Jacob de
Puis and Jean Fouchier made the annual journey to the Fair, as
did Jean Vaugris, Sebastien Gryphius, and Henri Estienne. The
amount of French literature available for purchase in Frankfurt
must, indeed, have been substantial. Jean Vaugris (1480–1527), a
commissioner and book dealer from Lyons, visited the Frankfurt
Book Fair regularly between 1510 and 1525.

> On arrival in the city, a book dealer like Vaugris had
> to arrange to have the crates he brought with him
> installed in the sales and storage area he rented or
> maintained on a permanent basis. He would then
> have to unpack the 24- or 25-sheet bundles of pages
> of the still unbound books, put them in order, and
> finally stack the titles he wanted to sell in front of the
> door with prepared placards ready for display. But
> even then, his work was far from complete since he
> had other books, either those sent under contract
> through the main publisher he worked with or those
> obtained on his own initiative. For these particular
> books, he had to make all transport arrangements as
> well as inform himself about the state of the market
> so he could make suggestions about the choice of
> future new publications once he returned home.[13]

Book printers, publishers, and dealers from the Netherlands were
also heavily involved in these business dealings and were joined later

by those from Belgium. The most prominent names among these were Willem Vorstermann, Johann Beller, and Christoph Plantin. Lodewijk Elzevier of Amsterdam was also a regular visitor to the Fair.

Besides book dealers, at the Frankfurt Book Fair both domestic and foreign libraries were able to obtain the books they sought in order to increase their holdings. For example, from a book dealer's widow, Duke Johann Albrecht von Mecklenburg bought up the entire inventory of her late husband's shop for the library of the future University of Rostock. The Elector Prince Ottheinrich of the Pfalz endowed the Heidelberg library with the sum of fifty florins to be applied to purchases at every Frankfurt Book Fair. From 1593 onwards, Queen Elizabeth I of England regularly arranged for books to be bought at the Frankfurt Book Fair for the Bodleian Collection at Oxford.

The personal recollections of Michael Harder provide us with an insight into the range and type of books being sold at the Frankfurt Book Fair towards the end of the sixteenth century. Harder was an employee commissioned in 1569 by the widow of a publisher named Gulfrichs to sell off a portion of the company inventory for a collective group of heirs. A surprising total of 5,912 titles would be offered for sale at that particular Fair, and it must be remembered that Harder represented only one Frankfurt publisher. As a sales area, Harder used the available space within the Carmelite Monastery. Here, on a single day, April 6, 1569, he sold a grand total of 234 books to M. Baudin, a book dealer from Lyons.

And, even in those days, the turnover in individual titles varied considerably. Especially notable is the high percentage of prose versions of German epic ballads from the Middle Ages, such as Wigallois vom Rade's prose version of the thirteenth-century German work that described the life of a Knight of the Round Table.

The titles of popular romance fiction were also intended to serve as an alluring form of sales advertising. As a case in point, we find *Emperor Octavian, how he banished his wife and two sons to a life of misery; and how, amazingly, they were once again reunited in France with the good King Dagobert.* Or for further titillation: *The true story of how a man called Hug Schapler, a humble butcher's son, became a powerful King of France.* Such well-loved "popular fiction novels" as *Fortunatus,* which related the experiences of the lucky owner of a sack of gold that never empties, were also much in demand, as was the tale of *Till Eulenspiegel,* whose crude pranks were always greeted with applause among the public.

An insight into the extent and nature of commerce associated with the Fair is brought to light in the notes of the Antwerp printer Christoph Plantin and his son-in-law Moretus. The *Big Frankfurt Book,* so named by Plantin, is displayed in the Plantin Museum of Print in Antwerp, and contains meticulous notes about the printers' participation in the Spring Fairs of 1566 and 1579:

> To get to the Lenten Fair of the year 1566, the 46-year-old Christoph Plantin travelled in a wagon from Antwerp to Cologne, while his son-in-law made the trip on foot. From Cologne to Frankfurt, they both travelled by ship. On the return journey, they once again travelled by ship to Cologne, then proceeded on foot to Maastricht, and finally took a wagon from there to Antwerp. Their total travel costs including freight, customs, and gratuities came to 131 florins.
>
> Six packing cases of books went to the Lenten Fair for the Plantin Company; they contained 5,212 copies of 67 various works. Sales amounted to 1,625 florins; purchases came to 1,625 florins. At the end of the fair, a storehouse holding 1,617 copies of 240 works remained in Frankfurt. On Plantin's death, the goods in the Frankfurt storehouse were valued at 8,024 florins and these were acquired by his son-in-law Moretus for only 4,824 florins.[14]

An Intellectual Centre

Not only printers and book dealers gravitated to Frankfurt. Increasingly the city was becoming the intellectual centre of the time, although surprisingly Frankfurt did not boast its own university until 1914. Aside from the many book dealers, professors from most European universities sent on buying trips by their respective administrations met with one another at the Book Fair. Librarians from state-run and ecclesiastic libraries also gathered here, along with poets, archivists, mathematicians, and clerics, such as the theologian Philipp Melanchthon (1497–1560), the famous humanist and reformer, and his adversary, Matthias Flacius Illyricus. All spent time here, partly to examine and acquire the latest publications for sale, and partly to settle with their publishers or to negotiate the publication of new works and to exchange information with colleagues.

The little Frankfurt street that runs north from the Leonhard Church to a small corn market was already known as Buchgasse (Book Lane) in 1518, and it developed gradually into a contact exchange

Print stalls at the Frankfurt Fair at the corner of Sandgasse, April 1835.
Watercolour by Mary Ellen Best from The World of Mary Ellen Best
by Caroline Davidson, Chatto & Windus, 1985.

for intellectuals. Philipp Melanchthon, for example, conferred with his publisher, Thomas Anselm of Hagenau, at his shop on Buchgasse while attending the Easter Fair in Frankfurt. The book dealers located there could give out the Frankfurt addresses of scholars such as Ulrich Zasius, Johannes Agricola, Johannes Praetorius, and Johannes Sturm. And the art market was located here as well. Not only books, but also paintings, drawings, copperplate engravings, and wood carvings were being sold. In 1540, Agnes Dürer came to Frankfurt to put the works of her deceased husband, Albrecht Dürer, on the market.

In 1494 the Basel lawyer Sebastian Brant (1458–1521), later lawyer for the City of Strasbourg, launched his satirical work *Ship of Fools*. He represented the thoughtless progress through life of an assortment of foolish people, sometimes in a critical fashion and at others in a sarcastic vein. To a certain extent, Brant's book became the first "bestseller" of the Frankfurt Book Fair. In 1497, a Latin translation appeared, then a French version, and finally it was translated into English and printed by Jakob Locher in Lyons. The Frankfurt Franciscan monk Thomas Murner took Brant's *Ship of Fools* as a point of departure for a series of lively, popular sermons that he delivered to his Frankfurt congregation of barefoot friars. In 1512 Murner, who numbered among the first of Frankfurt's publishers, released his *Guild of Rogues*, a series of shorter dialogues in which the rogue's wicked expressions are answered each time by the monk's critical preachings. The dialogues were later published under the catchword *Patentia*.

In 1523, the book *Pantagruel* appeared, a burlesque mixture of humanist scholarship and satirically expressed ideas relating to reform, combined with the well-known folk tales of "the terrible giant Gargantua and his son Pantagruel" by the Lyons doctor François Rabelais (circa 1494–1553). The first part of his story ends with a promise: "You will have the rest of the story at subsequent Frankfurt Fairs."

The notorious bloodbath in Paris on the night of St. Bartholomew's feast day in 1572 led to the slaughter of thousands of Calvinists (Huguenots) throughout France and resulted in a large wave of Protestant emigration. Andreas Wechel, a Huguenot and a leading

French publisher, made the decision to abandon Paris for Frankfurt and brought a substantial number of French authors with him. This unforeseen and important influx from France contributed greatly to the internationalization of the Frankfurt Book Fair.

In 1591 the controversial Italian author and philosopher Giordano Bruno (1548–1600), a man purported to be "the most sublime and universal mind of his era,"[15] visited the city of Frankfurt. Andreas Wechel had invited Bruno to be his personal guest, but the city council, which had to approve the visit, blocked this gesture of hospitality. From the council minutes, we learn: "Gordanus Brunus of Nola, student of natural science and philosophy, has asked that his request be approved to spend a few weeks here at the book-printing house of Andreas Wechel. But his request is denied and he is told to take his money elsewhere." The firebrand from Nola was not welcome. The council's perception was that wherever he stayed, unrest followed. As an alternative arrangement, Andreas Wechel paid for Bruno's lodging at the Carmelite monastery. While there, Bruno received an unexpected visit from a book dealer from Venice, who brought with him an invitation from a certain Venetian nobleman requesting instruction in the art of memory. In accepting this invitation, Bruno unwittingly sealed his own fate, as he was later denounced by his host, Mocenigo, as a heretic and left to the tender mercies of the Inquisition. After languishing for eight years in various prisons awaiting his sentence, Giordano Bruno was finally condemned to be burned at the stake in Rome. We are never told of Andreas Wechel's reaction to this act of treachery that had its beginnings at the Carmelite monastery in Frankfurt, but it is not difficult to imagine his considerable distress.

As for developments in the art of printing, it was not Gutenberg but Christian Egenolff (1502–1555) who became the first established printer and publisher of books in Frankfurt. Egenolff, also the manufacturer/producer of the lead letters used in the printing process, had originally set up his own business in 1528 in Strasbourg but moved it to Frankfurt two years later. In the twenty-five years of Egenolff's activity as a printer and publisher, more than four hundred works were produced on his premises. His strongest competitor in Frankfurt was Peter Braubach. The émigré from Paris Andreas Wechel should also be included, along with Sigismund Feyerabend (1528–1590). On the other hand, Frankfurt figured among the leading European printing and publishing cities for only a relatively short period, from 1530 to 1590.

Poem of Praise to a Fair

In 1574 the Parisian humanist and publisher Henri Estienne (Henricus Stephanus) (1528–1598) composed his famous Latin poem of praise to the Frankfurt Fair (*Francofordiense Emporium sive Francofordiense Nundinae*) and dedicated it to the Frankfurt City Council. Estienne had left his native city of Paris for religious reasons in 1551 and immigrated to Calvinist Geneva, where he operated a printing and publishing company for many years. As a notice in the Frankfurt catalogue of 1593 indicates, he also owned an affiliated print shop in Lyons. In Estienne's ode to the Frankfurt Fair, he first speaks of the impressive abundance of merchandise to be found there before moving on to a description of a "second fair":

> I now come to a second fair which may be perceived by some as an extension of the one discussed thus far, and so I take my leave of Mercury's Fair [Mercury was considered to be the patron saint of business enterprises] in order to sing the praises of the Fair of the Muses. For the Muses summon to Frankfurt their book printers and book dealers and instruct them to bring along poets, speakers, storywriters and philosophers....
>
> When all are assembled there, it is hard to believe that all of this is taking place in the German city of Frankfurt. In reality, it should be happening in that city where once bloomed the most celebrated intellectual life in all of Greece.

One would do well, perhaps, to designate Frankfurt's Book Lane, dedicated to literary traffic and occupied by book printers and book dealers, as the Athens of Frankfurt.[16]

This was, in short, Estienne's hymn of praise to the Frankfurt Book Fair.

FRANCOFORDIENSE
EMPORIVM,
SIVE
FRANCOFORDIEN-
SES NVNDINAE.

Quàm varia mercium genera in hoc emporio proftent, pagina feptima indicabit.

HENR. STEPHANVS de his fuis nundinis.

Impiger extremis merces non fumis ab Indis, Sed piger hafce potes lector habere domi.

ANNO M. D. LXXIIII,
Excudebat Henricus Stephanus.

Reproduction of the title page from Henri Estienne's 1574 poem of praise for the Frankfurt Fair.

In terms of the wholesale book trade, however, Frankfurt was not the important centre that Leipzig was destined to become, since the publishers and book dealers of those days were primarily interested in retail sales. There was not yet a close-knit network of well-stocked book dealerships, and the acquisition of new publications was actually quite difficult. The most compelling reason that so many travelled to Frankfurt was that they viewed the book as a medium for intellectual and cultural exchange. Once again in Estienne's words:

> So what comes out of this "Fair Academy," as I have designated it earlier, is the fact that those who come there can gain something in Frankfurt beyond what they can obtain from any library. For here, each person can hear the voices of many learned men who have come together from many academies; here one can hear them philosophizing as earnestly as if they were transported in time to the groves of the Lyceum in Athens where Socrates and Plato once held sway....

A great humanist and admirer of the Frankfurt Book Fair, Estienne returned from Frankfurt to Lyons for the last time in March 1598, heartsick and on the brink of death. His monumental multi-volume work, the *Thesaurus Linguae Graecae*, had used up all his resources, and its anticipated success had eluded him. Presumably it was for this reason that his editor finished a copy of the lexicon and published it. At the time, this unauthorized publication (a pirated edition) was perceived as a scourge on the book trade. It would be another few centuries before legal protection for intellectual and economic property was enacted. Even in those days, the timeworn argument was put forward that readers were better served by these cheaper editions, when, in fact, this attempt at persuasion only served as a means of disguising something long referred to as the profit motive.

Fair Catalogues

The earliest Book Fair catalogues contained no comprehensive listings of the participating printer-publishers. They were regarded, rather, as partial lists of some of the participating suppliers. Nonetheless, on the whole, they gave quite an accurate picture of the contemporary book market in that they were a clear indication of what was being sold and reflected various fields of interest. Oriented towards the classical faculty divisions at the universities, they provided a systematic guide to the new publications in theology, jurisprudence, medicine, and literature. There followed a small section of German-language books, once again in systematic order, and finally "history, stories, and tales." This last category represented what might be considered the "mixed" element of the book market.

In 1564 Georg Willer, a book dealer in Augsburg, published for the first time a "Book Fair Catalogue" for the Lenten and Fall Fairs, but it was by no means complete, and of the 256 books he listed all were works he had bought in France and then taken to Augsburg. Starting in 1592, Nicolaus Bassée, a Frankfurt printer, published a comprehensive edition incorporating all previous Fair Catalogues. Since these predecessors of today's publications' catalogues were hastily prepared and often printed while the Fair was taking place, they contained no details identifying publishers or point of origin. A mere six years later such private initiatives were summarily forbidden by the Frankfurt City Council. From 1598 until 1750, a Frankfurt Fair Catalogue appeared annually as the official publication of the Frankfurt City Council. What more effective way to ensure that nothing escaped the watchful eye of officialdom!

The Book Fair Newsletter

The flowering of the Frankfurt Book Fair at the end of the sixteenth century also gave rise to a novel and interesting means of conveying information to all and sundry: the Fair newsletter. Following the example of a similar initiative in Cologne, these appeared every six months in Frankfurt from 1591 until early into the nineteenth century. Although they began as broadsheets or flyers, they eventually evolved into quasi-newspapers, which appeared periodically and were aimed at a cross-section of educated readers. These highly popular *Relationen*, or newsletters, chronicled the major events of the previous six months. The interested fairgoer could gain an overview of military events and war-related matters (about one-quarter of the contents), inform himself about political and ecclesiastic changes (a second quarter), and find out about economic developments and legislative changes. The reader could then go on to discover a wide assortment of miscellaneous news items ranging from genealogy to news of the nobility and — last but not least — reports on the most gruesome and unusual crimes, worldwide natural disasters, and signs of wonders such as comet sightings. The Frankfurt newsletters dating from 1591 to 1806 were accordingly bound into five-year volumes, which rendered them invaluable as permanent chronicles of their time.

The Frankfurt newsletters belong also to the early history of illustrative journalism: portraits, city views, and maps were liberally used to embellish the written news. The artistic value of copperplate engraving not only underscored the written descriptions of sieges and city conquests that so often appeared but also contributed to the visual enhancement of the information given.

Book dealers at the Fair were undoubtedly the first to receive the Fair newsletters. Not infrequently the newsletters were treated as saleable merchandise and taken back home. Certainly, they played a significant role in the developmental process of scholarly historical research.

Pleasures of the Fair

A sometimes exhausting tradition at Frankfurt Book Fairs, which has been preserved to this day, can be traced back to those early times. An excerpt from the travel journal of printer Joshua

Mayn reveals that he stopped in Frankfurt while travelling from Holland to Zurich:

> On September 8, 1551, we were travelling on the Main to Frankfurt, that widely famed city, known in all countries. There we met the honourable Christoff Froschauer [his step-father], the venerable citizen and printer from Zurich, who put us up in his lodgings for several days. Since I could be of service in his bookstore, because I had grown up in such bookshops and was able to deal effectively with foreigners in Latin and French, he was loath to let me go until the Fair had ended. It was difficult work loading and unloading books, and I could not get away to visit the city, which offers much of interest during the annual fairs.... I was able to quench my thirst across the river in busy Sachsenhausen before returning to my labours in the shop.

Goethe's favourite view of Frankfurt from the River Main.
Reproduction of an engraving by Anton Radl, circa 1815.

It goes almost without saying that the tradition of revelry has continued undiminished to the present day. There is an old saying that Frankfurt has more wine in its cellars than water in its fountains. And the nearby vineyards along the Rhine remain as attractive to today's Book Fair visitors as they were to those who came to Frankfurt in the days of Joshua Mayn. As one visitor wrote to his wife in 1597, "May the good Lord grant me a safe journey home and the opportunity of refilling my cup when I can once again drink in Frankfurt's many pleasures in the years to come."

Chapter 4

A Meeting of Minds on Buchgasse

ooks offered for sale twice yearly were stored in the vaulted stone cellars of the prosperous-looking houses on Frankfurt's famous Buchgasse. This was the gathering place where scholars, authors, printer-publishers, and book dealers could meet and discuss a broad range of topics on the assorted issues of the times. Following the Lutheran Reformation, Protestants were pitted against the so-called papists who clung to Catholicism and had galvanized themselves into a "counter-Reformation" in a struggle against all things Lutheran.

Johannes Nas (Nasus), a Franciscan monk, was among the most critical and embittered polemicists against Lutheranism. At one point he had joined the Lutheran camp, but in 1552 he returned to Catholicism after reading *De imitatione Christi* (*The Imitation of Christ*), attributed to the Augustinian prior Thomas à Kempis (circa 1380–1471). Having joined the Franciscan order as a lay brother, he went on to train as a priest and eventually became both a popular preacher and the controversial "author of inflammatory works." In one section of his six-part *Centuriae controversarium*, he went so far as to declare the concept of marriage espoused by Luther as being nothing less than a form of concubinage.

Obviously this virulent attack was not about to go unanswered by the Lutheran faithful. Matthias Ritter the Younger, a pupil of Luther, Melanchthon, and Martin Bucer and a preacher in

DIALOGVS,

Das ist/ein Gespräch/

Von dem Ehrrührigen

vnd Lästerlichen Vrtheil/Bruder Joann
Nasen zu Ingolstatt/daß alle Lutherische Weiber
Huren seyen. Wie er inn seiner vierdten
Centuria geschrieben hat.
Gestellt/
Durch Matthiam Ritter.

Getruckt zu Franckfurt am Meyn/ durch
Nicolaum Basse. M. D. LXX.

Title page of Matthias Ritter's Dialogue against Johann Nas in 1570.

Frankfurt since 1552, struck back in 1570 with a scathing *Dialogus* relating to the dishonourable and malicious judgement passed by Brother Nas of Ingolstatt that all Lutheran women were whores.

In terms of the Reformation, the *Dialogus* belongs to the "conversational" style of literature that emerged in the final period of consolidation. This particular form harks back to the Middle Ages, and was popularized by Erasmus of Rotterdam and Ulrich von Hutten, whose dialogues had shown that even difficult contemporary issues could be rendered more comprehensible by employing a conversational format.

Through the use of a three-way conversation, Ritter undertook to restore the honour of the Reformer's ideal of marriage with astonishing objectivity. It is also devoid of any of the polemic that is characteristic of a number of other controversial writings of the sixteenth century.[17]

Being a long-time resident of Frankfurt, Ritter was thoroughly familiar with the Fair. He also knew many of the people who met there and was well aware of the attraction of the Fair's atmosphere. With this publication, in a sense Matthias Ritter became an important reference, in that he created one of the few descriptions that provide contemporary details about the events at the Frankfurt Book Fair of that time. The *Dialogus* takes place at the Book Fair of 1570, where three former school friends meet and eventually find themselves in the midst of a heated debate:

Siegfried:	Hello, there, Wolfgang! Where are you off to in such a hurry?
Wolfgang:	I'm headed for Book Lane to see what new things the foreign printers have brought in for this Fair.
Siegfried:	I, too, wanted to go there. May I tag along with you?
Wolfgang:	I would have thought you'd already been there.
Siegfried:	I've had other things to do, so I haven't had time until now. But it's still early. I'm not even sure the shops are open yet.

Wolfgang: I thought of that, too, but I didn't want to count on it. You know how things often go. The Fair starts early and is over before you know it. Anyone who doesn't get there early misses out.

Siegfried: That has certainly happened to me before, but it won't be long now till we're there. There's nothing much to see around here.

Wolfgang: Let's go a little further along. Look! Over there, there are already a lot of shops open.

Siegfried: But there aren't any books displayed. And there are no people in the lane. It must just be servants who have been sent out ahead.

Wolfgang: There, at the corner, one of the vendors has put up a display.

Siegfried: That's a new store. Let's go and see what's being offered there.

Wolfgang: Do you know him, the man sitting inside?

Siegfried: I should, but I can't quite seem to place him.

Wolfgang: Isn't it Reinhart?

Siegfried: You're right. That's exactly who it is.

Wolfgang: Hey there, Reinhart. Have you become a book dealer?

Reinhart: Wolfgang, I'm so pleased to see that you're well and are back here in our midst. And you, too, Siegfried. Thank God, I'm meeting some of my old friends again. Come, sit down here and we can catch up after such a long time. It seems you two have both become successful gentlemen, but here I am — still a poor working man!

Siegfried: It truly doesn't look that way to me. I take it that these books are all yours?

Reinhart: They belong to me and to those who believe in me.

Wolfgang: But old friend, how come you've ended up in this business? I thought you were going to become a doctor.

Reinhart: Have you never heard that a failed student makes a good book dealer?

Siegfried: Being a good farmhand, is what I've heard somewhere.

Reinhart: That may be what those who have never studied say about it. But I have at least learned a little Latin.

Siegfried: All right, but you had such a good start, if only you had kept on.

Reinhart: It wasn't meant to be, I guess!

Wolfgang: What new things have you brought?

Reinhart: I'm still waiting for the new books to arrive. They're on the way. I hope the drivers will be here in one or two days. If you find something you like in my shop, then I'll give you a discount for old times' sake.

Wolfgang: Yeah, sure, the customary one or two pennies more than the others....

Reinhart: I'm far too honest for that. But I have something new here that has never before been available.

Siegfried: What kind of a book is that? *Quarta Centuria* by Brother Johann Nas. He's a monk, I believe.

Wolfgang: Let me look. That must be the book a good friend of mine from Braunschweig showed me. My friend, take a look at Chapter 24. If I remember rightly, it should contain a Latin and therefore Roman Catholic conclusion. Give me the book. There, I've found it in Chapter 45, and it is indeed the book I was referring to. My friend, how could you sell me this book? Have you read what's in it?

Reinhart: I have read a little here and there when I had nothing else to do, and I certainly noticed that he is totally opposed to the Lutheran position. Should I not sell it for that reason? I have to carry books that can be sold if I am to earn a living.

Wolfgang: You didn't think that way when we were all together in Wittenberg.

Reinhart: In those days I didn't even want to know the price of corn. This is another place and time. Both my parents have died and I now have to look after feeding myself along with my wife and child.

Wolfgang: Do you honestly want to devote your time to selling books like this and abandon your devotion to the Good Lord whom you once acknowledged so wholeheartedly?

Reinhart: I can certainly see that you haven't changed. Anything that doesn't fit in with your way of thinking has to be immediately damned and denied. What does it matter to me what's in that book? I'll leave that to the authors and poets to decide. I'm here to sell books. Why shouldn't I offer books that people are clamouring for?

Wolfgang: If things were as they should be, you would realize how this book's content affects you, personally. And this monk should certainly know what is appropriate to write about and what isn't.

Reinhart: How come?

Wolfgang: Do you really have to ask? Don't you know what happens to those who distribute invective? And the consequences for the buyer?

Reinhart: But this is not invective!

Wolfgang: No? Listen to this: *Summa summarum, Lutherana Meretrix.* In the final analysis he is saying that all Lutheran women are whores. You can certainly understand that. Even though I haven't read this book all the way through — as I said — a good friend showed me these words in his copy. I don't doubt that there are more similar passages in it.

Reinhart: No, no, Wolfgang, that is just a lot of talk. If you were to label it invective so quickly, no one would be allowed to write anything any more without weighing every word first. What would become of me and my colleagues? We would have very few new books to sell. You can also find Lutheran tracts where one or two words would be offensive to Papists. To my mind it all comes out even in the end.

Wolfgang: I doubt very much that you'd find such audacious blasphemy in the writings of a Lutheran teacher who, to my certain knowledge, has quite a different reputation among us, than this monk has among Papists.

Reinhart: Good Lord, we're simply talking about references to women. Do you want to defend women this way? Siegfried, tell me, did Wolfgang here get married?

Siegfried: Yes, not even a year ago. And he got himself a very pretty and virtuous wife.

Reinhart: Aha! I thought as much. That must be the reason he's taking up the cause of women so earnestly.

Siegfried: That may well have something to do with it. However, be that as it may, I still find these words horrify me, and I believe every honourable man — as we all aspire to be — must be similarly affected by them. The way in which these thoughts have been expressed is far too crude and, in my opinion, it cannot be excused or tolerated.

Reinhart: Really! I am very surprised that these few words have upset you to such an extent.

Wolfgang: You are so dazzled by the idea of making money that you can't see the harm involved. Whether they are shameful or honourable publications doesn't seem to make any difference to you. Siegfried, my friend, try to make Reinhart be a little more reasonable. You're less emotional than I am.

Reinhart: All right then, for the sake of peace between us, I will go along with you gladly. Anyway, at the moment I have nothing better to do.

Siegfried: I'm not expecting you to make a momentous declaration. If someone were to call your wife a whore, would you then understand what we're talking about here? This monk thinks he can call all Lutheran women whores. It seems to me that is pretty plain language.

Reinhart: And so? Just because someone calls you something, that doesn't make it true. Remember the old saying about sticks and stones…?

Siegfried: Are you bringing up that pathetic argument again? If it were acceptable, then why is it that God's law as well as the Imperial laws forbid the use of inflammatory words, lies, invective and blasphemy? And even the unwritten law inscribed in every man's heart forbids each of us from doing this. No one enjoys having unsavoury things said about him. And whatever a person resents having done to him, should govern how he treats other people.

Ritter's literary "dialogue" continues at length in the same vein, involving vigorous debates on various allegations made by Brother Nas, until the three friends eventually decide to go their separate ways, promising to resume their discussion at the next possible opportunity.

Chapter 5

The Frankfurt Book Fair in the Seventeenth Century

A contemporary of Shakespeare's, the English travel writer Thomas Coryate (1577–1617), visited Frankfurt in 1611. Among other things, he recorded the following impressions:

I went to the book dealers' street, where I saw such an immeasurable wealth of books that I had to marvel at it. For this street surpassed the displays of books to be found at St. Paul's in London, the rue St. Jacques in Paris, the Merceria in Venice, and literally everything that I have ever seen on my travels, by so much that it seemed to me to be the epitome of all the most significant collections of books in Europe. That particular street is not only famous for its book trade per se, but also for every aspect of the arts and sciences, as well as the presence of many highly advanced printing establishments. Printing has been developed so extensively in the last few years that Frankfurt stands in the forefront of any other city in Christendom in this respect, not even in comparison with Basel, which I earlier praised so highly because of its outstanding achievements in this art.[18]

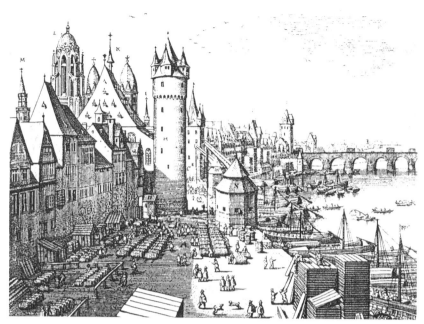

View of the quay on the River Main, Frankfurt. Copper engraving by Matthias Merian, 1646.

At long last, Englishmen appear to have discovered the attractions and advantages of the Frankfurt Book Fair. In the bibliographic work of Georg Draudius, the *Bibliotheca exotica*, there are 312 English works listed together with their publishers and printers that were brought to the Frankfurt Book Fair for sale between the years 1561 and 1620.

Beginning in 1598, Sir Thomas Bodley is on record as having had books purchased in Frankfurt for the new Oxford University Library and had drawn his librarian's attention to the Frankfurt Book Fair Catalogue of 1602: "There is a large volume printed *in quarto* which includes the Frankfurt Fair Catalogues from 1564 to 1592, available at Norton's." From 1608 to 1618, the year that marked the beginning of the Thirty Years' War, the book dealer John Norton had an English edition of the Frankfurt Fair Catalogue printed. Somewhat later, possibly in 1620, a separate edition of the catalogue was printed with an appendix of the new books published in English, which eventually became the predecessor of the English National Bibliography. A further Frankfurt Fair Catalogue was published in 1646 by the Richard Whitaker Company in London. The extent of the demand for English-language copies of the Book Fair Catalogue is indicated by the fact that Whitaker ordered six crates of books from Frankfurt publishers in 1649.

The great German mathematician and astronomer Johannes Kepler also used the Frankfurt Book Fair to sell copies of his books. From 1623 to 1627 he maintained a dogged struggle to get his *Rudolphinische Tabellen* printed during the difficult times brought on by the Thirty Years' War.

> As the supervisor of the publications program for technical literature, he was successful in getting a 568-page manuscript printed. He negotiated his way through exceptional political circumstances, dealt with personal problems, arranged for the necessary paper for printing, inspected the cut of the special typefaces for the symbols, the setting of the type, and consorted — as a travelling salesman — with other merchants in order to promote the finished product at the Frankfurt Book Fair.[19]

The trade in books published in Frankfurt proceeded to soar to unimagined heights, but the general trend of the times was in the opposite direction.

> While the number of books printed in North Germany before 1590 was only one-third of the total printed in German cities to the south and west, the proportions gradually changed. In the decade between 1611 and 1620, the two groups were almost evenly matched. In fact, at the time, Frankfurt was actually surpassed by its younger competitor, Leipzig, which boasted an average annual output of 225 publications. Frankfurt

was next with 178, followed by Cologne with 140, Wittenberg with 78, Augsburg with 42, Strasbourg with 38, Magdeburg with 33, the university city of Rostock with 30, Basel with 29, Nuremberg with 27 published items.[20]

Then, from 1618 to 1648, Germany became deeply embroiled in the Thirty Years' War, which first broke out in Prague, the capital of Bohemia, because of a perceived violation of Protestant rights that involved the revolt of the Protestant aristocracy. For Germany, this was a catastrophic war that had dire consequences for the book trade in general and Leipzig in particular. During these difficult years, Leipzig produced only one Fair Catalogue and book production sank to an all-time low.

Frankfurt was considerably less affected by the war than Leipzig. The imperial city of Frankfurt was occupied for four years by Sweden starting in 1631; however, it was stricken by a severe plague in 1635, which, in turn, was a factor in the cancellation of the Fair that year. In 1630, despite the difficult times, 135 new books had been produced by Frankfurt publishers. Within the next five years production once again increased and almost reached the high point of 1610, whereas Leipzig's recovery was perceptibly slower.[21]

With the end of the war in 1648, the Frankfurt book trade once again prospered. In fact, for a brief period — when it came to books and printing — Frankfurt's position was uncontested as the foremost city of central Europe. In the eleven years from 1649 to 1660, no fewer than 1,272 titles were produced. The Frankfurt Book Fair also figured largely in the international book trade.

According to one historian, however, "Conditions changed substantially during the Thirty Years' War and worked to Germany's considerable disadvantage. Between 1632 and 1680, the Dutch book trade was the principal player and leading power at the Frankfurt Book Fair."[22]

The Dutch also distinguished themselves in their unabashed production of pirated editions. At the time, there was scarcely a major publication in Germany that was not copied in Holland. Of the remaining foreign exhibitors, the French from Geneva, Lyons, and Paris remained faithful to Frankfurt; the Venetians had already kept their distance even before the war; and the English appeared only sporadically. In the final analysis, however, it appears that the book fair in Frankfurt survived the dramatic events of the first half of the seventeenth century relatively unscathed.

The Frankfurt Tax

By 1662, the contentious issue of imperial-Catholic book censorship, which will be further explored in the following chapter, had reached into the heart of the book trade when the emperor in Vienna decided to assume full authority over the Frankfurt City Council for regulating the printing industry. In March of that year, an edict from the Imperial Court was posted, by order of which "all aspects of the book trade, as well as the books themselves, were to be assessed a tax," and further that "the book trade was forbidden to Jews because they would contaminate the book business."

Back in Vienna, only twelve publishers supported the emperor's scheme to impose stringent regulations governing the book industry in Germany. Among them was a plan involving a tax ordinance that would effectively impose a uniform selling price. Needless to say, most participating publishers at the Frankfurt Book Fair declared themselves vehemently opposed to these unwelcome restrictions. In fact, they threatened to boycott the Fair should the tax be implemented. The countless variables of the book trade — the royalties, the types of editions, the prices of paper and printing, the cost of patents, the expenses involved in travel, customs and freight charges, the uncertainty of sales, the differing degrees of outlay for business expenses — all made it totally impossible to allow for a policy of fixed pricing.

At the Spring Fair of 1671, a written protest was issued, accompanied by a list of the opposed participants representing 204 companies from 84 cities. Among these, 35 were cities located outside Germany, and the remaining 49, which included the German-speaking cities of Switzerland, were counted as German. Even book dealers and publishers who had listed no titles in the official Fair Catalogue were among the signatories. The unrest among book dealers continued into the spring of 1672, when the emperor was finally convinced of the difficulties involved in enforcing the book tax. In the face of the book dealers' steadfast resistance, the imperial plans were thwarted and a major threat to the Book Fair's future was successfully averted.

The Leibnitz Initiative

Other attempts at reform that were intended to support and further develop the work of book dealers took place primarily in the two main book centres of Frankfurt and Leipzig. The Mainz philosopher Gottfried Wilhelm Leibnitz (1646–1716), for example, proposed the establishment of a German scholars' society and a universal library that would be based in Frankfurt. In 1668 Leibnitz also proposed the publication of a supplement to the Fair Catalogue, which would outline the content of particularly noteworthy books. He named this catalogue *Nucleus Librarius*. On October 22 of the same year he divulged his plan to Emperor Leopold I, but his letter remained unacknowledged. Undeterred, he wrote again on November 18, 1669, requesting exclusive imperial permission for this publication and appealing for financial support. Much to his chagrin, this second request fared no better than the first. In an appendix to his letter of proposal, in Latin he wrote: "One difficulty still remains: how to accomplish the publication of this Catalogue of New Books simultaneously with the Fair for which it is destined. I think I have found a way to achieve this: the summary of books could possibly appear towards the end of the Leipzig Fair which immediately follows the one in Frankfurt. Usually most of the books and publishers go on to the Leipzig Fair from Frankfurt, or at least those who deal in them do."

In his appeals to the emperor, even a man with a mind as great and independent as Leibnitz's was obliged to submit to the formal conventions of the time. As a precaution to his "all-illuminating, all-powerful, and most invincible emperor," he recommended the following measures:

> In order that no manuscripts deemed offensive, revolutionary, or illegal be promulgated at the Fairs or between them by word of mouth, a stringent warning should be added: that in the year that this proclamation is issued, no such book may be offered for sale in Frankfurt by any book dealer. In this respect no distinction may be made as to whether the book is newly published or re-published, and the punishment for offering such a book for sale shall fall on the book dealer who has published the book. Therefore, in Frankfurt, as I say, no such book may be offered by dealers unless a copy has been submitted previously for the preparation of a report on, and abstract of, its content.

Leibnitz's attempt failed because of a complete lack of political will on the part of the imperial authority to support or further the interests of the Frankfurt Book Fair, which was perceived as both troublesome and fractious. Or, more realistically, was it not the fact that the book trade had evolved into a far-reaching Protestant force that did not conform to the interests of the Roman Catholic Church and its undiminished ties with the emperors in Vienna? Frankfurt and its book trade posed a potential threat, although there was still influence to be exerted through the Frankfurt City Council by virtue of its close relationship with the Imperial Court. For its part, Leipzig was already removed from this conflict, as the Catholic emperors had long since lost their influence there.

Newspapers and Calendars

A particularly striking example of the popularity of pamphlets that depicted current events and were already sometimes referred to as "newspapers" is Grimmelshausen's seventeenth-century novel *Simplicius Simplicissimus*. In graphic detail, the author describes the observations of his hero, who works at the Fair as a hawker. "How would it be," he reflects, "if you were to become a newspaper hawker in your old age, selling little calendar pamphlets in various cities?" Grimmelshausen then proceeds to comment on the current craze for pamphlets and newspapers and includes a satirical jab at their sensationalized content: "And since this was around the time of year when these were just coming off the press, I would go in all possible haste to a well-known city and seek out a comfortable inn, so I could reflect in peace there on the contents of various newspapers recounting their sad tales of murders, or sea battles, or other such things."

At the time, the Venetian conquest of the Turks off Candia in June 1668 was the topic of the moment. Grimmelshausen's hero buys up a full complement of newspapers recounting the events of the sea battle and then attempts "to relate the course of events … in a ballad, and to sing it at the earliest opportunity in the public marketplace." Fortune smiles on him when he immediately finds a printer who agrees to print this newly created masterpiece and at the same time to sell both the hero's pamphlets and his song. The sales process is depicted in an illustrative woodcut that is accompanied by the protagonist's detailed description: "The innkeeper explained immediately to me that I didn't have far to go since his inn was only steps from the public market. I could put my wares on a small table that he was willing to lend me for that purpose. After that I was free to stand comfortably unchallenged on a bench singing out the praises of my totally invented newspaper to the passing throngs...."

That publications such as this were also sold in Frankfurt in a similar fashion was substantiated earlier by Max Mangold, who mentions singing newspaper hawkers on board a market ship.

A number of sales-related jingles describing the antics of singing hawkers at the Frankfurt Fair in the seventeenth century have since come to light, and these provide further evidence not only of their existence but also of the prevailing cynicism with which they were regarded by educated observers of the time.

Crisis in the Frankfurt Book Trade

The first signs of the decline in status of the Frankfurt Fair were to be found within the local book trade itself. From the early sixteenth century until late in the seventeenth century, Frankfurt had been a dominant force in both publishing and retail book sales. In particular, the latter half of the seventeenth century appears to have been the high point of Frankfurt's book trade.

Yet within one brief decade, a radical change took place that would wreak havoc on a grand scale. Between the years 1680 and 1690, virtually every publishing house in Frankfurt collapsed. The blame for this catastrophe was laid on "usurious interest rates" said to have been charged by two Jewish moneylenders in Frankfurt, David zum Schiff and Nathan Maas zum Goldenen Strauss. It seems that several of the best-known publishers in Frankfurt owed these individuals vast sums of money. Among their number were the heirs of the Catholic Schönewetter Publishing House, who saw their debt climb in a few years from 1,800 thalers to 16,680 thalers. Christoff Wust, who printed bibles, had to surrender 24,000 thalers' worth of published works to these same creditors, and the highly regarded Merian Publishing Company had a similar experience.

The reaction to these economic reversals was a call for state intervention coupled with an anti-Semitic backlash. A 1765 excerpt from *A Detailed Discussion of the Two Famous Imperial Fairs Held Annually in the Imperial City of Frankfurt-am-Main* declares:

View of Judengasse, July 1835, watercolour by Mary Ellen Best, from
The World of Mary Ellen Best *by Caroline Davidson, Chatto & Windus, 1985.*

The Jews in the book trade were arrogantly profiting to such an extent that the competing book producers and dealers were unwilling to tolerate the situation. Their complaints eventually brought about the 1688 and 1695 ordinances to be passed by the council, completely barring Jews from the book trade. As a concession, they were allowed a short time to dispose of the books in their possession, but they were directed not to acquire any more books and to close down those storage premises they had outside the Buchgasse. They were also permitted to transfer as many books as they needed to sell. As a result, those whose business dealings were adversely affected appealed the ruling....[23]

The control of the Frankfurt publishing houses by the Jewish moneylenders was, however, only one of a number of related factors and not the underlying cause of their economic ruin, just as, in the final analysis, the excesses of the imperial-Catholic Book Commission were not solely responsible for the eventual collapse of the Frankfurt Book Fair. The real culprits were primarily the complications brought on by the wars instigated by Louis XIV and the repercussions of the War of the Spanish Succession, both of which provoked the general decline of business activity in Frankfurt. Needless to say, the Fair also felt the repercussions of this reversal of fortune. Between 1691 and 1718, there were no less than twenty-two complaints registered in the records of the Frankfurt Book Commission that cite "war-related events" and the resulting instability that created difficulties when it came to mounting the Fair. For example, a note on file from the period contains a declaration to the effect that most of the book dealers stayed away because of the perceived dangers created by the War of the Polish Succession. The fact remains, however, that around the turn of the century, despite the concerns of those involved in the survival of the Fair, between 110 and 150 publishers still offered their books for sale in Frankfurt

A Traveller's Account of a Visit to Frankfurt

Before embarking on the story of the final collapse of the old Frankfurt Book Fair, perhaps one last attempt should be made to envisage conditions that have long since ceased to exist. The travels of a priest from Einsiedeln, who recorded his impressions in a little book entitled *Report of a Trip to the Frankfurt Book Fair*, should serve as an instructive guide. After a twelve-day trip on horseback from Einsiedeln in Switzerland, via Zurich, Basel, Strasbourg, and Heidelberg, Father Joseph Dietrich arrived in Frankfurt on March 26, 1684:

> We came to the watchtower on the outskirts of Frankfurt, and the watchman on duty inquired about the purpose of our trip, however did not ask for passports, and allowed us through. Once inside the city we were, however, required to show our passports. Any person who failed to produce one had to swear an oath that he came from a place that was free of communicable diseases. A coachman then drove us to a good spot from where we could easily reach our lodgings. I was the first to alight with my servant and went in search of the Carmelite monastery, which took me some time to find....

A letter of recommendation ensured that Father Dietrich would be lodged along with his servant in the monastery. After having settled in, the two set off to find a suitable place to sell the books they had brought with them. This proved to be more difficult than anticipated, since the bell signalling the opening of the Fair was about to toll:

> On March 27th, I got up at five o'clock with my servant, who had taken a small room near mine, went to the Church, read Holy Mass, completed other duty prayers and meditations. Then I went out to the marketplace to find a storage space or a

room for our books, but I did not find anything. I went through the lane several times from one end to the other, looking desperately for a vacant booth; but everything was already taken and in the end I returned in disappointment to the Monastery....

Undaunted, Father Dietrich later resumed his search and finally met a Cologne book dealer of his acquaintance:

I greeted him politely, spoke with him about the invoice our director of typography Father Bernhard Kälin had given me, and he answered me in a friendly manner, wishing me good luck, but could do nothing further on my behalf. The good man complained that he had suffered at least 4,000 thalers in losses the previous year because of unprecedented rainfall that had flooded his storage cellars to the height of a man in water. He went on to inform me that most of the Einsiedeln books had been ruined and requested an extension in meeting the terms of his debt.

In desperation, Father Dietrich decided to rent a cheap little room that could be reached only by mounting a spiral staircase to the fourth floor:

I paid the rent immediately, and began unpacking the books. These had been stored partly in the shop of Herr Bodner from Zurich. Another portion had not yet arrived but was expected the next day. I got everything upstairs with the assistance of my servant, and that of a hired porter. Then I set about arranging the books so that it began to look like a bookshop.... In the afternoon, we got busy with the unpacking which was made more depressing by the discovery that our books had been badly packed, and some had been damaged. At 7:30, we returned to the Carmelite Monastery to partake of the daily Lenten meal, for which I had bought myself some bread for a couple of coins because the Monastery only offered black bread which gave me heartburn…. On March 28, we had a barber come to shave us…. Immediately thereafter we went to our frigid book room. In order to cut down on our work due to the extremely cold weather, we organized the books in all possible haste and then sent for book dealers to be brought to us in our rented premises.

According to Dietrich's account, "On March 29th we had very cold weather with a relentless north wind, which blew not only all day long, but also through the night, even into my room, causing me significant discomfort because of the ill-fitting windows. All night long there was such continual rattling and banging that I got almost no sleep, while I lay freezing beneath the covers. In the morning we found some snow in the streets, but not much."

In addition to the weather, the Fair's early opening date created other problems not only for the booksellers but also for those visiting the Fair. As a result, a few decades later the Frankfurt Council attempted to change the dates of the Spring Fair.

Father Dietrich also reported on the market ships:

Afterwards I walked to the Main which flows past the city on the right: there I saw ships such as we have never seen in our country. They have been fitted with high masts, almost like a galley-ship, and carry a few hundred people plus a variety of merchandise. The vessels are covered and extend to lengths of 70, 80, and even 100 feet long. There is even a kitchen on board. They are drawn along partly by horses, particularly the market ship from Mainz which has no rudder, and instead uses poles to help the ship move along the river. The market ship arrives in Frankfurt every evening around six and has to take on board everyone who has a pass. At ten in the morning, it sets off again from Frankfurt towards Mainz, arriving there around six o'clock, except when there is a headwind. It takes on board neither horses nor cattle, only people: and each passenger pays 4 Imperial batzen. A single boatload can bring in 60, 70 to 100 batzen, over and above the merchandise which must always be paid for.

Finally, the bell tolls to close the Fair, as it has done on every day of the Fair, and Father Dietrich begins his journey back to the monastery in Switzerland. "At eight o'clock the bell of the Cathedral tolls for half an hour. Thereupon all shops are closed and the streets cleared. Directly afterwards, a shot is fired from a large cannon; thereafter the tower watchmen play a brief but well-executed interlude on the cornet and trumpet. I was quite delighted."

Market ships at anchor on the River Main close to Frankfurt.
Watercolour by Julius Christoph Eymer, circa 1870.

Chapter 6

~~~

The Issue of Imperial-Catholic Book Censorship

In early January 1486, the Elector Prince and Archbishop of Mainz Berthold von Henneberg, in his capacity as the Holy Roman Empire's arch-chancellor of Germany, issued a "penal order" known as the Censorship Edict, instituting the censorship of foreign-language publications translated into German. To ensure the efficacy of his edict, he appointed four respected professors from various faculties of the university to act as official censors. In addition, the senior cathedral theologian and two councillors appointed from the city council, along with the four academics, were charged with the responsibility of inspecting all books offered for sale within the diocese.

> Since the God-given gift of the art of printing was invented in our golden Mainz, we have the absolute right to protect its reputation and meet our obligation to preserve it from all contamination.... In the case of Frankfurt, the books offered for sale must first be inspected and approved by a respected theologian, and one or two duly appointed representatives from the City Council, in addition to various professors and qualified experts.[24]

Stalls along the River Main, Frankfurt Fair, April 1835.
Watercolour by Mary Ellen Best.

Prior to the princely archbishop's edict, the pope had left the censorship of any and all written works to the universities. In the era of handwritten books, there had been only rare instances of confiscations. After the invention of printing, however, opposition to Church doctrine was growing and with it the proliferation of so-called heretical texts.

The Council of the Free Imperial City of Frankfurt wasted no time in aligning itself with the archbishop. In response to a communication from "Our gracious gentlemen from Mainz," the council proposed the appointment of certain suitably qualified individuals as censors for the City of Frankfurt. In the end, the rise of the great critic and reformer of the papal church Martin Luther ensured that the matter of book censorship received the attention it deserved.

Martin Luther (1483–1546)

The Congress of Princes, a gathering of the German sovereign Electors where the new German emperor was to be chosen, had been called in June 1519 in Frankfurt-am-Main. At that meeting, Karl von Kastilien was unanimously elected Emperor Karl V (1500–1558). Karl was subsequently crowned emperor in the Cathedral of St. Charles in Aachen. With that ceremony, the young sovereign, who spoke not a word of German, was thrown into the problem-ridden realm of imperial German politics at a time when the future of all the European states was a maze of uncertainty. The prevailing social structures and legal systems were being increasingly jeopardized due to the limiting power exerted by the ruling monarchies. Modernization had brought change on many fronts, including methods of conducting business, waging war, and developing means of transportation, in addition to the communication of news, all of which allowed for the mobilization of state power in previously uncharted waters.

But, for Germany, the year 1519 had a special significance brought about by other unprecedented events. It was the year of the "Great Debate." From June 27 to July 16, a lengthy public debate took place in Leipzig between Johann Eck, a prominent church scholar, and the controversial reformer Martin Luther. Along with his friend and fellow monk, Andreas von Karlstadt, Luther was challenged by Eck to engage in a public discussion involving the dissemination of his inflammatory views. Two years earlier, Luther had had the temerity to publicly call into question the authority of the Church of Rome as part of his personal crusade for religious reform.

How easily the course of history could have been altered had Luther not chosen to follow his own inner voices. Contrary to his father's wishes, instead of becoming a lawyer, Martin Luther had entered the Augustinian monastery at Erfurt in 1506 and was consecrated as a priest the following year. After a lengthy period of theological studies at the universities of Erfurt and Wittenberg, he obtained his doctorate and was then in a position to assume the chair for the teaching of the Old and New Testaments. Before long, he began making a name for himself as an increasingly prominent theologian. Over time, however, it also became apparent that Luther had begun to doubt the value of the "accepted basic works," preferring instead to rely on the strength of his own inner conviction and the grace of God. Having weighed the consequences of publicly expressing his new-found views, in 1517 he openly challenged the infallibility of the pope as proclaimed by the Church of Rome. This, in turn, led to the passionate public debate two years later with its historic and far-reaching consequences.

> Neither Luther himself nor the many humanists, theologians, and princely advisors who then began to peruse and disseminate his written works could have foreseen what would follow as a result. Certainly no one anticipated a schism within the Church. Nor would anyone have even imagined the establishment of an entirely independent church. The overwhelming majority of German public opinion was with Luther, to whom they imputed their own hopes for reform — whether national or political. The fact remains, however, that scarcely anyone remotely understood the depth and radicalism of Luther's theology.[25]

The reaction of the Church and conservative theologians was surprisingly slow, but finally, in the summer of 1520, a threat of excommunication — *Exsurge Domine* — was issued against Luther. This, in turn, created a public outcry that subsequently led to the convening of the Imperial Diet at Worms in 1521.

The question of Luther's position towards the Church was not officially on the agenda of the general assembly held in Worms. Instead, there were various complaints about taxation and the legal encroachments of the Roman curiae into Germany. In this anti-Roman atmosphere, the Dominican prior from Augsburg,

Johann Faber, declared that steps had to be taken against Luther's intolerably presumptuous statements. It was unthinkable that an ordinary citizen should dare to reprimand the pope. While Erasmus of Rotterdam still believed that the "Luther Tragedy" could be resolved by a court of arbitration, the papal nuncio proceeded immediately to have an arrest warrant issued for Luther. Finally Luther was brought before the Imperial General Assembly. He was not allowed to argue his case. His only option was to recant. As evidence of his heresy, his books were laid out on a table, and he was asked whether or not he was willing to recant. Luther's reply, delivered first in German, then in Latin, made his position abundantly clear: "The Pope is the power which has devastated, ruined and destroyed the Christian world with his iniquitous teachings and evil example. For no one can contest or disguise the fact that by the laws of the Pope and his teachings governing humanity, the consciences of men are being held captive and their lives mortally endangered. Many have been martyred and tortured, in the most contemptible way."

When asked repeatedly whether he would recant, Luther countered with the famous response, "If I cannot be persuaded and convinced by the evidence of the Holy Scripture or by plain reason, then I still believe in what I have written and the Word of God. I cannot and will not recant because it is wrong and dangerous to act against one's conscience. May God help me, Amen!"

The emperor, a staunch Catholic, undoubtedly fearing for the welfare of the realm, desired nothing more than to denigrate Luther and his teachings: "I do not want to see him again. He has his believers, but I consider him henceforth a notorious heretic...."

The possibility of a settlement that was mutually satisfactory — one that might have led to a much-needed internal reform of the Church — was soon destroyed when the emperor issued his renowned Edict of Worms that outlawed Luther as a heretic and banned the reading or possession of his writings. Whether by his own volition or under duress, Luther withdrew from public life to Wartburg Castle near Eisenach, where he worked on his translation of the Bible into German. This work proved to be a historic and cultural achievement of the first magnitude, which would also have an impact on the book trade. Gradually Luther's work received increasingly broader exposure — largely because of new developments in the realm of printing. On August 18, 1520, his pamphlet "Address to the Nobility of the German Nation" was published in an edition of four thousand copies, and was sold out so quickly that another edition had to be printed only five days later. At the Frankfurt Book Fair, fourteen hundred copies of the debate between Dr. Luther and Dr. Eck were sold in three days. By the summer of 1520 approximately 370 editions of Luther's 300 published manuscripts represented about 400,000 individual copies.

> With the increased need for religious reading material, to which Luther's spiritual movement gave impetus, a powerful change occurred in the actual production of books. Luther turned to the use of the smaller, more accessible format of pamphlets for his writings on Church and political topics, thereby substantially increasing circulation. By any standard, the dimensions of his literary output were unprecedented.
>
> As soon as a new Luther pamphlet was published, it was immediately and eagerly seized upon by the printers in Basel, Augsburg, and Nuremberg, in order to make copies that were frequently published without naming the place of origin. Ten or more editions of many of these texts were published one after the other. Luther's work entitled *German Theology*, of which seventy different editions have been documented, serves as an excellent example of the prevailing volume of productivity.[26]

Erasmus of Rotterdam wrote somewhat sourly to King Henry VIII of England in 1530: "For Germans there is scarcely anything available for sale other than Luther's writings and those of his opponents." Luther's appearance in Frankfurt also had an inestimable influence on local politics. It posed a major problem for the city council, whose membership was recruited mainly among wealthy Frankfurt citizens of noble birth, merchants, and property owners, who made a handsome profit on the houses that they had frequently built for the express purpose of renting them to Fair visitors. As an imperial coronation site where the emperors were elected, the City of Frankfurt had enjoyed the assured protection and goodwill of the emperor and for centuries had fared reasonably well as a result of its political loyalty. Even the Fairs themselves had benefited from imperial protection. But with the appearance of Martin Luther, who stopped twice in Frankfurt en route to Worms, this political advantage suddenly came into question. The Book Fairs made Luther's vast literary output readily available to the people of Frankfurt. Yet in 1524, he called Frankfurt "the hole through which homegrown silver and gold, minted here in our homeland, flows out of Germany." In criticizing Frankfurt's role as the centre for the transfer of money and goods out of the country, he could be assured of the support of Frankfurt's largely impoverished population. As a result, the city council was faced with the difficult task of maintaining the balance between the Catholic royal houses and the predominantly Lutheran population of Frankfurt.

On Easter Monday 1525, an "uprising of the guilds in Frankfurt" expressed the outrage of the people for the first time. Primarily it was directed against the dogma-ridden Catholic clergy, but the powerful city regiment that, in the public mind, was associated with wealth and privilege was also targeted. The uprising was quickly quelled — as was the simultaneous peasants' revolt in southwest Germany — by an alliance of princes, and the Frankfurt City Council was reinstated to continue in its traditional role. The underlying problems, however, were far from being resolved:

> The Frankfurt Council had become predominantly
> evangelical for political reasons. Concern to preserve
> its status as a Fair city and as the site for the election
> of Germany's kings was an obstacle to any significant

change. However, in the light of developments in other major Protestant municipalities, the worrisome possibility of reform eventually had to be addressed. In the early summer of 1526, his personal concern over the inroads being made by the Reform movement prompted the Archbishop/Elector Prince of Mainz to exert pressure on the Frankfurt Council, by threatening that the Emperor would withdraw the privilege of holding the Fair in that city should any further signs of disloyalty occur.[27]

In order to fully understand the council's indecision and its waffling approach to the issues that would soon come to the fore, Frankfurt's dilemma must be duly recognized.

A War of Words

The State and Church authorities were challenged not only by the very real threat posed by the Reformation but also by other troublesome developments. At this point, no regularly published newspapers, periodicals, or magazines existed, leaving the books and pamphlets available at Frankfurt's Easter and Fall Fairs as the only existing means for the propagation of new ideas.

In the early part of the sixteenth century, *The Hand Mirror* by the Dominican priest Johannes Pfefferkorn of Cologne (1469–1522) was offered for sale at the Easter Fair. This publication contained the author's defence of Emperor Maximilian I's success in the burning of all Jewish books. These views were almost immediately refuted by Johannes Reuchlin (1455–1522), a noted Hebrew scholar of the time, despite the fact that Reuchlin himself was not Jewish. In his harshly critical response entitled *Der Augenspiegel*, he deplored the folly of this destructive and unchristian policy. Because it insulted the Imperial Majesty, a royal proclamation officially banning this publication was posted on the door of St. Leonhard's Church at the south end of the Buchgasse.

In *The Nightingale*, a controversial book of verse penned by former Heidelberg deacon Wilhelm Klebitz (Cleovitus), the emperor, who was generally rather tolerant in matters of religion, perceived an attack on the imperial constitution. In 1557, he ordered the Frankfurt Council to proceed immediately to arrest and charge the Frankfurt printer Hans Schmidt. The lines of demarcation were being drawn for the battle to come.

The rapid expansion of printing, the increasingly successful Reformation movement, and finally the Peasants' Revolts engendered a plethora of polemic texts and pamphlets that the Catholic imperial censorship regulations were no longer able to effectively control. Finally, in 1559, Pope Paul IV issued an *Index librorum prohibitorum* in which he listed publications deemed injurious to the True Faith. Henceforth the ownership, sale, or even reading of any of these publications would lead to excommunication.

The Imperial Book Commission in Action

Ten years later, on August 1, 1569, Emperor Maximilian II commanded the City of Frankfurt to set up a book commission to fulfil two specific functions: to prevent the possibility of the publication or distribution of any of the prohibited heretical texts, and to ensure that His Imperial Majesty would be the honoured recipient of a complimentary copy of every new book that came into print.

In its haste to act swiftly in response to the imperial command, on September 16 and September 18, six weeks after receipt of the emperor's order, the Frankfurt Council summoned all local and foreign publishers and book dealers to City Hall. Each of them was further requested to deliver copies of their catalogues and to present their licences to operate. This was tantamount to demanding a general inventory of the Book Fair — and placed those affected in an intolerable position. Fortunately, as luck would have it, the council, in its enthusiasm to appear decisive, had made what proved to be a fateful blunder. It asked the emperor to exempt it from the supervision of the book dealers because it would "cost more in time and labour." Instead, as a practical alternative, the council suggested that the emperor could send, not only his own royal advisor, Jakob Ochseln von Schlettstadt, but also several other learned gentlemen to personally oversee the administration of the plan. And thus — with the flourish of a pen — the Imperial Book Commission was created, although seven years would pass before any further action was taken.

It was not until after Maximilian's death in 1576 that his son Rudolf II (1552–1612) concluded that the time had come to act upon the opportunities presented by the Imperial Book Commission originally set up by his father. Writing from Prague on March 23, 1579, he reprimanded the Frankfurt Council for its failure to exercise its responsibility to eradicate "inadmissible texts" and appointed Johann Vest from the Imperial Court in Speyer to act as the first imperial book commissioner to Frankfurt. Commissioner Vest proved to be a loyal subject who took his responsibilities in the Counter-Reformation very seriously. When the emperor set him the task of dealing with the suppression of contentious texts, Vest was ably assisted by Johann Steinmetz, dean of St. Bartholomew's Cathedral, whom the emperor appointed for this purpose. Johann Steinmetz prepared a report on the Fall Fair of 1579 for the Imperial Court in Vienna. The report sheds a good deal of light on the occurrences marking that particular Fair. Three questions were put to all participating printers, publishers, and book dealers:

1. Are Imperial Printing Permissions in evidence?
2. Have the regulation dues been discharged; that is, have the required copies of all books been submitted?
3. Have printed catalogues and other related materials been made available and submitted to the Censorship Authority?

The report listed seventy printers and publishers in Frankfurt, thirty book dealers, and twenty others who usually attended the Fair. "The large mid-European market remained strong and unchallenged in its position, particularly in the southwest portion of the Empire with its German-speaking neighbours.... In many cases printers and publishers did not come to the Fair themselves, but were represented by commissioners."[28]

In all imperial communications following Rudolf II's 1579 decision to enforce the terms of his father's edict, it was emphasized that the Imperial Book Commission did not itself impose strictures. Instead it would fall to the Frankfurt City Council to undertake the administration of the censorship regulations, including confiscating materials and pressing charges when necessary. On the other hand, the imperial authority was reluctant to relinquish its supremacy over Frankfurt in this regard, despite the fact that since 1629 the council had supported and ratified all censorship recommendations. As a result, the situation became an endless source of irritation, which did not augur well for the status of the council politically, nor for the interests of the book trade as a whole.

Valentin Leucht

On March 20, 1596, Rudolf II once again delegated Johann Vest to visit and investigate the Book Fair, but ill health made it impossible for Vest to accept this responsibility. A suitable replacement would have to be found and, in due course, Valentin Leucht, senior papal legal advisor and imperial bureaucrat, was appointed in Vest's place a year later. Leucht would soon become respected as a wise and highly effective book commissioner: "He was gentle, intelligent and a cautious Book Censor, who clearly strove to implement the Emperor's wishes — in this case, by conducting a thorough inspection of the Book Fair catalogues and ensuring the admission of Catholic book publishers in an obviously unprejudiced manner."[29] Who was this exceptional man, and how was he able to represent so clearly the interests of the elector prince and Catholic archbishop of Mainz, as well as the imperial national regiment within a Lutheran city state?

His origins and career illustrate impressively the religious and political situation in the ecclesiastic territories on the Main in the last third of the sixteenth century. Superficial religious peace reigned as a result of uncertain power relationships and a widely relaxed Church discipline guaranteed to the Catholic side — and to a number of comfortable clergy in religious establishments and small orders — the untrammelled enjoyment of their relative freedom from external interference. For decades the strict ritual of spiritual renewal, known as the *Tridentium*, had been observed only in certain circles on paper. Then, gradually, powerful bishops were able to prevail over the lax atmosphere in the religious orders that they controlled. But, realistically, the clergy could be reformed only by new recruits. Valentin Leucht was among these. Early on, he became the author of numerous German religious tracts. His extensive output (thirty-nine publications in several editions) was unparalleled in his time. Martin von Cochem, a prolific and widely read religious author, also used Leucht's works as models and a source of inspiration. Before Leucht's time little or no Catholic literature had existed in Germany.

Leucht was the driving force that established the office of book commissioner as an institution ratified by the emperor. On February 17, 1597, he wrote to Johann Vest in Speyer in his capacity as the titular book commissioner, asking him to petition the authorities to confirm the appointment of himself and his commission and to give him special diplomatic powers to pursue those who remained recalcitrant and disobedient. The desired confirmation and special powers were immediately forthcoming, "in order that book printers and dealers would be governed by fear." The success of Leucht's year of efforts to achieve legitimate status for himself and the commissioners marked the beginning of growing conflict between the emperor and the council over control of the Book Fair.

Fair Catalogues

Initially the Frankfurt Council prohibited the publication of any private Fair Catalogues, such as the one printed by Georg Willer of Augsburg, in reaction to the Imperial Court's activities, and set about publishing its own official catalogue for the Fall Fair of 1598.

> As the sixteenth century drew to a close, the significance and status of the Frankfurt Book Fair had become an established fact. The power struggles for influence over book production and, above all, control of the book trade began in earnest. With the consolidation of political blocks — determined along territorial and religious lines — and the beginning of the Catholic counter-attack to the Reformation, the activity of the Censorship authorities gained significance on both sides....[30]

Initially envisaged as a means of facilitating the marketing and sale of books, the Fair Catalogue developed into a device for ensuring further suppression of undesirable publications. To Valentin Leucht, however, even this was insufficient to the need. Beginning in 1606, under the sponsorship of the elector prince and archbishop of Mainz, a special "Catholic Fair Catalogue" was planned. Both catalogues were published simultaneously in 1619 after Leucht's death. The political situation in Frankfurt appears to have become especially favourable for the Imperial Book Commission and its supporters. "The uprising in 1614 of the frustrated lower classes could only be suppressed with imperial assistance. It also remained a festering thorn in the side of the dissolute aristocracy whose power was being threatened. But without any effective control over the masses, they were dependent on imperial assistance, for which much would be expected in return."[31]

The Troublesome Issue of Censorship

"We decree that you censor diligently in this regard..."

Despite the high cost of licences, the book dealers had complied with the terms of the emperor's decree, including the submission of three complimentary copies of all books printed with imperial permission. However, towards the end of Emperor Rudolf II's reign, the situation began to change. Throughout the censorship of all books offered for sale at the Frankfurt Book Fair, the political campaign waged by the Catholic Church against the Protestants should have been adequately strengthened. On March 15, 1608, however, in a decree issued from Prague, a free copy of every book printed without an imperial licence would have to be submitted. This measure was clearly not instituted for fiscal reasons; rather, its purpose was to demonstrate the royal intent to impose an even greater degree of imperial censorship. Moreover, an inventory was required of all books in storage that were going to be brought to the Fair, as well as proof that they had all undergone the requisite royal censorship process.

The fourteen articles in this decree were read aloud to the printers and book dealers in Frankfurt at the next Fall Fair. Without exception they were required to swear to abide by all of them. Anyone who refused would be forced to close up shop. Not unexpectedly, the participating dealers from Protestant regions were incensed by this cavalier announcement. On February 17, 1609, enclosing a copy of the offensive decree, the book dealers from Leipzig, Wittenberg, and Jena petitioned their elector prince, Christian II of Saxony, requesting his protection and assistance. Would he consider interceding on their behalf and ask that the emperor excuse the Saxon book dealers from the required proof of censorship and from the submission of free copies? In addition, they asked him to exert all possible influence in order that the Frankfurt Council might continue to "afford them their Freedom of the Fair." The Saxon book dealers were adamant that the new decree was "in contravention of the Fair Freedoms, obstructed free enterprise, and hindered the book trade." It was, therefore, contrary to the interests of the Imperial Majesty. Initially there was no reaction from Saxony; however, when the Elector Prince Friedrich wrote from Heidelberg on March 18, 1609, to his Saxon counterpart, declaring that he, too, was of the opinion that the decree placed Protestants at the Frankfurt Fair at a distinct disadvantage, the Saxon government found the will to support the interests of the petitioners.

The book dealers of Saxony and Thuringen had based their arguments primarily on the fact that — in accordance with imperial orders — there was already a mandated book censorship in the jurisdictions of their respective elector princes. Censorship in Saxony was carried out by the universities; the supervision of the book dealerships was divided between the university and the respective city councils of Leipzig and Wittenberg.

Finally, the Elector Prince Christian II took it upon himself to write to Emperor Rudolf II. In his letter of June 19, 1609, he referred to the existing laws in his jurisdiction that precluded the proliferation of heretical literature. Would the emperor consider excusing the Saxon book dealers and printers from complying with the latest decree? The book dealers and printers from Saxony were further advised to refuse compliance pending the outcome of a legal assessment of the validity of the imperial decree as it applied to them.

The grateful book dealers of Leipzig, Wittenberg, and Jena thanked the elector prince for his intercession and requested him to inform the Frankfurt Council of the situation by making use of the good offices of the Leipzig Council. However the Saxon councillors may have expressed themselves to their colleagues in Frankfurt, the Frankfurt Council abandoned any further attempt to implement the emperor's decree. For the time being, His Imperial Majesty remained silent — in the not ill-founded hope of more opportune times on the horizon. These were not long in coming. The political troubles and exigencies of the Thirty Years' War soon weakened the City's ability to oppose the royal decree and presented the Empire with new and even greater opportunities for intervention.

From 1629 on, in its dealings with the Frankfurt Council, the tone and attitude of the Imperial Book Commission changed dramatically. Without consulting the council, the commission publicly posted an imperial edict in Frankfurt that effectively circumvented the jurisdictional authority of the council and relegated directly to the Imperial Court in Vienna any and all outstanding licensing disputes. As well, it expressed its intention to implement the required submission of free copies of all books brought for the first time to the Fair. As a result of this precipitous attempt to exert imperial control over the Frankfurt Council, the book commissioner's authority was seriously undermined. Little by little an impasse with far-reaching consequences was taking shape.

Georg Friedrich Sperling — The Enforcer

On July 16, 1661, Georg Friedrich Sperling was appointed as Ludwig von Hörnigk's replacement to the position of book commissioner because of von Hörnigk's disappointingly mild attitude and apparent inability to implement the wishes of His Imperial Catholic Majesty. It was deemed that Commissioner von Hörnigk's perceived ineptitude had directly contributed to "signs of disorder and negligence in the Book Commission," as cited in the imperial decree naming Sperling as the new commissioner. Although von Hörnigk remained nominal senior book commissioner until his death six years later, from the moment Sperling seized the reins, there is absolutely no question that his subsequent actions and attitude hastened the decline of the Frankfurt Book Fair.

> Sperling exceeded all his predecessors in ruthlessness and arrogance. In the twenty-four years of his tenure, he succeeded in making himself universally despised on a personal level, but — worse still — over time, the Imperial encroachments made at his behest were so damaging that the

Frankfurt Book Fair was literally destroyed on his account. When Sperling himself was at last replaced on March 16, 1685, and the Abbot of Our Lady's Monastery, Kaspar Vollmar, was named as his successor, Frankfurt's position as centre of the book trade was already beyond redemption, leaving Leipzig as its worthy successor....

Sperling belonged to that special breed of man destined to win the heart of the Imperial Court in Vienna. Without scruples and undeterred by violence, he went about his business ruthlessly. And he always knew precisely how and when to strip away the last vestiges of Frankfurt's independence. Any misfortune that was visited on the city's book trade could either be traced directly to his initiative or was the result of a direct order issued by him.[32]

Sperling strictly enforced the ruling about the submission of free copies of all new books, required since 1642 by the elector prince of Mainz, in addition to the five copies demanded for the emperor. And, as if this were not enough, still another copy had to be submitted to Sperling himself. "Sperling proceeded with great zeal in his efforts against the book trade. In the most brazen fashion, he let his intent to further the political aims of the Church be known; he seized all Evangelical theological works, while even the most contemptible examples of Catholic libel and slander remained sacrosanct...."[33]

As the Sperling situation became increasingly intolerable, on December 6, 1669, the evangelical princes and dignitaries of the realm sent a further complaint to the emperor about the peremptory confiscation of books other than those covered in Sperling's mandate, but it was all too little and too late.

At the Fall Fair of 1678, the Frankfurt Council was finally galvanized into action and retaliated by seizing three hundred copies of an anonymous text containing despicable insults aimed at the Evangelical Church. The offending texts were the property of the heirs of a Cologne publisher. True to form, Sperling intervened at the Vienna Court on behalf of the Catholic publisher. The following March, he demanded the return of the confiscated copies and at the same time forbade the council to make any further independent confiscations.

At the behest of the Frankfurt Council, the Protestant princes and dignitaries of the Empire finally took up the cause on April 22, 1679, and demanded the energetic prosecution of the case by the imperial authorities of Sperling and the publisher's heirs.

From Bad to Worse

The greatest displeasure of the Vienna Court was reserved for the political publications that were produced on printing presses in Holland and this, in turn, caused it to renew its long-standing attempts to censor the Frankfurt Book Fair Catalogue. The suspicion, initiated by Sperling, that the Frankfurt Council secretly supported the book dealers who were threatened with confiscations caused the court to urge its commissioner to proceed in a most energetic manner by specifically targeting imported books. This, too, became a contributing factor in the eventual decimation of the Frankfurt Book Fair — the end result of the single-handed misuse of power on a grand scale.

Frankfurt's famous Hotel de Russie. Watercolour circa 1832, artist unknown.

Chapter 7

〰

The Gradual Decline of the Book Fair in Frankfurt

At the end of the last day of the Fair, book dealers were required to close down their shops and storage areas. From this day forward, no further business involving books would be permitted until the next Fair in the spring or the fall. The Fair participants — whether they were dealers or printers — warehoused a portion of their goods (when it was not worth their while to hold their own storage area year-round) with a friendly book dealer, and took their new acquisitions, or respectively their own new publications, back to their home city or on to the next fair. Since the Middle Ages, the book trade had been governed by the principle of buying and selling books only at accredited fairs. It was, in fact, this very principle that had brought Frankfurt to its pre-eminent position in the book trade. With the decline of commerce in unbound folios, which had long represented the major portion of trade, and the increasing numbers of bound books, the book dealers were now in a position to sell their new publications between fairs.

The transition from periodic exchange commerce, which was limited to the fairs, to continuous commission trading was effectively a *fait accompli*. In contrast, however, the dealers of the old imperial book trade who were concentrated in Frankfurt were having a difficult time abandoning the outdated practices to which they had grown accustomed. Instead, they looked backward with pride at their illustrious history and insisted that their storage areas remain closed between fairs and that during non-fair times, no business was to be conducted. "For more than twenty years they persecuted Friedrich Böttcher, a travelling book dealer from Jena who did business between fairs and offered books for sale in various places during fair times. They castigated him as a person without honour, who respected neither God nor authority, a man addicted to serving his own insatiable greed to the continual and serious detriment of his fellows."[34]

This insistence on clinging to outmoded, unproductive business practices was one of the causes of the ruin of Frankfurt's local book trade. Indebtedness to Jewish moneylenders should be seen as a consequence rather than a cause. The Leipzig businessmen, who were more flexible, were already laying the groundwork for the eighteenth century, when Leipzig would become the commissioning centre of the German book trade — a position that Leipzig retained for almost another two hundred years.

The Gregorian Calendar

With the introduction of the Gregorian calendar into Protestant lands, which included Frankfurt, the Frankfurt Book Fair found itself in further difficulty. This new way of measuring the year required the loss of eleven days in order to even out the irregularities of the former Julian calendar. When one went to bed on February 17, 1706, one awoke the following morning on February 28, which, of course, wrought havoc with the dates of the Fair.

The Frankfurt Council proposed to the Leipzig Council that both cities delay their fair dates. Leipzig categorically refused. Frankfurt, still convinced of the tremendous importance of its Fair, went ahead on its own and delayed the Fair by three weeks in order to avoid the spring floods. The opening day of the Fair moved from the first Sunday before Easter (*Judica*) to the first Sunday after Easter (*Quasimodogeniti*). As a result, the dates of the Frankfurt and the Leipzig Fairs overlapped one another, creating yet another problem. Previously the book dealers had been able to use the time between fairs for travel from one location to the other. No doubt the Frankfurt Council had hoped that the change in timing would prove to be a distinct advantage to its own Fair; however, many merchants and dealers, forced by the overlapping dates to choose between them, chose the Leipzig Fair in preference to Frankfurt.

The end result was that, far from reinforcing its position, the Frankfurt decision had hammered still another nail into the coffin of its ill-fated Fair. Even Emperor Karl IV's approval in 1726 to move the opening date back one week did not alter the Fair's decline in any appreciable way. On the other hand — however significant the Frankfurt Council's decision may have been for the future of the Fair — the real causes of the shift towards Leipzig lay elsewhere.

The Reformation had unquestionably moved the spiritual and intellectual centre of Germany out of the Catholic south to the Protestant north. The increasing use of German as the national language displaced Latin. To make matters worse, the centre for trade had gradually shifted from west to east, substantially undermining Frankfurt's status in general and its Fair in particular. The trade route along the Rhine had been superseded by the route along the Elbe leading to and from the port of Hamburg. French, Spanish, English, and Dutch merchandise came into Germany through Hamburg, as well as products from the colonies. Along with Germany's major seaport of Hamburg, linked by the Elbe, Leipzig and its Fair achieved new significance; in effect, the two cities became interdependent and complemented one another in many ways.

The Frankfurt Fair deteriorated along with its affiliated book fair. In 1719, the Frankfurt chronicle noted that many bookshops had been converted into wine bars and taverns. By 1723 the once-imposing Frankfurt Fall Fair Book Catalogue was composed of only twenty pages. In Frankfurt there were a few desperate attempts to stave off the inevitable. The incumbent imperial book commissioner, the Cathedral's dean, von Scheben, asked the emperor to withdraw future Fair privileges from all book dealers who did not include the Frankfurt Fair among those attended. In addition, he set up a warehouse for north German publishers for books on commission, but this closed almost immediately, most probably because of opposition from Frankfurt book dealers.

Franz Varrentrapp, a Frankfurt publisher, in a particularly desperate act, tried to circumvent the Imperial Book Commission and attempted to set up a rival book fair twenty kilometres away in Hanau. Initially the local government refused him permission, suspecting a "copiers' fair," but in 1773 the crown prince of Hessen approved a renewed request because of Frankfurt's pronounced and obvious decline. This, in turn, was countered by Philipp Erasmus Reich, now a Leipzig book dealer, who nurtured a long-standing animosity towards Frankfurt and Varrentrapp.

Philipp Erasmus Reich, renowned Leipzig book dealer and outspoken critic of the Frankfurt Book Fair, 1764.

In 1775 Philipp Erasmus Reich, with the co-operation of the Frankfurt Imperial Book Commission, obtained an imperial prohibition order against attendance at the Hanau Fair by any Frankfurt book dealer. Franz Varrentrapp disregarded the edict and arrived in Hanau, but only fourteen book dealers appeared on the scene. In 1776, still another Hanau Fair took place, but with even fewer participants. The fate of this short-lived attempt to compete with Frankfurt was effectively sealed.

In fact, the final bell on the Frankfurt Book Fair had already rung two years earlier. For the Easter Fair in 1774, Philipp Erasmus Reich travelled through Weimar, Erfurt, Eisenach, Fulda, Gelnhausen, and Hanau, before returning to Frankfurt for the last time. He convinced the remaining north German printers, publishers, and book dealers — including some from southern Germany — to remove Frankfurt from their itineraries and instead come directly to Leipzig. On his return to Leipzig, he wrote in obvious satisfaction, "At the last Book Fair, along with various other friends from Frankfurt-am-Main, I took my final leave and more or less personally wrote off the Book Dealers' Fair located there."

Part Two

~~~

Leipzig's Era of Supremacy (1764-1861)

An 1840 set of copper-engraved images relating to Leipzig's historic past.

Chapter 8
Leipzig's Historic Role

In the pitched battle between Germany's two major book fairs in the eighteenth century, Leipzig emerged victorious. And, for participating publishers and printers, the city would remain in the forefront for almost a century. Like Frankfurt, since the Middle Ages Leipzig had gradually become a major centre of the book trade. Strategically, it opened a door to visitors from the east, while Frankfurt had been more accessible to those arriving from the west and south. Although admittedly incomplete, records of the time indicate that fairs were already being held in Leipzig in 1268. And from 1475 onwards, the existence of commerce in books at the Leipzig Fair has been carefully documented.

In spite of early efforts to make Leipzig the centre of the book trade, it would be another three hundred years before this became a reality. While the printers and publishers coming from far and wide had enjoyed enormous success in Frankfurt, since 1478 the European dealers in handwritten manuscripts remained predominantly in Leipzig. In the first two decades of the sixteenth century, however, increasing numbers of publishers from Nuremberg, Augsburg, Rostock, and even Basel had begun to appear in Saxony's city on the River Pleisse.

The Reformation and the soaring book production that followed in its wake helped both cities. Yet Leipzig could have come more rapidly to the fore in the rivalry between the two fairs had it not been for a setback contained in the order issued on February 10, 1522, by the Catholic Duke Georg of Saxony, as a result of the Edict of Worms, forbidding the proliferation of Luther's writings. This prohibition was fortuitously cancelled in 1539 by the duke's successor, Heinrich the Pious, and in the years that followed, the number of visitors to the fair in Leipzig increased accordingly. As well, commerce with the east became increasingly profitable, and this was yet another factor in Leipzig's growing success.

By the mid-sixteenth century, production in the city's publishing houses was also on the rise; however, Frankfurt continued to maintain its pre-eminent position as the recognized centre for scholarly and scientific publications, thanks largely to its long-standing ties to so many foreign countries. But when it came to commerce in domestic books, Leipzig was forging ahead, and by 1586 it surpassed Frankfurt for the first time. A few years later, in 1595, a catalogue of the Leipzig Book Fair was published to enhance Leipzig's position in its ongoing competition with Frankfurt.

There is no question, however, that the Thirty Years' War (1618–1648) had a severely negative impact on the economies and book trade of both Frankfurt and Leipzig as well as those in the southwest. Frankfurt also suffered from the withdrawal of the Catholic book trade, which had chosen to patronize the fairs held in Salzburg and Prague, where Catholicism was still firmly entrenched. To make matters worse, Frankfurt's economy was adversely affected by the ambitious wars of Louis XIV along the Rhine and also by the War of the Spanish Succession. Leipzig, on the other hand, remained undisturbed to reap the benefit of its rival's misfortune.

Because of the unsettled political and economic climate in Frankfurt, foreign publishing houses were keeping their distance, and, as a result, an increasingly greater share of the market gravitated towards Leipzig. However, with the introduction of commission trading, which was the real key to Leipzig's success, the publishers themselves gradually began retreating into the background. A few publishers had already engaged independent book dealers or other Leipzig firms to handle their books on a commission basis, but before long the proprietors of larger book retailing warehouses realized the distinct advantages to be gained by following suit.

> A prime example of commission trading was the business operated by the former wine merchant Pantzschmann, who had founded a publishing company with Ludwig Horncken and Gottfried Hittorp of Cologne with subsidiaries in Wittenberg and Prague. It was only a matter of time before the sale of books was no longer confined to the Fairs themselves, since a brisk trade in books was also being conducted between Fairs.[35]

The character of the Leipzig Book Fair changed even further during the course of the eighteenth century with the introduction of procedures that no longer required the personal presence of the book dealer at the Fair. Instead, he would send a representative or simply give his order to another book dealer on his behalf. Given the fact that the fairs took place only twice a year, and the public demand for books was on the rise, the dealers were quickly persuaded that it would be to their advantage to accept book orders between fairs. The obvious solution presented itself with the introduction of commissioned sales representatives. The book dealers generally maintained a warehouse and sales area in Leipzig for one or more publishers, and were now in a position to fill any and all orders that might be placed with them between the two annual fairs.

Leipzig's "cash or even trade" policy also resulted in another new development that evolved in the form of "conditional sales" or "sales on consignment." A business could choose to operate using traditional and accepted practices based on small capital outlay; however, under this alternative arrangement, the acquisition of new publications meant book dealers had to pay in cash — even if the publisher were willing to extend credit until the next fair. The publishers or their agents on commission rapidly established the practice of selling their books conditionally, or on consignment. The books then remained the property of the publisher until the dealer had sold them. And, for his part, the book dealer had until the next fair to pay the publisher for the copies he had sold. He could then send back the unsold copies, or — with the publisher's agreement — he could arrange to have them put on a new conditional account, if he thought he could sell them in the course of the coming year.

The Leipzig Book Dealers' Fair

Since the beginning of the sixteenth century, the Leipzig Book Dealers' Fair had been held in the area encompassing the Nicolai Church, Ritter, University, Grimmaischen, and Nicolai streets, as well as the Neumarkt or New Marketplace. Here the so-called foreign dealers rented stalls for themselves and hung out their brass nameplates. At the stroke of seven in the evening, the city watchmen ensured that the stalls in front of the storage-sales areas were closed, and in the adjacent accounts office, activity was temporarily suspended. Behind the scenes, however, business still continued and accounts were meticulously recorded.

By the middle of the sixteenth century, accounts were usually settled on a half-yearly basis. They were calculated from the Easter to the Michaelmas (or Fall) Fair, and once again at the following Easter Fair. Later, in the second half of the eighteenth century, as attendance at the Fall Fair gradually diminished, all accounts were settled on an annual basis.

For the "foreigners" who attended the Fair (anyone from outside Saxony), the experience often proved to be both time-consuming and strenuous. In 1714, a certain Herr Elers, representing a book dealership attached to the orphanage in Halle, recorded his personal impressions of a day at the Fair: "Business begins at 5 a.m. Not only do you receive visitors at this ungodly hour, but you must also be prepared to make visits yourself. These visits kept me fully occupied until 8 p.m., when I was so exhausted that I could scarcely control the movement of my tongue after an entire day of what seemed like an endless series of calculations."

The Leipzig Book Dealers' Fair made its particular mark of distinction in the eighteenth and nineteenth centuries, when it gave birth to a system that was considered to be among the most advanced and finely tuned in the world. It was a system that, in fact, still distinguishes the German book trade to this day.

The Birth of a Model System

In the early stages of the developmental phase of the German book trade, Philipp Erasmus Reich (1717–1787) had already begun making a name for himself as a leading Leipzig dealer. Among other things, he undertook an attempt to institute order into the chaos of the book trade, which had evolved as a by-product of the Fair itself. At the Easter Fair of 1765, he founded the first Book Dealers' Association, which immediately attracted the membership of fifty-six dealers. One of the newly established association's principal objectives was to find effective ways of dealing with the pressing question of illegal pirated editions.

In his inaugural speech at the founding ceremonies of the association, Reich expressed the unspoken concerns of many of his colleagues, namely the unimpeded and widespread production of unauthorized copies of books. It was a practice to which printers and publishers appeared to be either oblivious or showed no particular awareness of any wrongdoing: "Theft is universally considered as a punishable crime, but unauthorized copying is not yet recognized as such, nor are there any appropriate consequences, although it is no less a crime on the part of the perpetrator, and the effect and consequences for the victim are no less than that of a violent robbery." In Reich's opinion, the biannual Frankfurt Book Fairs had become the "copiers' Fair of the Empire" because so many of the pirate printers appeared there to do business — with the tacit approval of the imperial book commissioners. In 1773, as a result of persistent pressure on

Reich's part, an order was issued by the government of Saxony that forbade the sale of pirated books or trade in unauthorized copies at the Leipzig Fair. This was effectively a major triumph for Reich and his campaign against pirated editions.

Reich was also in complete agreement with the major Leipzig publishers on the policy of "cash or even trade" policy established in 1780. The Frankfurt tradition of exchange trading — at least as far as the Leipzig market was concerned — was no longer viable.

The Exchange Association

For a number of reasons, the lifespan of the Book Dealers' Association founded by the imperial government was relatively short. Among the competing participants at the Leipzig Book Fair, the time was not yet ripe for activities in the common interest. Finally, the dealers present at the Fair in 1788 began to discuss the possibility of creating a general collection and accounting centre in order "to cut down on the annual business paperwork and where an annual general assembly could receive written proposals for actions in the common interest, and unanimous decisions could be taken." At that time, Johann Gottlob Immanuel Breitkopf estimated that roughly three hundred foreign book dealers came each year to the Leipzig Fair, and their business at the Fairs generated the princely sum of approximately one million thalers.

Three years later, in 1791, a publisher identified only as Herr Göschen decided to pursue the obvious merits of establishing a central counting house. The following year Paul Gotthelf Kummer, a like-minded Leipzig publisher, went one step further and set up an accounting office in premises rented for the duration of the Fair on the second floor of the well-known Richter Coffee House, which even Schiller had patronized and praised its popular punch. On April 10, 1792, Hungarian-born Carl Christian Horvath, who would later become the honorary president of the Book Dealers' Exchange Association, enthusiastically endorsed Kummer's foresight: "I embrace you as a true friend for having rescued me from all the endless and tiresome running around that we have been subjected to in the past and I remain in all sincerity...."

A certain Herr Johann Philipp Palm, a dealer from Erlangen, offered his own words of wisdom in the hope that "more good than just the facilitation of book business during the Fair will be the end result," and added that it could well lead to "the clarification of many points of confusion and disorder through open discussion and a united effort." Another book dealer, Friedrich Severin from Weissenfels, insisted that the thorny issue of pirated editions should be dealt with immediately. Here Reich's recommendations were once again brought forward and proposals made that went well beyond establishing an accounting office and an improved organizational structure for all future fairs.

There were, as always, critics who were very much opposed to such an undertaking, and they also made no secret of their views. Friedrich Nicolai from Berlin put forward in writing a detailed argument citing the inevitable indiscretion, controversy, and unpleasant scenes that could be avoided by maintaining the status quo. The foreign dealers were particularly concerned that local dealers in Leipzig would not participate, and "were responsible almost exclusively for the Fairs' hectic pace and not remotely interested in easing the lot of those dealers who had to travel 60, 80, 100 or more miles as well as risking life and limb." The following year, when the local dealers heard the news that Herr Kummer's troublesome proposal on behalf of the foreigners had fallen flat, they were hard-pressed to contain their delight.

In 1795, Carl Christian Horvath (1752–1837) from Potsdam, a dealer named Ernst from Quedlinburg, and a Herr Kaffke from Stettin joined forces to review the matter once more. The three leased the Auditorium Theologicum at the university on the lower floor of the Paulinum, in the heart of the book dealers' quarter. Their rent amounted to one hundred thalers annually plus an additional twenty for service and storage of the books during the Fair's Exchange, known as the Börse. (Tradition has it that the word Börse originated from Van der Beurse, the surname of a noble Belgian family. In the past, international merchants had made a habit of meeting in front of the Van der Beurse house in Bruges in order to determine prices and rates of exchange.) For the use of space in the rented auditorium in Leipzig, each book dealer had to pay Horvath one thaler; however, since profit-sharing was not part of the arrangement, Horvath was later accused of having lined his own pockets at the expense of his fellow dealers.

Friedrich Johann Frommann from Jena, for many years a member of the board of directors and several times its president, as well as the historian of the Exchange Association, penned a detailed description of the Horvath enterprise:

> The whole room was furnished with tables, each with two chairs, even the balconies were wide enough to take a long row of tables around the edge. On entering the room, you turned immediately to the right towards the single window which overlooked the Pauline courtyard. Here old Horvath had set up his table in order to collect the one thaler entry fee. On a chart, the name of the company the payee represented was written in Horvath's clear hand and endorsed with his stamp. This chart was held in safe-keeping from one Fair to the next and duly stamped on each subsequent occasion.
>
> Many Exchange dealers had pre-selected designated tables for their personal use. When each individual had found his man, taken a seat, and opened his account books, the usual routine began: "My side" … "Your side" … "Agreed" or "Not agreed." In cases when no agreement could be struck, the disputing parties went into conference at a special arbitration desk, however this seldom led to a settlement, with the result that they were then directed to: "Pay according to your account book and make up the difference when you get home." When the accounting was completed, the amount of the outstanding balance was noted,

then the rate of exchange applied to the amount in ducats or Louis d'or. But even then, the matter was not yet concluded, for each would then bring out his list of new publications, and the other would indicate what he thought he could sell. These orders were then promised for delivery before the close of the Fair and finally the two parties would enter into friendly conversation about business in general and other matters of mutual interest.

By the beginning of the nineteenth century, the number of book dealers in Leipzig had trebled since 1726. In 1806 there were fifty-nine dealerships, twenty-three printers accounting for a total of about ninety presses, three type manufacturers, and forty copperplaters. Four years later, in 1810, the Leipzig Book Dealers' Fairs recorded the participation of 280 foreign dealers.

Until 1824, the Exchange in the Paulinum remained a private enterprise controlled by Horvath, but changes were imminent. On April 30, 1825, under the leadership of Friedrich Campe from Nuremberg and B.F. Voigt from Jena, the foreign book dealers turned the Exchange into a co-operative enterprise after founding an association that adopted a constitution incorporating its own specific regulations. This action definitively marked the birth of the Exchange Association, an alliance of professionals within the book trade — an association that, in fact, continues to exist to the present day. The same year also marked the official prohibition in Saxony of all pirated editions.

The issues dealt with by the association included the development of copyright laws and the publication of reference bibliographies. Horvath was elected honorary chairman and Friedrich Campe became chairman along with B.F. Voigt and J.L. Schrag. The newly founded association did not, however, immediately adopt the name "Exchange Association." Until 1830 only the 645 foreign book dealers were eligible as members, the book dealers in Leipzig having already formed their own association. At the Easter Fair of 1830 the executive (C. Duncker and Wilhelm Perthes) of the foreign dealers invited their Leipzig colleagues to a general meeting, and the following year the organization became known as the Joint Exchange. Then, at long last, in 1832, it permanently acquired the official name "The Exchange Association."

At the Easter Fairs of 1833 and 1834 the relationship between the two associations was such that the book dealing accounts in Leipzig were payable on a yearly basis and the exchange was open year-round to both associations. The first issue of the *Exchange News for German Book Dealers*, which still operates as a major professional journal, appeared on January 3, 1834. The *Exchange News* was first published by the Leipzig Book Dealers' Association, but ownership was acquired in 1835 by the Exchange Association. The first *Addressbook of German Book Dealers* was published in Leipzig in 1839. By 1842, Leipzig boasted 73 commissioned agents employed by 1,242 foreign book dealerships and the Exchange Association had 700 registered members.

The End of an Era

By the middle of the nineteenth century, the existing book fair system — almost unchanged since the Middle Ages — had clearly outlived its usefulness. The business of running a fair was becoming less and less viable. With a rapidly expanding road network coupled with the development of postal and communication systems, as well as the construction of the first railroad, the future of the Fair was far from secure. No longer did merchandise have to be transported over difficult and dangerous roads in order to reach the marketplace. The emerging communication systems could be used for placing orders and the railroads for the direct delivery of merchandise. Many railway lines already converged at Leipzig, but from 1839 to 1859 additional rail links were established between Leipzig and most of the major cities in Germany.

In 1840 the *Exchange News* complained that book retailers were no longer coming to the Leipzig Book Fair because there was scarcely any business for them there. The report went on to say that the only reason for attending was "to finalize the previous year's accounts and withdraw the balance." It went on to say that fewer and fewer senior company officials came to settle their accounts at the Exchange in person, preferring, instead, to send a designated representative — sometimes even a very junior employee — to do this on their behalf.

A partial solution to the attendance problems was achieved when Leipzig introduced the concept of so-called prototype fairs: "Modern mechanized mass production permitted a standardization of products, in contrast to handmade articles, with the result that careful scrutiny of the product was more or less superfluous. It was sufficient simply to have the model and nothing more."[36] By the end of the century, this transition to exclusively prototype fairs assured Leipzig a premier position among German fairs, and before long it was recognized as a leading centre throughout Europe.

The book trade, however, had long since become independent of the original Leipzig Book Fair. Instead, it had created a thriving production and business centre that acted, in effect, as an adjunct to the Fair. At the main commission headquarters of the German book trade in 1881, 142 agents represented 6,136 employers. Attendance at the Fair became a matter of who could still attract whom, and for what purpose.

By the second half of the nineteenth century, communication between branches of the book industry had become the main function of the Fair. In a spirit of good fellowship, connections were made not only among the like-minded but also among the representatives of special-interest publications. Eventually, the traditional term "book fair" was replaced by the more specific "book dealers' fair."[37] It was a sign of the times.

During the course of the nineteenth century, no real book fair of any consequence existed in Frankfurt, nor, for that matter, was its rival in Leipzig far behind, as the old century gradually advanced towards the new.

The German Book Dealers' House

The dedication of the German Book Dealers' House in Leipzig on April 28 and 29, 1888, which was presided over by His Majesty King Albert of Saxony, took place with all the pomp and ceremony for which the nineteenth century is renowned. As a rather amusing footnote, the list of those invited to attend the evening's celebratory banquet did not include the names of any women (including wives) since space for this gala event was at a very high premium. In any case, the business of dealing in books was, to all intents and purposes, an exclusively male domain. This, too, would change radically before another century had come and gone.

As a mark of its support and generosity, the City of Leipzig had recently donated a building site to the Exchange Association in the Great Johannis Garden on Hospital Street, but only on the condition that the property would revert to the City should the Exchange move or use the building for other purposes. Before any further conditions could be imposed, a building was immediately erected on the site in the style of a sixteenth-century north German city hall.

In the traditional sense, a book fair site had not actually existed in Leipzig since 1861. Almost all German publishers had set up their own commission and delivery outlets in the central part of the city. And many Europeans — among them Dutch, Swiss, Baltic, Austrian, Hungarian, and Czech — had established themselves in similar facilities. Their books were shipped out to all German-speaking lands, and also to eastern Europe — in particular to Poland and Russia, as well as the Baltic countries. The fact that special book trains left Leipzig on a daily basis is an indication of the amount of commerce generated by the book trade, in spite of the absence of an actual fair site.

Attempts at Renewal for the Leipzig Book Fair

Shortly before the outbreak of the First World War, an attempt was made to revive the former glory of the Leipzig Fair tradition.

From May 6 to October 18 of 1914, the first International World Exhibition of the Book Trade and Graphic Arts (BUGRA) was greeted with great enthusiasm — until news of the assassination of the Austrian crown prince, Archduke Franz Ferdinand, and his wife in the Bosnian capital of Sarajevo brought the event to an abrupt halt. With the commencement of hostilities, the Russian, French, and British pavilions were immediately dismantled, and shortly thereafter the fairgrounds became a centre for the training of militia. For the next four years, the production and sale of books were sidelined as trench warfare took its universal toll.

It is a real testimony to the resilience of the entrepreneurial spirit that less than a year after the 1918 Armistice, discussions were already underway to revive the Leipzig exhibition. A special book fair was planned in conjunction with the so-called BUGRA exhibition. But a series of disagreements between the Exchange Association and the German Book Trade Association failed to be resolved, and in the end the Book Trade Association independently mounted the first BUGRA exhibition in Leipzig in 1919. As a result, the Book Trade Association became the driving force in the revival of the Leipzig Fair tradition. Continued opposition from the Exchange was due to the fact that most of its members were still rooted in their conservative nineteenth-century convictions and simply would not be moved towards change in any way, shape, or form.

Despite the achievements of the nineteenth century, this ongoing dissension proved to be a distinct disadvantage for Leipzig's future. For one thing, the association did not see itself capable of meeting the new challenges of the book market — the book clubs and other merchandising tactics that were so foreign to the time-honoured ways of conducting business. Then, too, along with the social, political, and economic upheaval that came as the aftermath of the First World War, an alarming new American concept was introduced into postwar Germany in the form of widespread advertising and marketing of literary works. This new wrinkle came as a highly unwelcome intrusion that the old time book dealers felt bound to resist as vigorously as possible.

"Modernization" and "Americanization" had quickly become the catchwords of the era. The evolving mass market for books called for the use of bold new tactics. Among these were an acceleration of the production process and the introduction of shorter time frames for turnover and re-financing. The recipe devised by the American automotive giant Henry Ford and the theories of Frederick Winslow Taylor offered the best hope to maximize production and output.[38]

On April 19, 1919, editor Emil Thomas of the *Exchange News* wrote about the unrest in the various branches of the book trade in a review of its participation in the Leipzig model or prototype fair. This amounted to a plea to the Exchange Association to mount an independent exhibition dedicated only to books and all those involved in their production: publishers, manufacturers of paper and typesetting equipment, printers, graphic artists, producers, book binders, artists, and illustrators. Instead, a miniature BUGRA Fair was mounted within the Leipzig Prototype Fair in 1919, but without the support of the Exchange Association.

The modest success of this first BUGRA Fair led to another meeting in the Book Dealers' House among the chief representatives of the Exchange Association, the Book Trade Association, the Leipzig book dealers, and the Leipzig Fair Management to discuss the participation of the book trade within the Leipzig Prototype Fair. Finally it was decided to mount another BUGRA Fair during the week of "Kantate" Sunday (the fourth Sunday after Easter) that would be held more or less in conjunction with the regular Spring Fair. Later in the year, the so-called Christmas BUGRA would be mounted between November 24 and December 23 and would also include an exhibition with books for sale. The board members of the Exchange Association, who were also publishers, actually agreed with this plan, but at least one retail book dealer expressed steadfast opposition.

The first "Kantate" BUGRA Fair took place from April 29 to May 5, 1920, in the BUGRA Fair House at 38 Peter Street. This fair was planned to coincide with the financial year-end visits to Leipzig of the foreign book dealers and publishers. Six weeks prior to this — from February 19 to March 6 — a small-scale BUGRA Fair with three hundred exhibitors had taken place within the context of the regular Leipzig Fair. According to the director of the Leipzig Fair Authority, it was not particularly successful for the participating book dealers, but the concept of a book trade BUGRA incorporated within the biannual Leipzig Fairs continued until the Fall Fair in 1928. The following year, 1929, it was eventually cancelled because of general lack of interest. In fact, all further efforts and discussion concerning the revival of a book fair of any kind proved unsuccessful. Germany was on the threshold of political change that would dramatically alter its future for decades to come.

It was not until after the Second World War that dispersals and currency devaluation led to a clean slate for the book industry — at least in West Germany, where massive reconstruction was actively being undertaken. It was only a matter of time before the opportunity to renew the great German book fair tradition was set in motion.

Part Three

~~~

The Frankfurt Book Fairs
of the Twentieth Century

Chapter 9

Early Attempts at Revival

In Frankfurt, after the First World War, there were widespread concerns about the idea of reviving the old fair traditions. It was recognized, however, that the earlier success of the Leipzig Prototype Fairs had proved that this could become a viable option, and as a result the first International Frankfurt Fair took place from October 1 to October 10, 1919. Following the Leipzig example, it was conceived as a model or prototype fair and as such deviated radically from the previous combination of an annual market and an exhibition of commercial merchandise. For the next ten years, until spring 1929 when the worldwide financial crash made it impossible to hold any kind of fair or exhibition anywhere in Germany, most fairs opened their doors every spring and fall.

On July 27, 1919, the *Frankfurt News* greeted word of this new beginning in euphoric terms: "Finally, success! Everyone would like to applaud the fact that after years of effort by local dignitaries, a Frankfurt Fair is now assured...." Simultaneously there was a demand that a book fair again be established in Frankfurt:

> We must not forget that Frankfurt once, and indeed as early as the sixteenth century, was the hub of the German book trade, and, for that matter, of the European book trade as well. All the large book

printers and publishers visited our Fairs regularly. Leipzig has managed to sustain itself and enjoyed great success in attracting the book trade. Now it behooves Frankfurt to organize a concerted effort to bring the book trade back home permanently.

The Frankfurt Fair Authority possessed neither book trade expertise nor connections to the institutions of the industry that had long ago become concentrated in Leipzig. In addition, the past difficulties experienced by the Leipzig Fair were well known, as were their attempts to include the book business as an integral part of their fair.

Frankfurt, therefore, sought out another source with connections in the book trade and found it in the newly constituted German Association for Foreign Book Trade, founded in Leipzig in May 1919. This association was the brainchild of the well-known head of Insel Publishing Company, Anton Kippenberg. In Kippenberg's inaugural address, he clarified the association's objectives, stating, "We, as publishers, command significant economic resources, but we are also aware of our obligation to deliver the most valuable service to the German people as a whole through the proliferation of German books and literature abroad." It was, therefore, the main mission of the association to increase the export of German books after the enormous losses in foreign book markets caused by the First World War. The increasingly nationalistic public statements issued by the association may be attributed to the times. In any case, it seems that difficulties over the export of books were far from being resolved.

The marked animosity towards anything German, be it books, Baedekers, teaching materials, music, or whatever, was not especially engendered by fear of competition on the part of French and English publishers. Rather, it can be more directly attributed to the attitude of the French and English governments that wherever the sale of German books made any appreciable inroads, it could well be an indication that this was simply the thin edge of the wedge and that other German exports might readily follow. According to the relatively restrained statement issued in "Memorandum One" from the association, the challenges of winning over their former enemies would demand great fortitude.

The tone was significantly sharper in "Memorandum Two," entitled "The Battle in Foreign Countries Against the German Book — the most Representative and Distinctive Element of the German Character." The use of terms such as "hate campaign" and "poisonous assaults" are reminiscent of the propaganda that would later become an integral part of the Nazi Party's rise to power. In England, Alec Waugh's controversial book that took a conciliatory stance towards Germany created a huge furor. As one critic wrote, "Alec Waugh will certainly not enjoy the success of changing our opinion about the Huns ... nor will he make us want to shake the blood-spattered hand which wrought such unholy and immense suffering in the world." Commentaries of this nature were quoted by the German association as an indication of the desperate need to reverse the situation. A further example of what they were faced with is contained in another quotation emanating from France.

In the Bibliographie de la France, No. 27 (July 1919), the Hachette Company made an announcement in a two-page advertisement for its "Blue Guides": "The Baedekers have finally been driven out of France. It is not appropriate to help those who destroyed our cities and towns to guide our fellow citizens and friends to their destinations or ruins. The most powerful French tourist organizations have deemed it an honour to take over the guardianship of the industry." At the end of the advertisement, in large, bold letters spread over both pages, were these final words of caution: "To buy or sell the Baedeker Guidebook is to give money to Germany."[39]

Quite aside from the economic problems of the time, the struggle to promote the export of German books was bound to encounter similar attitudes in virtually any potential marketplace beyond the confines of its borders. As it stood, the situation scarcely presented a solid basis for a flourishing foreign trade within the context of an international fair. In any event, as an independent organization, the well-intentioned Association for

Foreign Book Trade managed to pursue its goals for a total of only three years and nine months. During its brief lifespan, however, it successfully organized book exhibitions such as "Het Duitse Boek" ("The German Book") in The Hague from January 7 to February 8, 1922, and another display at the International Book Fair in Florence, from May through July of 1922. It also published a journal, *The German Book*, which included periodic updates on the Frankfurt Exhibition Catalogue, and at one point it boasted that it had accumulated more than five thousand subscribers.

Sadly, in the Association for Foreign Book Trade, the Frankfurt Fair Authority had not found an ideal partner to help it in its attempts to revive the Frankfurt Book Fair tradition. On the other hand, word of these plans was the cause of great concern in Leipzig, where plans for its own fair were not progressing well. As a result, the association complained in a letter on July 23, 1920, to the Frankfurt Fair Authority's director, Herr Modlinger:

> The Leipzig Fair Authority made an official visit to us yesterday, and vehemently demanded to know why our Association was conducting propaganda in foreign countries on behalf of the Frankfurt Fair Authority. It was — they alleged — absolutely absurd that an Association based in Leipzig should promote the interests of the Frankfurt Fair Authority in this way…. Then today the representative of the Saxon government came to us complaining that we had not informed them about our intentions in Frankfurt and enquired whether we could not cancel our exhibition plans there.

Nonetheless, "The German Book," a bravely ambitious undertaking, opened for the first time in 1920 within the Third International Frankfurt Fair from October 3 to 20 in the Viktoriahaus (the Victoria School, Hohenzollernplatz, located approximately where the Marriott Hotel stands today). It was clearly not a commercial exhibition in the traditional sense and was essentially based on the premise of making the cultural character of the book useful for political and economic reasons. The 1920 edition of the periodical *Book Trade and Graphics Record,* Vol. 9/10, contained the following description:

> The exhibition was designed to open a special door for the German book. This last and most powerful weapon left to us, does not take life but renews it.... In the great struggle against the economic upheaval that has followed the end of the War, it is an opportunity for us to make a show of strength, not as means of spreading political propaganda, but as a vehicle for displaying Germany's intellectual history and knowledge....

Within the exhibition, the majority of the books were arranged according to publisher. Beyond this, there was a so-called Milieu Display, designed to stimulate interest and possible sales among book buyers. This section consisted of a wide variety of individual "libraries," each decorated with appropriate furnishings, among them "The Library of the Middle-Class Home," "The Library of a Lady," "The Music Salon," "The Children's Room," "The Literary Writer's Room," "The Work Room of a Theatre Director," "The Library of an Engineer and Architect," "A Booklover's Library," and "The Sixteenth-Century Scholar's Room" — the latter made up from the stock of antique dealer Josef Baer. The library concept was an imaginative attempt at innovation that attracted at least a modicum of attention and approval. But its success was fleeting at best. With the onslaught of the Great Depression and the rise of National Socialism, the future success of Germany's book fairs became little more than a distant dream as the spectre of an impending war once more threatened to engulf the world.

Poster announcing the Grand Opening of the 1949 Frankfurt Book Fair.

Chapter 10
ᨍᨍᨍ
The Frankfurt Phoenix

The Second World War broke out in September of 1939, and almost six years would pass before the German surrender to the Allies on May 8, 1945. Just prior to this, on April 17, Leipzig was occupied by the Americans. Two months later, with the division of Germany into military zones, the city was handed over to the Soviet Military Administration. Before pulling out, however, the Americans arranged for a group of Leipzig publishers to leave in a convoy bound for Wiesbaden in the American sector of occupied Germany.

Before the end of the war, seven hundred book dealers still existed in Leipzig. Although an attempt was made in the first decade after 1945 to re-establish Leipzig and its fair as the book capital of the German Democratic Republic, the centre of the East German publishing industry gradually shifted to Berlin. In 1946, the Soviet Military Administration in Germany granted permission to the Leipzig Exchange Association to resume business, and the opportunity was immediately taken up, with the result that the first Leipzig Peace Book Fair was mounted in the newly reconstructed Fair Palace that same year, with twenty-eight Leipzig publishers participating. At the next Leipzig Book Fair, in the spring of 1947, seventy publishers from the Soviet-occupied zone participated, along with twenty from the other zones, as well as publishers from ten other European countries and even from Mexico and Uruguay.

There was, however, a notable absence of Western publishers — especially from the United States — publishers who had made a point of turning down the invitation.

A year later in 1948 between May 8 and May 23 a similar undertaking took place in a newly established Frankfurt Exhibition housed in the old Frankfurt Exchange that had come through the wartime bombing of the city relatively intact. The organizers' plan was to establish Frankfurt's superiority over other competing West German cities in a bid to become the new transshipment centre for the book trade. Among those actively involved in this postwar initiative were the commissioned agents who were now exclusively based in Frankfurt. Given the circumstances, this attempt could be considered quite successful, but the currency reform of June 1948 and its effect on buying power held severe implications for the future of the book business in West Germany. This was clearly demonstrated the following autumn at the Frankfurt General Fair. Among the 1771 exhibitors represented in Frankfurt at the first "German Mark" Fair, only a few publishers and book dealers took the risk of setting up exhibits and, in fact, their presence was scarcely noticed. It was clear that the book market urgently needed reorientation and new opportunities to expand and flourish.

The Book Dealers' and Publishers' Association of the State of Hessen in the neighbouring city of Wiesbaden had been considering the idea of mounting a book exhibition in 1949 during the Goethe memorial year as a means of reviving the book market in Frankfurt. Perhaps the strongest advocate for the revival of the Frankfurt Book Fair was Alfred Grade, the association's president of the board, and a former book dealer from Halle.

In March 1949, a Frankfurt Fair Committee was formed that included Grade, publisher Walter Gericke from Wiesbaden, Frankfurt book dealer Dr. Bergmann of Blazek & Bergmann, Gottfried Löbmann, a senior executive of Dietrich Publishing, and the publisher of the *Frankfurt Exchange News*. This publication had been set up in Wiesbaden two years after the war's end, since Wiesbaden was one of the few cities in

Germany that had escaped heavy damage. Mayor Walter Kolb of Frankfurt was supportive of the idea, and Deputy Mayor Walter Leske, previously from Leipzig, was equally enthusiastic and also familiar with the concept. In May, the so-called First Fair Committee attempted to rent St. Paul's Church (Paulskirche), which had been recently rebuilt in honour of the centenary celebration of the first German Parliament. It was only after considerable and lengthy negotiations that the committee was successful in acquiring the use of the premises.

The Frankfurt Exchange Association and its predecessor, the Professional Union of German Publishers' and Book Dealers' Organizations, now based in Frankfurt, did not initially endorse the Frankfurt Fair initiative. On the other hand, its president, Vittorio Klosterman, was later instrumental in re-establishing the Frankfurt Book Fair by personally guaranteeing a bank loan for that express purpose.

At the June meeting of the new Exchange Association, which took place in Cologne, it was to be decided where the general meeting of all members of the individual book dealers' organizations in all jurisdictions was to be held. Alfred Grade travelled to Cologne, but was denied the opportunity, despite written and oral requests, to speak about the Frankfurt project. Instead the association endorsed an exhibition of 160 southwestern German publishers to be held in Stuttgart.

Even the *Exchange News*, No. 63, of August 23, 1949, scarcely mentioned the Frankfurt Book Fair, which was to take place September 18 to 25 in St. Paul's Church, while full coverage was given to the exhibition in Stuttgart and still another in Hamburg. It is difficult to find an explanation for the antipathy of the Exchange Association and the West German publishers towards the Frankfurt initiative. Perhaps it was simply that the lobby in favour of the competing cities was stronger because they had more regional book dealers. What's more, at this point, the number of publishing houses in and around Frankfurt was relatively small, and the original Frankfurt Book Fair tradition was still overshadowed by Leipzig's more recent prominence.

Gradually members of the First Fair Committee abandoned the concept of a Frankfurt Book Fair in favour of the potential of rebuilding closer to home. The Frankfurt undertaking seemed destined for failure. Against all odds, by the middle of July, just eight weeks before the opening of the Frankfurt Book Fair, Alfred Grade found that he could count on one hundred exhibitors. At this juncture, Grade's enterprise also benefited greatly from the co-operation of Heinrich Cobet, co-owner of the Frankfurt Book Room, who agreed to serve on the Fair Commission. Cobet was an enthusiastic champion of the concept and had extensive and important connections that would be very helpful in this first postwar enterprise. When Alfred Grade became bedridden for a lengthy period following a serious fall in his shop, the full weight of the preparations was taken over by none other than the tireless promoter of the Book Fair, Heinrich Cobet.

As a first step, Cobet brought Wilhelm Müller to Frankfurt to serve as the first official director of the Frankfurt Book Fair at a monthly salary of DM 350 with a promised bonus of DM 500 if the Fair proved to be a success. The two men had once served together in Nazi-occupied Paris churning out propaganda for the German Army, and it was through this wartime connection that Cobet had become aware of Captain Müller's great organizational talents. Josephine Diehl, an employee in Grade's bookshop, was taken on as the director's only assistant, and together in their makeshift headquarters the two worked tirelessly night and day to accomplish their goal. What they desperately needed was a substantial increase in the number of exhibitors.

According to Müller, the Fair "office" had been creatively furnished with two crates and a suitably broad plank from Cobet's antiquarian shop, plus two broken-down chairs and an ancient typewriter. But results were what really mattered, and in this regard, the efforts of these two optimists were crowned with success. And thanks to astute budgeting, they were in a position to cover the estimated outlay of DM 30,000. They were able, as well, to establish equitable policies for displays, and remarkably these same policies and principles remained in place into the 1980s. All fittings, equipment, and furnishings were included in the rental costs for a booth. This lent a uniform appearance to the displays, which were available in four sizes and priced accordingly: DM 100, DM 140, and a select few at DM 280 and DM 320. These display policies also allowed smaller publishing houses, who often devoted themselves to younger, avant-garde authors, to feel they could hold their own beside their larger competitors.

When Alfred Grade was asked twenty-five years later to offer his explanation for the remarkable success of the Frankfurt Book Fair, he replied, "I have given the answer a few times over the years that the technical limitations of the Paulskirche space determined the democratic spirit of our actions and that it is this same spirit that has been the true source of the Fair's success."

Grade's answer is, in fact, only a part of the real story. There is no question that the circumstances he describes helped to determine the special character of the Frankfurt exposition, but the decisive factors that led to its meteoric rise in stature as the leading book fair in the world lie elsewhere. Following the currency reform, the beginnings of the unparalleled economic growth in the West German Republic and the consolidation of the book market were both hugely important elements in the growth of the Fair. But these same factors also applied to competing fair initiatives in other West German cities. There was, however, another fortunate circumstance that played an important role in setting the Frankfurt Book Fair on its own unique path towards future prominence.

When the first Frankfurt Book Fair was opened on Saturday, September 17, 1949, in St. Paul's Church, book lovers had already had a week's time in the neighbouring town hall — the Römer — to visit a book exhibition mounted by the Syndicat National des Éditeurs (National Union of Publishers), which the High Commission in Germany for the Republic of France had already planned, and, at Cobet's request, arranged to coincide with the opening of the Book Fair in St. Paul's Church.

In his opening speech, André François-Poncet, the high commissioner of the French Occupation Zone, took as his central theme the role of the book in reviving and renewing bonds between the two peoples, and how very necessary it was to foster cultural co-operation between France and Germany. Only a few days later, at the opening of the Book Fair, the living proof of his words about the importance of books was there for all to see. More than 200 German exhibitors displayed some 8,400 titles to roughly 14,000 visitors at the first Frankfurt Book Fair in St. Paul's Church.

Exhibitors at Frankfurt's first postwar book fair in St. Paul's Church, 1949.

Moreover, in addition to France, a second European country was also exhibiting in Frankfurt in early September 1949. From September 1 to 16, just one day before the opening of the Frankfurt Fair on the seventeenth, a group of Swiss book dealers held an exhibition in the Frankfurt Exchange building. Heinrich Cobet had tried to convince the chairman of the Swiss book dealers to hold this exhibit within the timeframe of the Book Fair, but to no avail. In spite of this, the revival of the Frankfurt Book Fair was very carefully observed, with the result that the following year Switzerland sent forty-four exhibitors — the largest foreign publishing contingent at the Fair.

Undoubtedly reports about the first Frankfurt Book Fair in both France and Switzerland were a factor in bringing its existence to the attention of the book trade in other countries. In any event, much to the surprise of the organizers, without any targeted promotion, the second Frankfurt Book Fair attracted 100 foreign exhibitors in addition to 360 German dealers and publishing houses. The signs were hopeful that the Frankfurt Book Fair was destined for an international future.

In addition, the Exchange Association abandoned its initial reservations. Immediately after the conclusion of the first Frankfurt Book Fair, the chairman of the Exchange Association wrote asking the local association of Hessen to make its wishes known with regard to the Book Fair. Without waiting for a reply, the executive decided unanimously that "in the future, the Frankfurt Book Fair will be conducted under the auspices of the Exchange Association," and further agreed to set up a standing committee for displays with Fair Director Wilhelm Müller acting as business manager. The committee was to "deal with all questions relating to displays and, as well, with exhibitions of German books in foreign countries."[40]

Even the *Exchange News* declared itself willing and able to print a report of the event. Director Müller duly reported on the finances of the Fair with the impressive figure of over two and a half million Deutschmarks in registered turnover by exhibitors. At the same time, he made public a few letters he had received that clearly reflected the positive attitude of the participants. Perhaps more significant, however — from the standpoint of the German book trade — was the report in the *Exchange News* published by the Exchange Association of Leipzig, which described the success of that city's long-time rival. In the commentator's opinion, it looked as if Frankfurt could well be in a position to once again assume the leading role in the centuries-old rivalry between the two book fair locations.

The article of October 15, 1949, began appropriately with a description of the alleged success of the Leipzig Fair. It had celebrated its conclusion only a few weeks earlier with the declaration that,

"Although temporarily hampered by economic and political factors, as the site of a Book Trade and Fair, Leipzig can never be overlooked by those involved in the trade." This was followed by a mention of the experiences of the "East Occupation Zone publishing houses" during their visit to Frankfurt. Since they had decided only at the last minute to participate in the Frankfurt Fair, the majority of the Leipzig exhibitors could not be accommodated in Paulskirche and had to find display space nearby in the vicinity of the Platz der Republik. Only four publishers from the Soviet Occupation Zone could be accommodated within the main exhibition in the church.

After a lengthy and positive review of many of the new titles released by West German publishers, the real thrust of the article suddenly became very clear. At the close of the Frankfurt Book Fair, according to the author of the article, it was obvious that the West German book trade had already launched itself in new directions. These initiatives veered from the traditionally conservative book trade principles that had governed the competition in the 1920s, towards an emphasis on creating a stronger market economy. In Leipzig, by contrast, the old principles were still in place and destined to remain so for several more decades.

The author then provided some truly alarming examples of the new trends in evidence in Frankfurt, citing one West German publisher whose titles included Churchill's memoirs, Montgomery's *El Alamein to the River Sangro: Normandy to the Baltic,* Eisenhower's *Invasion,* and Sir Samuel Hoare's popular *Ambassador on a Special Mission* — four American-style bestsellers presented in a discreet black volume. As a final word of caution, the article warned of the serious danger facing the entire West German book trade. Unless they quickly changed direction, they were on the brink of sinking into the "superficiality of mere trading in books."

It goes without saying that no amount of criticism from Leipzig, the old book trade capital, could undo what had taken place in Frankfurt in the autumn of 1949. Four years later, the British publisher Sir Stanley Unwin opened the Frankfurt Book Fair of 1953 with the slogan "A Frankfurt Phoenix has risen from Leipzig's ashes."

In retrospect, it must be noted that the success of the "Phoenix" was based almost entirely on the efforts of three determined men of vision with an unshakeable belief in the importance of their endeavour: Alfred Grade, Heinrich Cobet, and Wilhelm Müller.

Alfred Grade, a survivor of Buchenwald, had brought his own vision of a book fair to Frankfurt from Leipzig. His roots were in the workers' movement of Saxony, and he had managed a "workers' book dealership" in Halle, where, after 1933, he supported the introduction of socialist literature and was eventually interned in a Nazi concentration camp. Grade's dream was to create a western Leipzig in Frankfurt. He believed in co-operative ideals and was convinced that, taken one step at a time, the whole enterprise would come together successfully.

For his part, Heinrich Cobet was precisely the man the project needed to bring it to fruition. He was of a conservative turn of mind and had, since his youth, been convinced of the important role of the book in the scheme of things. "What really interests me and why I entered the book trade is not because of the book trade, but for literature itself — out of a certain sense of national purpose. After 1918, when Germany was laid low along with the hope that it could ever rise again, it came to me that literature was a decisive element. I went to Eugen Diderichs in Jena and he took me on...."[41] Cobet then studied with Johann Goldfriedrich as a trainee and completed his "Praktikum" with Walter Schatzki in the latter's bookshop in Frankfurt. "At the same time I could not bring myself to abandon university and the study of literature which I considered the life-breath of the nation. So I went to Heidelberg and from there to Paris to study the sociological aspects of the history of literature."[42]

In Paris he came to know the sociologist Karl Mannheim, under whom he prepared his dissertation: "The Psychology or Phenomenology of Writing as the Basis for the Sociology of the Book." When Mannheim left for the London School of Economics, Cobet followed. There Mannheim introduced him to Douglas Waples, professor of the History of Literature and Libraries at the University of Chicago. According to Cobet, "The Frankfurt Book Fair was really founded in conversation with Douglas Waples and Karl Mannheim in London's Rencourt Hotel." There are those who recall that Cobet possessed a certain flair for the dramatic, but in any case, it is true that Waples, who was working on the internationalization of the book trade, later met with Cobet several times in Frankfurt before the Second World War to consult with him about the German book trade as well as the work of the German National Archives of Literature. After the Allied victory, Douglas Waples went on to become chief of press and book publication control in the American sector, which had its headquarters in Frankfurt. Although unsubstantiated, it may well be that it was from Cobet that Waples acquired the list of the publishers whom the American troops brought with them to Wiesbaden in 1945 after their withdrawal from Leipzig.

There is no question that the combined efforts of Cobet and Grade in these difficult times were an important stroke of luck for the Frankfurt undertaking. Cobet had the connections with the occupation forces, and Grade, a "clean record." This, in itself, was also important in those days of non-fraternization, when every move had to be approved by the occupation authorities. Both men were visionaries, but they also knew enough to maintain a sense of equilibrium and practicality. Yet, in a very real sense, without the addition of the Fair's first director, Wilhelm Müller — the third and vital element in the mix — it is quite conceivable that the "Frankfurt Phoenix" might never have taken flight. In the end, it was Müller's organized pragmatism and energetic sense of purpose that made the difference between failure and success.

Despite the opening remarks made at the Fair in 1953, Frankfurt did not, in fact, rise from the ashes of the Leipzig Book Fair. It was, rather, the catastrophic destruction of the graphics quarter and the book dealers' centre in the night bombing raids of December 4, 1943, to which Sir Stanley Unwin referred in his image of "Leipzig's ashes." Unwin had himself learned the book trade in Leipzig and was an admirer of the German system. In the national consciousness, Leipzig had undeniably been not only a geographical site, but also a representation of the sentiments and a mindset that dated back to the nineteenth century.

The fact that it was Frankfurt and not Leipzig that was able to successfully revitalize its book fair cannot be attributed solely to the relative degree of devastation in each city, nor even to new political complexities. The Leipzig tradition had already sacrificed its evolving strength, just as Frankfurt had done in centuries past. This time, however, Frankfurt was on firmer footing.

Max Niedermeyer, chairman of the region's Publishers' and Bookdealers' Association (left) with Heinrich Cobet, the co-founder of the new Frankfurt Book Fair in 1949.

Chapter 11

~~~

Moving Forward in Frankfurt

Following its postwar resurgence, Frankfurt's name had once again become synonymous with "book fair." The Frankfurt Book Fair tradition, which had slipped into oblivion during the Leipzig years, was once again riding the wave of success.

In the words of one observer:

> This altered situation influenced the decision of the Exchange Association to hold its Annual General Meeting of all members of the regional associations in conjunction with the Frankfurt Book Fair. A similar proposal from Hessen's local association had been put forward only the previous year, but it had been rejected and the AGM was held in Stuttgart. Now, however, the guaranteed co-ordination of time and place has increased attendance substantially.[43]

On May 3, 1950, in a persuasive circular, Wilhelm Müller called for participation by all publishers at the Second Frankfurt Book Fair. Although the same letter announced an increase in fees for the rental of stands, by the end of the same month more than 318 publishers had sent in their completed and binding participation forms. It was already clear to those responsible that the available space in Paulskirche would no longer be sufficient. In the end it was decided to make use of three of the ground-floor halls in the neighbouring Römer Town Hall, which the City guaranteed to restore in time for the Book Fair.

This event had been planned specifically as a fair for German publishers, whose displays would be organized according to speciality. The spontaneous and growing interest among foreign publishers remained an unknown quantity. It had already been necessary, despite the extensions of available space, to further limit the dimensions of each stand to a frontage of 2.25 metres. More construction work was needed and agreed upon in order that one hundred additional foreign exhibitors from seven countries could be accommodated — forty-four from Switzerland, thirty from France, twenty from Austria, two from England, and one each from Holland and Sweden. In addition, there were two American publishers represented, and the Fair organizers were still faced with a lengthy waiting list. The internationalization of the Book Fair, whose future extent and influence remained largely unsuspected, was definitely moving forward.

Shortly before the opening of the Second Frankfurt Book Fair, when all problems seemed to have been resolved, the construction workers went on strike for higher wages. To make matters worse, the reconstruction of the historic Römer Town Hall was far from completed. Windows were left unglazed and some of the walls remained unfinished. The roof was provisionally covered with canvas, yet it was impossible to delay the opening. Even the hope of mild fall weather failed to materialize. Instead, it poured rain every day, and this was accompanied by November-like temperatures and a ferocious wind that rattled the canvas roofing. Outside, pedestrian and vehicular traffic was a disaster. Inside, throngs of visitors elbowed their way through the unfinished building. Some got stalled on the stairways and others failed to make it into all the exhibition areas. And even when they did, they were forced to keep on the move because of the structural inadequacies and unseasonable temperatures.

Happily, the reputation of the fledgling fair was not damaged by these adverse conditions, and the following year saw almost all exhibitors flocking back, along with a good many newcomers who were keen to participate.

The opening celebration on the afternoon of September 20, 1950, was attended by thirteen hundred guests: book dealers and publishers, representatives of the federal government, the occupation authorities, as well as designates of foreign consulates and embassies. Carl Hanser, chairman of the West German Exchange Association, expressed his pleasure at the first-time attendance of so many foreign publishers: "We believe that this is a visible sign that the barriers which have restricted Germany are now slowly being removed. It is our hope that the political and economic difficulties which still inhibit the publication of books will soon change for the better."

Already a dire warning of the possible demise of the book accompanied the opening celebration of Frankfurt's second Book Fair when Erwin Stein, the minister for culture and education in Hessen, spoke passionately "of the dangers to the book — and therewith to people's minds — presented by the media: film, radio and illustrated magazines. With the systematic repression of the book in favour of these media, an intellectual and spiritual conformity threatens to engulf large sections of the population."[44] It was a recurrent theme that would echo through the coming decades, but for the moment, the press was greatly impressed by the abundance of books on display. According to official statistics, some 28,000 books were exhibited, 5,000 of which were new publications. Karl Korn of the *Frankfurter Allgemeine* wrote:

> The first and enduring impression of this 1950 Frankfurt Book Fair is that of well-ordered confusion. The boldest collection of photo-montages could never manage to reproduce the effect of 15,000 book titles representing close to 400 publishing houses. Since walking through the

corridors and foyers of St. Paul's Church and the Römer building across from it, I have been left with the impression that I am being pursued by books, books and more books.

The reporter from the Leipzig *Exchange News* was, however, more than a little pessimistic in his article:

> The publisher who exhibits in this city [Frankfurt] is already in the top layer of the underworld and caught up in a two-fold dilemma. The law of "free enterprise," imported from America, has undercut the established retail price and held a knife to the throat of the publisher. He, in turn, would gravitate towards the best price in the hope of making the most profitable deal, while the Fair was awash in mindless "made in USA" publications, bestsellers, blockbusters, untruthful trash, and the subtle poison of neo-fascist propaganda....[45]

Discounting the fact that much of this type of criticism was simply a question of political posturing, what such critics failed to acknowledge was the fact that the merchandising aspect of the book was paramount and that it had proven to be a highly saleable item. All previous attempts to insist that book fairs were vehicles for bringing culture to the people were finally given up as a lost cause. Fairs are — first and foremost — centres for commercial sales and can only function effectively when there is merchandise to be sold. What they can also offer, however — when the circumstances are favourable — is an overview of the cultural and scholarly climate of the times, as well as an important venue for new trends in literature and art.

The Second Frankfurt Book Fair was a recognized success. An estimated 38,000 contracts for orders were drawn up by the 460 exhibiting firms during the six days of the 1950 fair, which represented about 6 million Deutschmarks in sales. A questionnaire circulated among the publishers revealed that 15 percent declared themselves entirely satisfied with the volume of business generated at the fair and 50 percent stated that they were generally satisfied, but 35 percent expressed dissatisfaction. This did not, however, prevent their immediate pre-registration for the following year, indicating that the degree of disenchantment was lower than it might have been.

Relative market position was yet another factor in determining a publisher's participation in any book fair, but, admittedly, information of this nature is rarely broadcast to the world at large. Soon it became apparent, however, that the value of participation could not be measured in terms of sales alone, but also in terms of the quality of the information gathered. For many of those involved in the book trade, the mere fact of having attended the Frankfurt Book Fair became a powerful motivator.

Chapter 12

~~~

The Frankfurt Peace Prize
and Expansion to the Fairgrounds

Perhaps no one will ever discover precisely what it was that inspired the prominent German playwright and poet Hans Schwarz to establish a literary peace prize in 1950. Was it a form of postwar malaise or possibly his own intense horror over the crimes of the Nazi regime? While the source of Schwarz's motivation remains obscure, the fact remains that he managed to convince a handful of publishers to join in the presentation of the prize to its first recipient, German-Norwegian author and editor Max Tau, in June of that same year at a private residence near Hamburg.

Max Tau, born in 1897 in Beuthen, Upper Silesia, had long promoted German and Scandinavian authors in his capacity as editor-in-chief with the prestigious Jewish publishing house of Bruno Cassirer in Berlin. Being Jewish himself, Tau made the timely decision to immigrate to Norway in 1938 and eventually obtained Norwegian citizenship. After 1945 he once again resumed work as a senior editor, this time for the Norwegian publisher Grundt Tanum in Oslo. His autobiography, which later appeared in two volumes, *Das Land, das ich verlassen musste* (*The Country I Had to Leave*) and *Ein Flüchtling findet sein Land* (*A Refugee Finds His Homeland*), and his novel, *Denn über uns is der Himmel* (*Together under One Sky*), stand as testimonials to his humanitarian spirit, his critical intelligence, and his ceaseless efforts towards world peace and mutual understanding among people everywhere. These were the very qualities that distinguished him as the ideal recipient of the first Peace Prize. In *A Refugee Finds His Homeland*, Max Tau wrote: "My heart always went out to those who had sacrificed their fathers and lost their sons. From my innermost soul arose the hope that the bereaved would be granted the strength to find the inherent good in Man in order to bring inner peace to themselves and to the world at large. Only peace will make it possible for the individual to grow from within, to flourish and thrive."

In Oslo, Max Tau had found in Johan Grundt Tanum an empathetic employer — as he had with Bruno Cassirer in Berlin. Tanum allowed him to maintain his literary principles, focusing on works that encouraged the cause of mutual trust and understanding among nations. It was almost certainly due to Tau's influence that Grundt Tanum was the first Norwegian company to include a number of publications in German after the Second World War featuring such well-known authors as Waldemar Augustiny, Hans Werner Richter, Peter Bamm, and Albert Schweitzer.

In awarding the first literary Peace Prize to Max Tau, the honour was being conferred on a man who "has made an outstanding contribution to the fields of literature, scholarship and art, and also towards the realization of peace." At the award ceremony 130 invited guests heard Adolf Grimme, then general director of the Northwest German Radio, make the official presentation to Max Tau, and the entire event was broadcast throughout Germany and beyond. The response of listeners in Norway, Tau's adopted homeland, was one of particular enthusiasm and pride at the honour bestowed on their countryman.

The obvious success of this event inspired the organizers to consider making the Peace Prize an award that would embrace the entire world of book publishing. Friedrich Wittig, one of the founding members of the Hamburg Peace Prize initiative and a member of the Frankfurt Fair Committee, introduced the possibility to the Exchange Association, which agreed to assume responsibility for the endowment. At the suggestion of Max Tau, his friend Albert Schweitzer would be the next recipient.

President of the Federal Republic of Germany Theodor Heuss (left) presenting the 1951 Book Fair Peace Prize to Dr. Albert Schweitzer.

The name of the prize, however, became the source of heated discussion in the committees of the Exchange Association. There was a propaganda war going on between two political systems, and the word "peace" had already been misused in many contexts by East Germany's GDR (German Democratic Republic). Opponents of the name of the prize were of the opinion that use of this terminology implied a certain solidarity with the GDR. The infighting finally ended when Walter Hallstein, state secretary of the Foreign Office, declared that he had nothing against the title "Peace Prize," and on July 8, 1951, the decision of the executive was recorded: "The first official Peace Prize of the German Book Trade will be awarded in a ceremony at the Frankfurt Book Fair 1951 to Mr. Albert Schweitzer." The *Exchange News* was asked to assist in soliciting donations from members to further endow the award. Within a few weeks the fund already stood at DM 10,000.

The first president of the Federal Republic of West Germany, Theodor Heuss, agreed to make the presentation on Sunday, September 16, 1951 — just three days after the opening of the Frankfurt Book Fair — and praised the prizewinner as "an individualist with a strong sense of freedom." Since then, the ceremony for awarding the Peace Prize has seldom taken place without the participation of the president of the Federal Republic. In fact, the prize performed an important function as the catalyst for the creation of a cultural-political framework for the Book Fair. No longer would the Fair have to bear the burden of achieving commercial success on its own.

By the middle of May 1951, orders for booths already stood at 430 and requests from France and Holland had not yet arrived. It was foreseeable that once again there would be serious constraints on the amount of available space. As one of the original stalwarts of the Fair, Heinrich Cobet wanted above all to keep the event within the distinguished halls of the Römer building and the St. Paul's Church. It was his firm belief that expansion out towards the fairgrounds would seriously detract from the cultural aspects of the Book Fair and open the door to commercialization.

It soon became clear, however, that the mounting interest among the six hundred registered exhibitors would require more space, and that the renovations to the display rooms were far behind schedule. Steps would have to be taken to avert disaster. On June 10, 1951, a provisional decision was made to erect two tents in the Römer Square.

Originally, it was planned that the foreign exhibitors were to be located in Paulskirche, which was considered to be the best possible space, but the Austrian and Swiss contingents strenuously objected to being separated from the German publishers, which only served to make matters worse. Then there were difficulties with the tents, or more specifically the foundations. With great foresight, Fair Director Wilhelm Müller finally negotiated directly with the Frankfurt Fair Authority for access to the fairgrounds as an alternative solution. He knew, of course, that if this solution did not succeed in satisfying the needs and wishes of the exhibitors and visitors, Frankfurt's future as a book fair site could be in serious jeopardy. He was willing to take the gamble.

There were, however, already firm bookings for the space on the fairgrounds, as endless negotiations continued between the City, the Fair Authority, and the Exchange Association. The repeated threat of having to move the Book Fair out of Frankfurt finally prompted the decision to advance the Book Fair by one week, and a reasonable rental arrangement was obtained for use of the fairground's Congress Hall, the Handicrafts Hall, and other additional on-site space. Another crisis averted, with precious little time to spare.

At the opening of the Third Frankfurt Book Fair on September 13, 1951, a more elaborate celebration was planned in connection with the Peace Prize. In the auditorium of the fairground's Congress Hall, René Phillipon, chairman of the French Exhibitors' Committee, extended greetings from the French book trade; then, after a short introductory speech, Josef Knecht, chairman of the Exchange Association, declared the Fair open.

Of the 602 exhibitors, about two-thirds were West German, but there was substantial representation from other European countries, as well as four U.K. publishers and two from the U.S., plus a return exhibitor from East Germany. All expressed satisfaction with the new venue and expanded facilities. This was especially pleasing to book retailers for whom special sessions were included for the first time.

By 1951, the German book trade in general was experiencing a strong increase in domestic and foreign sales despite continuing restrictions on foreign trade. It had become increasingly important to meet and get to know business connections personally. Publishers discussed possible projects with authors, began to make co-operative plans with other publishers, and negotiated for their own publications in other formats: paperbacks, newspaper serials, and book club editions. Now they could also propose translations of their books to foreign colleagues.

By 1951, virtually every facet of the book publishing industry seems to have developed a new-found sense of energy and purpose.

Authors, publishers, those who wrote, those who promoted, critics, booklovers, paper producers, printers, and binders all became caught up in the moment. On the subject of fairs, author and publisher Ernst Heimeran commented, "The most noteworthy aspect of the modern fairs is that they do not concentrate, as before, on exhausting conversations among colleagues discussing supply and demand. Now people socialize, exchange opinions, learn all sorts of new things, make new acquaintances, renew old ones, become excited and generally feel fulfilled." At the Frankfurt Book Fair of 1951, a phenomenon had begun taking shape. Eventually it would result in something known as "the book family." Over the coming years, the satisfying sense of belonging that evolved from being a part of this unique community generated countless initiatives and relationships that owed their genesis to the Frankfurt Book Fair.

Chapter 13
~~~
## The Book Family

The Frankfurt Book Fair had now incorporated all the elements necessary for its successful development. After the formative years from 1949 to 1951, there were few remaining doubts about what lay ahead, as each year more and more exhibitors and visitors flocked to Frankfurt. The record was speaking for itself.

In 1952 publishers representing eight different countries totalled 857, of which 484 were German and 373 were foreign exhibitors. There was also a headcount in excess of 22,000 visitors. Then the following year, a new display hall was added, doubling the space for exhibits.

From 1952 to 1957, the number of exhibitors had increased from 857 to 1,384. The foreign representation expanded from 373 to 737 and eventually included twenty-one different countries. After a compromise was reached between the East and West German Exchange Associations in 1955, there was also a dramatic increase in participation from the East Zone, the Soviet Union, Hungary, Czechoslovakia, and Yugoslavia. And during this five-year period, the number of visitors to Frankfurt doubled from 22,00 to 44,000.

By now, the German book trade was in full agreement that the Frankfurt Book Fair had become a permanent fixture. Gradually a unique sense of solidarity had taken hold and flourished. The Fair had long since evolved from simply being the site of the general meeting of the Exchange Association, which now met annually in the Kantate Auditorium of the newly reconstructed Book Dealers' House on Grossen Hirschgraben. Now myriad groups and sub-groups of the book trade gathered in their annually prebooked meeting rooms — representing, among others, such disparate groups as the Working Committee for Schoolbooks, the publishers of books for young people, and book retailers in any number of specialized fields. There was also space designated for the use of the increasing numbers of international literary agents who were flocking to the Fair.

On "Fair Sunday" it had become customary for those attending the Fair to set aside time to go to St. Paul's Church for the Peace Prize ceremony. Recipients of the award included philosopher Romano Guardini, the German-Israeli Professor Martin Buber, the Swiss historian Carl J. Burckhardt, and authors Hermann Hesse, Reinhold Schneider, and Thornton Wilder. Unfortunately, St. Paul's could not possibly hope to accommodate the large number of book dealers and publishers who came in droves to attend this prestigious event. Every year twice as many tickets were ordered as there were seats available, and increasingly the organizers had to cut back on more and more of their members.

In 1957, even the temporary additional seating for 193, which had been permitted in the past, was refused by the local police. The allocation of tickets had become a nightmare for those responsible. It was obvious that somehow a solution had to be found. Finally, a breakthrough! The Peace Prize ceremony had been televised annually since 1953, and the suggestion that the prize-giving could be simultaneously broadcast into the Kantate Auditorium of the Book Dealers' House was greeted with enthusiasm. Although lacking the unique experience of attending the event in person, it did provide expanded seating and at least a degree of consolation to those who would otherwise have to make do with nothing.

These years of solidarity among book dealers also owed much to one of the Fair's greatest supporters — West Germany's highly respected president, Theodor Heuss. Since his Peace Prize presentation speech in honour of Albert Schweitzer in 1951, a Book Fair without the participation of "Papa" Heuss would have been unthinkable. He made a habit of spending some time with his publisher friends at their respective stands, enjoying a glass of wine or exchanging a quip or two while puffing on his ever-present cigar. Anecdotes about these legendary Heuss walkabouts eventually became part of the history of the early years of the Book Fair in Frankfurt.

Everywhere an atmosphere of festivity prevailed as people exchanged greetings, expressions of thanks, and opinions about the importance of the book and the pleasure of meeting one another here. On the occasion of the opening of the Fair in 1953, there were more than a dozen speakers. The following year fifteen speakers representing all aspects of the book trade at home and abroad vied for the attention of the audience.

Although the customary publishers' receptions had not yet been instituted, there were plenty of opportunities for informal socializing throughout the duration of the Fair. An annual evening reception for foreigner publishers was held in the Kaiserkeller in the Friedrich-Ebertstrasse, and later in the Hotel Frankfurter Hof, where the tradition of hospitality dictated that sufficient food and drink were available at relatively moderate prices. People could also dine at the Palmengarten restaurant without breaking the bank. Those in a more exuberant mood could kick up their heels at the Fair Ball, where copious quantities of reasonably priced wines from the local vineyards were on hand. In the fairgrounds' main restaurant, dinner music was provided by Willy Berking and the Frankfurt Radio Orchestra.

To continue a Leipzig tradition established in days gone by, a card index of registered visitors was maintained at the information booth at the entrance to Congress Hall. Every Book Fair participant was listed and access to the list came with the package. The original feeling of being part of a family gathering prevailed for quite some time, although there were clear signs that the balance of business done at the Fair was gradually shifting to the foreign exhibitors. The unique sense of camaraderie that characterized the first two decades of the Book Fair did not really disappear entirely until 1968, but growing indications of the transition to a different kind of fair were already in evidence as early as 1957.

Quite aside from the discussion concerning East German

publisher participation, that same year an international conflict attracted a great deal of attention. For the two previous years, the People's Republic of China had been among the exhibitors, but when the Fair Authority indelicately designated a part of their display "Books from China-Taiwan," the indignant representatives of the People's Republic withdrew in protest. In fact, it was not until 1975 that China was enticed to return without risk of simultaneously provoking a walkout by Taiwan. The ramifications of international politics had become an unavoidable by-product of attendance at the Fair, and this particular incident was merely the first of many to follow in the years ahead.

The question remains, was the stress brought on by the unfortunate "China incident" the final straw that drove Wilhelm Müller to tender his resignation as director of the Frankfurt Book Fair? True, he had no background in books or book dealers, nor did he have experience in international business. He had, however, been largely responsible for putting the Fair on the map, and after Frankfurt's ninth book fair in 1957, having completed what he had set out to accomplish, he made the difficult decision to bow out. Eventually Müller returned to journalism after accepting a position as the editor-in-chief of a small newspaper, but there is no question that he left part of his heart at the Book Fair. As he wrote sixteen years later to his successor, Sigfred Taubert, "Leaving the Exchange Association was not easy for me. I have often asked myself whether I was right to decide to return to my former profession. And for years I have avoided the Book Fair that I built up, in order not to be overwhelmed by memories."

Taubert was cut from a rather different cloth. Born in Stavanger, Norway, in 1914, he learned the book trade in Leipzig through his involvement in antiquarian book dealing and publishing. After a training period in Helsinki and wartime military service, in 1945 he began working at a West German book dealership and was active as a freelance writer until 1951. A year later, Taubert became an employee of the Exchange Association, where he concentrated on market analyses for the book trade and published *Books and The Book Trade in Figures*. In 1954, he became head of press relations for the Exchange Association, and he remained in this position until his appointment as Müller's successor and director of the Exchange Association in 1957.

Like his predecessor, Taubert devoted himself totally to the development of the Frankfurt Book Fair. By the end of his eighteen-year tenure, he had acquired a wide network of personal friendships, but he had also created important connections that developed and multiplied as time went on. The mark of his success was that he took what was still, in principle, a regional German book fair and turned it into a highly visible international event. Without Taubert's tireless promotion, things could have taken an entirely different direction. There is no question that Sigfred Taubert was the person largely responsible for bringing the world's most important publishing houses and publishers to Frankfurt's doorstep.

In Taubert's seventh year as director, the Fair Authority was incorporated as the Exhibition and Fair of the Exchange Association Company Limited. Until then the Frankfurt Book Fair had remained a division of the Publishers' Committee, which appointed the Book Fair director and paid his salary. In 1964, Wolfgang Metzner, who was chairman of the Publishers' Committee and simultaneously chairman of the Foreign Business Committee, officially became the first chairman of the board of directors of the Frankfurt Exhibition and Fair Company, Limited.

*Ernst Rowohlt and Bundespresident Theodor Heuss (with cigar)*
*enjoying the 1953 Book Fair.*

# Chapter 14
~~~
East-West Turmoil

From the outset, the relationship between Frankfurt and the Leipzig publishing houses in the Soviet Zone — the ones who had opted to remain in East Germany — had been fraught with difficulty. The new beginning in Frankfurt had been viewed with considerable hostility. In spite of this antipathy, however, twelve Leipzig publishers decided to participate in the original postwar Frankfurt Book Fair of 1949. The majority of these had registered only at the last minute, with the result that all available display space in St. Paul's Church had been spoken for and it had been necessary for them to exhibit in the less convenient Platz der Republik space. Needless to say, this did not sit well with the visitors from the East.

Between 1952 and 1955, there were no further representations from East Germany, but in 1955 a total of forty-five publishers based in East Bloc countries — notably the Soviet Union, Hungary, Czechoslovakia, and Yugoslavia — took the necessary steps to make their presence known in Frankfurt. An agreement was struck between the East and West Exchange Associations to allow the display of "specialized and scholarly books" under the designation "Books from Inter-Zone Dealers."

In 1958 another agreement was reached whereby East German publishers would be allotted their own booths and their names were duly published in the Fair Catalogue, but an attempt to publicize the display using the designation "Books from the German Democratic Republic" was emphatically refused. Politically, the use of East Germany's official state name — the GDR — was both premature and unacceptable to the West. On the other hand, after their return from Frankfurt in 1958, the East German publishing contingent were pleased to report that their participation had been a political and economic triumph and had netted a total of DM 400,000 in imports and exports as opposed to DM 11,000 the previous year. These figures were indisputable proof of their success. They would return.

Once again in 1959, the prickly question of official nomenclature was raised. A display contract was inadvertently approved by Sigfred Taubert for a Leipzig firm — German Book Export and Import Limited — to exhibit under the banner "Books from the German Democratic Republic." This, in turn, provoked legal proceedings when the East German publishers demanded a court ruling that all their displays could therefore also be designated as "Books from the German Democratic Republic." In their opinion, a precedent had been established. On October 8, 1959, the court in Frankfurt ruled that the Frankfurt Exchange Association did not have the authority to sanction this. For the duration of this Book Fair, the East German displays were to be designated "Books from the Internal German Book Trade." The incident made it abundantly clear that unwelcome political hot potatoes would continue to fall into the lap of the Frankfurt Book Fair administration and, further, that it was ill-equipped to deal with such troublesome matters.

Since 1949, about 2.5 million people had fled East Germany, and this number was augmented by roughly 200,000 more each year. On January 5, 1959, the ambassador of the Republic of West Germany was reminded of the so-called Kruschev Ultimatum of November 27, 1957. In this document, the USSR had renounced the original agreement between the Four Powers about the Allied occupation of Berlin in order to force renegotiation of the status of the divided city. The resulting Geneva Conference of 1959 was to include the three Western powers, the USSR, the Federal Republic of West Germany, and the German Democratic Republic to the east. The conference agenda was to include the Berlin question, the reunification of Germany, a European security system, and disarmament — a daunting challenge at the best of times.

The Bonn delegation, led by West Germany's Foreign Minister Heinrich von Brentano, waived its status as a fully empowered conference participant in order to obstruct the recognition of the GDR, which had received the same status. For his part, Konrad Adenauer, the first federal German chancellor, wanted to include West Germany in the Western Alliance, making it the only voice representing all of Germany, and thereby continuing to isolate the GDR and withholding any official recognition.

Given the complexities of the questions under discussion among the participants, the Geneva Conference ended in August 1959 with few, if any, tangible results. In October of that year, the so-called German Democratic Republic of East Germany adopted its own official flag: a hammer and sickle surrounded by a laurel wreath on a black, red, and gold background. It became known in the West as the "splinter flag," since it represented a small object that had formerly been part of something much larger — and perhaps because splinters are also the source of pain and irritation.

East Germany's stand at the 1977 Book Fair.

Then on August 13, 1961, construction of the Berlin Wall was begun, with the unmistakeable intention of hermetically sealing off East Germany — its people, opinions, and information — from the surrounding world.

Against this highly charged political backdrop, the Frankfurt Book Fair was faced with the problem of finding a way to deal with the East German exhibitors on the one hand and the West German exhibitors on the other. At all costs, it was of the utmost importance to avoid shutting out the East German book dealers and publishers. As a result, a new policy of strict and specific guidelines for participation by East German publishers was devised. This caused subsequent fluctuations in publisher participation from the East Bloc countries, but by 1963 the numbers had risen to thirty-seven publishers, and a vastly increased display space offered them a much higher visibility than ever before.

Unfortunately, just as Günter Hofé, director of the Nation Publishing Company in East Berlin and representative chairman of the Leipzig Exchange Association, was about to set off for the 1963 Frankfurt Book Fair, he was taken into custody by the East German authorities. Even today, the reasons for this arrest are unclear, although records suggest that the legal groundwork for charges against Hofé was already being laid the previous year. In any event, the arrest led to a storm of protest that involved many of Germany's leading authors and lasted for several years. One indirect result of the ensuing turmoil was the founding of Wagenbach, a West German company that published literary works originating from the Soviet Zone that could not otherwise have been possible.

At the 1966 Frankfurt Book Fair, the East German publishers once again demanded that the so-called discrimination against them must not be allowed to continue and that the special conditions applying to members of the Leipzig Exchange Association be lifted. Their complaints, however, fell on deaf ears. The Fair authorities refused to relent and firmly maintained their position with regard to recognition of East Germany's official state name. A case in point was their rejection of an East German company that identified itself as the State Publishing House of the German Democratic Republic. Because of the inclusion of the words "German Democratic Republic" in the company's name, the firm was refused exhibition space.

The following year, Frankfurt's conditions regarding exhibitors were further altered as they applied to participants from East Germany. The new regulations were an even clearer affirmation of the Fair administration's steadfast determination to maintain its stance:

> German and foreign publishing companies may only exhibit at the Frankfurt Book Fair if they are duly inscribed in the business register of the place of publication. Excluded are those publishing companies whose business activities are founded on the expropriation of a German publishing house or similar measures, or of which a substantial proportion of the firm is the continuation of an unliquidated company, unless the owner is in agreement.

The East German objective of becoming a recognized country within the context of the Fair had now receded even further from the horizon.

The precise wording of this pronouncement was, of course, prompted by deep resentment on the part of publishers whose companies had been expropriated in the East and who had then re-established themselves in the Federal Republic. These publishers were primarily those who had left Leipzig for Wiesbaden with the American Forces after Leipzig became part of the Soviet-occupied zone.

From now on, the Frankfurt Fair administration would have to go through the list of applicants from the GDR for publishing companies operating under similar names to those in the Federal Republic. Then the West German owners of these publishing companies had to be asked whether they would approve the participation of their East German namesakes. If the answer was yes, then the applicant would be accepted. In 1967, the first year of the new regulations, almost all were initially refused. Later, however, fewer and fewer of these firms were excluded as they agreed to the right of representation among themselves. In the end, only ten firms from the GDR were refused admission.

It was predictable that East Germany would not take kindly to a policy that excluded any part of its "national" publishing production. So on June 25, 1967, the thirty-six approved publishers from the GDR refused to participate. A heated battle of words ensued between the GDR — represented more or less officially by its spokesmen — and the privately administered West German company that managed the Fair. The East German boycott remained firmly in place. Finally, with barely a month to go before the opening of the Fair, a breakthrough was achieved, and thirty-eight publishers from the GDR eventually arrived to set up their stands.

Among other incidents that created consternation was the issue involving the display of the "Brown Book." This was a publication of the East German State Company that contained attacks against the federal president of West Germany, Heinrich Lübke, including allegations of improprieties stemming from the Nazi era. On the third day of the Fair, the Fair director tried in vain to negotiate the removal of the Brown Book from the display shelves. Finally, on the last day of the Fair, a Justice Ministry official, armed with a confiscation order, arrived to transfer the offending publication into the hands of the Fair director. News of this perceived outrage prompted the entire GDR delegation to immediately remove themselves from the Fair in a flurry of protest.

Inevitably, the politicization of the Frankfurt Book Fair did not go unnoticed and was further reflected in the content and titles of a number of books. As an aftermath of the dramatic events of the 1967 Book Fair, the Frankfurt Fair Authority decided to make an attempt at reconciliation with the East Germans. It was, after all, important to improve relations with participants from the GDR, and by once again relaxing the conditions determining their participation, the Frankfurt administrators hoped to accomplish this.

At the 1968 Book Fair, the publishers from the East made a somewhat reticent appearance, and at the conclusion of the Fair they submitted a letter of protest to the Fair director citing particular grievances. To begin with, the list appearing on page five of the Fair Catalogue, which gave the names of all the countries represented, did not include any reference to the GDR. In addition, the national flags of all the participating countries were fluttering outside the Fair with the notable exception of the East Germany emblem. This was regarded as yet another discriminatory act and redress was demanded.

When it came to the issue of flags, however, their protestations appear to have had a rather unexpected effect. The Frankfurt Fair Authority decided to withdraw all national flags with the exception of the flags of the City of Frankfurt, the Frankfurt Exchange Association, and the Frankfurt Book Fair, which were raised for the duration of the Fair. For the time being the East Germans were mollified — at least on this particular point.

Since 1967 an important East German publisher had been assigned as an undercover agent to report his observations while attending the Book Fair using the pseudonym "Kant." Accordingly, in 1969, he informed his "handlers" that a number of prominent East German authors of belles lettres were being published by West German firms and that these same companies were making overt attempts to develop closer ties with East German publishing houses.

Kant's report highlighted the publications that were being featured and noted that "Our displays at the Fair were determined by the fact that this was the twentieth anniversary of the GDR and works of socialist literature from 1949–69 were the focal point. The display was dominated by our state emblem — a significant sign of progress over the previous situation. The economic result of this year's Frankfurt Fair must be qualified as good with a total intake of 83,393.55 East German marks."

In a follow-up report, Special Agent Kant went on at length about his concerns regarding the insidious infiltration activities being undertaken by West German publishing houses. He issued ominous warnings of the potentially dangerous political consequences this development might hold for the GDR, as well as possible psychological and ideological ramifications for those East German authors published in the West.

However, in spite of continuing discussions over who would be permitted to attend the Frankfurt Book Fair, the attitude of the GDR participants became less adversarial. To be selected as a member of the East German "travel unit" was a true mark of distinction and one accorded only to the most trustworthy "comrades." In addition, the authorities in the GDR had other reasons for limiting the list.

In 1971, Jürgen Gruner, the head of an important East Berlin publishing house, Volk und Welt, and a prominent figure in the East German literary community, had dared to complain about the incomprehensible restrictions on travel permits. The examples he cited included the lack of personnel to administer their stands; insufficient furnishings and equipment for the use of the staff on duty at the display space; and scheduled arrival times that failed to coincide with the opening of the Fair, with the result that there was less opportunity to circulate and become acquainted with the latest international literary works of special interest.

As his reward, Gruner was only permitted two days at the Fair in 1972, a restriction that severely limited his business activities. This was all the more surprising given the fact that the USSR had sent out clear signals that it wanted to expand its influence and display space. In 1975, space for only forty-six publishers was allotted from the exhibit area booked by the GDR. Thanks to the bureaucratic decision-makers on the other side of the Iron Curtain, this left several well-known East German publishers without any representation at the Fair. It was alleged that increasing the number of publishers would serve only to enhance the overall balance sheet of the Fair, while the GDR publishers themselves constantly criticized the Fair Authority's refusal to include East Germany's Brockhaus and BI publishing houses.

During the mid-1970s, the East German cohort found something new to complain about. This time it was the "de-politicization" of the Fair. Most West German publishers had removed political titles from their lists, since these were no longer in demand. And once again, there was irritation in the GDR towards the West German firm Luchterhand, which was described as the "most active" publisher in the Federal Republic in terms of taking on East German authors. The Luchterhand booth was evidently a particularly irksome sight for the GDR representatives attending the Fair. One-half was devoted to Solshenizyn and the other was reported as being slanted "overwhelmingly to literature from the GDR."

Another clandestine observer, code-named "Richard," who was also a leading GDR publisher, confirmed a less politically charged situation in his report to his superiors. In his opinion, "the GDR is recognized by publishers as an equal among the sovereign nations exhibiting, even by those from the Federal Republic. This is shown in the way we are dealt with; there are no tongue in cheek remarks; there is great interest in our literature; and this is demonstrated by the substantial amount of business transacted between our publishers and their West German counterparts."

The East German travel restrictions, however, remained in place. Only a select number of authorized publishers were permitted to attend the Fair. According to "Christian," who was yet another specially assigned observer for the East German authorities, the cohort was booked into the same accommodation and they also ate their evening meal together, often at a little place on the Mainzerlandstrasse. They combed their rooms for listening devices each day and checked their bureau drawers and luggage for signs of a search, but they were never able to uncover anything suspicious. Perhaps, by now, as the amount of business they generated at the Fair continued to grow, along with a general acceptance of their presence, their activities were no longer of any great interest to the authorities.

There were, however, other bones of contention. The anti-Marxist speeches delivered at the Peace Prize ceremonies were an obvious sore point for the GDR delegates as well as for others in the socialist camp. As a result the chairman of Leipzig's Exchange Association declined the invitation in writing on the grounds that this was the first official letter the East Germans had received from the organizers of the event.

The GDR authors who were a thorn in the side of the GDR leadership were also discussed in the special agents' reports. They did, however, express a certain relief that the works of the authors in question failed to excite much interest at their publishers' stands. Another report mentioned the fact that the media appeared to have avoided raising any issues that could be considered inflammatory.

Then came a report in the October 18 edition of the *Stuttgarter Zeitung* in 1977 that declared, "The Fair has certainly not lost its political dimension.... It becomes clear that the Frankfurt Book Forum continues to accurately reflect the contemporary concerns of literature."

The East German comrades felt themselves challenged once again by the Frankfurt Fair administration in 1984. Contrary to actual fact, they were under the impression that the Fair decisions were controlled by higher political powers. In a position paper for this particular Fair an official statement was released that stated:

> By order of the Board of Directors of the Frankfurt Fair Management Company, the motto of the 1984 Frankfurt Book Fair will be: "Man in a Controlled Environment." In the eyes of the Soviet Bloc countries and East Germany in particular, this central theme of the Fair, borrowed from the English writer George Orwell's (1903–1950) anti-communist work *1984*, constituted a provocation directed towards the participating socialist countries and young nation-states. Since the first appearance of *1984*, and particularly in recent years, this book has become a standard work for the ideological crusade against communism.

The objections went on to state, "The choice of this central theme for the Book Fair demonstrates conclusively the intent of the organizers to adopt a clearly anti-communist direction and objective for the Fair." Another related act of perceived provocation was the awarding of the Fair's 1984 Peace Prize to the Mexican writer Octavio Paz, a former friend of Orwell's and a virulent anti-communist. To add fuel to the fire, inflammatory statements were made at the opening ceremony of the Fair at which the chancellor of the Federal Republic, Helmut Kohl, was scheduled to speak. The position paper went on to conclude that the Book Fair must be seen as a presentation by the government.

For the East Germans, the selection of the recipients of the Peace Prize had always posed a problem. They were the only exhibitors who felt obliged to read a political motive into the award. This was particularly difficult in that almost all of the recipients were intellectuals who had, at one time, enthusiastically espoused the communist ideal but had distanced themselves from it later in life.

In the last decade preceding German reunification, these concerns were fortunately limited to matters relating to the Frankfurt Book Fair. Since 1973 annual meetings had been held involving the chairmen of both East and West Exchange Associations along with a senior director of the Frankfurt Exchange Association and the chairman of the Frankfurt Committee for Inter-German Business.

Peter Weidhaas, the incumbent director of the Fair administration at the time, recalls that in 1979 Klaus Höpcke, on his first visit to the Frankfurt Book Fair, asked Weidhaas to arrange an invitation for him to participate in this meeting. Höpcke had been cited by the West German commentator Bilke, in 1978, as an East German "bureaucrat of culture" and someone with great insight into socialist literature. The seating at the special meal that always accompanied the annual meeting was expanded accordingly to include Höpcke along with other important East and West German Exchange officials.

In 1980 an Inter-German Commission was set up to expand

book exchanges between the two German states. Members of this group met several times each year at the book fairs in Leipzig and Frankfurt, as well as twice in East Berlin. One of its primary objectives was to overcome the exclusion from the Frankfurt Book Fair of three East German publishers whose names were similar to those used by West German publishers. Finally, in 1990, an agreement was reached that allowed the publishers in question the opportunity to exhibit.

The second major focus of this work group was to enable Frankfurt to exhibit West German books in East Berlin, Weimar, Dresden, and Rostock; in return, East Germany would be allowed to participate in book exhibitions in Munich, Hamburg, and Stuttgart. This was realized in 1989 when a cultural agreement was signed between the Federal Republic and East Germany.

From 1989 onwards, an entirely different group of participants from the former East German territories — soon to be designated as new federal states — began turning up at the Frankfurt Book Fair. Hopeful young publishers, enterprising new book dealers, avidly curious librarians, and journalists, who had long dreamed of being able to visit the Frankfurt Book Fair, gradually became part of the mainstream.

One such journalist was Werner Köhler. As a Leipzig editor of literary and cultural publications, he had applied more than a dozen times for permission to attend the Frankfurt Book Fair. His requests were consistently refused and, instead, he was openly encouraged to attend the Moscow Book Fair. Now, however, at long last he could realize his dream. His reaction to everything he saw, heard, and did was enthusiastically reported to Saxon Radio, his employer at the time, and undoubtedly his detailed observations attracted a good deal of interest. Reunification had finally brought an end to the troublesome and turbulent years of a divided Germany.

Chapter 15
~~~
## In the Name of Literature

Although it constituted only a fraction of the books displayed at the Fair, literature was the centre of attention. Even an outstanding volume on architecture, an important economics publication, or new releases for youth or on the latest political topic were seldom accorded their due in terms of public interest. Literary publications were the yardstick by which the state of the book market could be measured. Over the years, the history of literature became synonymous with the history of the Book Fair.

On the heels of what was known in postwar Germany as the "rubble literature" of the 1950s, the literary authors of the Federal Republic set their sights more decisively on the present, although the experiences of the Nazi era were not entirely overlooked. As well, there were specialized books that became bestsellers, such as Werner Keller's *The Bible as Written History* and Pörtner's *Mit dem Fahrstuhl in die Römerzeit* (*To the Roman Era by Elevator*).

At the 1959 Fair, the names of three authors in particular attracted an enormous amount of attention. This was largely due to the fact that their novels singularly mastered an understanding of the past combined with incisive criticism of the present. Heinrich Böll's novel *Billiards at Half-past Nine* told the satirical story of a generation of characters that spanned fifteen years. Another highlight of the Fair that year was *The Tin Drum*, the prize-winning first novel of Günter Grass, a promising young author who belonged to the Gruppe 47 writers' association. When it came off the press *The Tin Drum* became an overnight sensation, and long before the opening of the Frankfurt Book Fair foreign publishers were actively vying for translation rights. The literary critic Walter Höllerer compared Grass to Grimmelshausen, Rabelais, and Balzac, but the City of Bremen refused to award him its literature prize because of his overtly permissive attitude towards sex.

A novel by a twenty-five-year-old East German author, Uwe Johnson, also attracted its own share of attention at the Book Fair. The themes of *Presumptions About Jakob* were the division of Germany and the inherent difficulties involved in finding an accommodation between two completely opposite worlds. Johnson also joined Günter Grass as a member of the Gruppe 47, referred to within Germany as "the Central Café of a literature without a capital."

On the international market, *In the Labyrinth*, a novel by French novelist and filmmaker Alain Robbe-Grillet, translated into German under the title *Die Niederlage von Reichenfels*, was a radical attempt to completely abandon traditional narrative subjectivity and create a comprehensively precise description of the objective world. The Italian writer and filmmaker Pier Paolo Pasolini also attracted attention with his book *Vita Violenta* (*A Violent Life*), which was set in the slums of the Roman suburbs.

That same year Heinrich Böll topped the bestseller list with *Billiards at Half-past Nine*, ahead of Rudolf Hagelstange's *Plaything of the Gods*, Giuseppe Tomasi di Lampedusa's *The Leopard*, Boris Pasternak's *Doctor Zhivago*, and Leon Uris's *Exodus*. Surprisingly, however, when it came to profitability, German-authored war stories and biographies outstripped all other competition.

Heinz G. Konsalik made a sensation by selling more than a million copies of his war novels, *The Doctor from Stalingrad* and *Straffbattalion 999*, based on his experiences as a war correspondent in the Soviet Union. Also successful in this category were Wolfgang von Parth's *Vorwärts Kameraden-Wir müssen zurück* (*Onward Comrades, We Must Fall Back*) and *Einen Besseren findest du nich* (*There Are None Better*), the story of an unknown soldier from the Great War. The popular novels of Johannes Mario Simmel continued to attract attention.

At the end of the 1950s there was also a noticeable trend towards autobiographies and biographies of personalities then regarded as "great men." In this category, popular choices were Konrad Adenauer's authorized biography by Paul Weymar and naturalist Bernhard Grzimek's *Kein Platz fur wilde tiere* (*No Room for Creatures of the Wild*). But in the 1960s the younger writers of West Germany no longer felt obliged to dwell on the Second World War and its aftermath. They gravitated, instead, towards themes relating to the present, and experimented with new forms of expression.

*Konrad Adenauer launches his book at the Fair in 1965.*

Martin Walser in his novel *Half-time* mercilessly criticized "the comfortable society," and Peter Weiss, a half-Jewish émigré to Sweden in 1934, visited the Frankfurt Book Fair for the first time to introduce his "micro-novel," entitled *Der Schatten des Körpers des Kutschers* (*The Shadow of the Body of the Coachman*). Arno Schmidt was another author whose work attracted a certain amount of attention amidst the general wheeling and dealing of the Book Fair of 1960.

A topic of discussion that dominated the Twelfth Frankfurt Book Fair in 1960 was the tragic death of the celebrated Algerian-French author and philosopher Alfred Camus. The Parisian publisher Michel Gallimard had been driving on a rain-slicked highway in southern France at high speed when the car left the road and struck a tree, killing both Gallimard and his passenger.

The philosopher Ernst Bloch was another author who made headlines in 1960 with the publication of the final volume of his seminal work, *The Principle of Hope*, which was published by Aufbau, an East Berlin press. The book was roundly criticized in government-controlled journals in the East and written off as an example of bourgeois thinking, based on the premise that Man, although incomplete, is on the road to an undefined but attainable Utopia.

The literary-minded public found another topic of discussion in the death of Nobel Prize winner Boris Pasternak at the age of seventy. His interment in his home community of Peredelkino near Moscow became the site of an impressive demonstration for artistic freedom that attracted more than three thousand participants. The protesters applauded a worker who demanded that the Soviet ban on *Doctor Zhivago* be lifted immediately since Pasternak had not been granted state permission to accept the prize and had been excluded from membership in the Soviet Writers' Union.

In 1961, a virtually unknown author stepped into the limelight when Ivo Andrić was awarded the Nobel Prize in Literature. In his most famous work, *Bridge Over the Drina*, Andrić related the history of his Yugoslavian homeland.

The same year, the novels of the controversial American author Henry Miller became the centre of attraction at the Frankfurt Fair. Miller's acclaimed first novel, *The Tropic of Cancer*, had been published in Paris in 1934; however, in the United States, where puritanical views were the rule rather than the exception, his books were considered pornographic and their publication banned. It was not until 1961 that a first edition of forty thousand copies, issued by the American publisher Grove Press, became an instant bestseller. Grove subsequently went on to successfully challenge U.S. censorship laws and precipitated the first "forced acceptance of banned books in the United States."[46]

A deluge of paperbacks descended on the Fourteenth Frankfurt Book Fair in 1962. More than one thousand paperback titles were published that year. Hardbacks were no longer in vogue as readers gravitated to the more portable alternative that could be carried virtually anywhere — in the streetcar, on train trips, in the park. And besides, a paperback was easier to read in bed. Belles lettres accounted for only 34.5 percent of book production, while translations of foreign works — mainly in English and French — gained ground and accounted for about one-sixth of West Germany's literary output.

Shortly before the opening of the 1962 Frankfurt Book Fair, a satirical monthly periodical, *Pardon*, made its first appearance. Among the contributors were a number of literary luminaries, including Günter Grass, and Erich Kästner, the noted children's author and satirist, was a member of the editorial board. In its preview edition, *Pardon* announced a writing competition — first prize: a week's vacation in East Germany; third prize: three weeks' vacation in East Germany!

Günter Grass's 684-page novel *Dog Years* made a sensation at the 1963 Book Fair. In the words of a prominent critic, its effect was like "a hailstorm of literary devices and provocative content." Like *The Tin Drum*, the novel was set in Danzig (present-day Gdansk in Poland) and centred on the Nazi years, while also exploring Germany's destiny and conscience. The ensuing controversy over the book and its author was fuelled by Grass's inclusion of figures from the contemporary scene in West Germany such as philosopher Martin Heidegger, publishers Gert Bucerius and Axel Springer, business magnate Josef Neckermann, and two prominent bankers.

The other novel of the year was Heinrich Böll's *The Clown*, in which he sharply criticized the developing differences between economic, cultural, and ecclesiastical power groups during the Adenauer era.

From the other side of the East-West border, novelist Christa Wolf's *Der geteilte Himmel* (*Heaven Divided*) also attracted a great deal of attention from visitors to the 1963 Frankfurt Book Fair. Given the political tensions of the times, Wolf's open criticism of the machinations of East German bureaucracy was nothing short of astounding.

At the same time, television was increasingly providing its viewers with an enticing alternative to books and reading. A second national channel, Das Zweite Deutsche Fernsehen, began broadcasting in 1963. In a 1953 survey, 43 percent of those canvassed claimed to have read a book in the previous two weeks. Ten years later, statistics indicated that the number of readers was declining at an alarming rate. The book trade's answer was to attempt to counteract the trend by expanding their paperback lists. In 1963, there were three thousand paperback titles available, and the majority of these could be purchased for an affordable price. During the course of the following year roughly one hundred more titles were added each month as part of a strategy to lure people away from their television sets and back to reading.

By 1964, it was obvious that certain authors were becoming more and more politically outspoken. Books by such notables as Heinrich Böll, Günter Grass, Peter Weiss, Rolf Hochhut, and Alexander Kluge were among those in the forefront. On the cusp of the radical student protest movements of the 1960s and '70s, these authors used their literary skills to criticize the country's disturbing preoccupation with economic growth and the smug self-satisfaction of the prosperous ruling class. At the same time, these writers rejected the prevailing tendency to treat the Third Reich as a collective traffic accident. To turn a blind eye was a form of denial that should not be condoned.

Suddenly fiction became the object of suspicion. Politically engaged authors countered this by basing their work on documentary material. A group of authors used this technique to good effect: Alexander Kluge in his *Battle Description–The Defeat of the 6th Army*, a detailed account of the Battle of Stalingrad in 1942–43; Rolf Hochhut's play *The Deputy*, about the attitude of the Vatican to the fate of the Jews at the hands of the Nazis; Heinar Kipphardt's docudrama *In the Matter of J. Robert Oppenheimer*, and Peter Weiss's play *Marat Sade*. The plight of the common working man also came in for its share of attention when Max von der Grün published his novel *Will-o'-the-Wisp and Fire*.

The most successful foreign work at the 1964 Book Fair was a book belonging to an entirely different genre. Foreign-language rights for *The Group* by Mary McCarthy were quickly snapped up, and the film rights were soon acquired by Hollywood.

In terms of German literature, the East-West conflict worsened in 1965. Four years after the Berlin Wall had been erected, increasing numbers of East German authors took up this theme. Their publications included Hermann Kant's first book, *Die Aula*; twenty-six-year-old Volker Braun's *Provocation for Me*, a volume of poetry; the poems of Rainer and Sarah Kirsch; and Wolf Biermann's ballads, poems, and songs about war, love, and everyday conflicts in Germany's East Zone.

*The Spy Who Came in from the Cold* by John le Carré, a thirty-four-year-old author and former British Foreign Service officer, topped the list of bestsellers at the 1965 Book Fair. Set in a divided Berlin, it was a captivating political thriller and, in the end, close to 5 million copies were sold worldwide.

In 1966 the Goethe Institute of New York invited eighty authors who had been sponsored by the Ford Foundation to attend a meeting of the Gruppe 47 at Princeton University. Since its beginnings in the postwar era, the group had met regularly twice a year, and over time a number of its members had become literary icons. Attendance at the group's meetings in Germany was by invitation only, and the organizers would send postcards listing the date and location to a pre-selected list. Writers in attendance would read from their unpublished manuscripts for criticism and discussion, and at the end of each meeting prizes were awarded for the most popular pieces. Predictably, however, the Princeton event was not without its moments of infighting and differences of opinion. For example, a contentious young Austrian writer, Peter Handke, who had just achieved notoriety through the publication of his first novel, *The Hornets*, took it upon himself to openly criticize the works of the so-called left-wing faction with the presentation of his play *Publikumsbeschimpfung* (*Offending the Audience*). In any case, the interest of the members gradually began to wane in the late 1960s, and in 1977 Gruppe 47 was officially disbanded.

In 1967, the tenth edition of *Kursbuch*, a quarterly review published by Suhrkamp, proclaimed that literature and aesthetics had become superfluous and ineffectual in their socio-political contexts. Increasingly, however, impassioned authors were writing about the political situation in the Federal Republic, the war in Vietnam, problems in the "Third World," and racial discrimination in the United States. The majority of the public, however, was not swayed by these literary digressions. An indication of this was the bestseller list, where top billing went to a heartwarming family saga, *Mornings at Seven*, by popular British novelist Eric Malpass.

For the first time, growing numbers of American authors had begun attracting readers of a more intellectual persuasion. These were writers who had chosen to champion the cause of the oppressed at every opportunity — authors such as Eldridge Cleaver, whose *Soul on Ice* had a great influence on the Black Power Movement in the U.S., and James Baldwin, who explored the loss of identity experienced by Blacks separated from their traditions. Allen Ginsberg dealt with corruption in American society, pacifism and humanity, sex and Eastern religions, in his volume of poetry, *Paranoia*.

Above all, however, it was literature that afforded the Frankfurt Book Fair its mark of distinction, setting it apart from other fairs. On the other hand, it remained first and foremost a commercial fair. As early as 1958, the Cologne publisher Joseph Caspar Witsch had summarized the dual character of the Book Fair. In his opinion, literature was not a pure ideal, independent of commerce. In fact, he maintained that the commercialization of literature was a necessary condition of freedom. He was also firmly dedicated to the belief that literature was a living monument to the strength of humankind — an eternal and effective voice of protest that touches every aspect of our lives.

*Günter Grass (right) and his daughter join friends over drinks in the usual Frankfurt atmosphere of enlightened discussion, 1988.*

# Chapter 16

## The Role of the Press

A tense relationship between culture and commercialism continued unabated. In essence, it was the same clash of interests that had contributed to the failure of the new beginnings in Frankfurt and Leipzig between the two world wars. When Leipzig fell so dramatically behind Frankfurt at the book fairs that followed the end of the Second World War, it was essentially the result of the fact that in Frankfurt commerce had taken the upper hand, while Leipzig had held fast to a cultural ideal.

In 1958, the highly respected literary publisher Joseph Caspar Witsch had publicly sought a reconciliation between the two opposing forces — the book and the book trade. His efforts were prompted in part by the fact that a new presence had come onto the playing field. Traditionally, participants in the Book Fair included publishers, book dealers, readers, and a few journalists — mainly local — who wrote reviews and commentaries on the Fair. Increasingly, however, by the mid-1960s reporters from a broader spectrum of newspapers and radio and television stations began to appear on the scene.

On September 17, 1964, the Hamburg daily, *Die Zeit*, reported that readers could spend six wonderful days in Frankfurt whether they visited the Fair or not: "For there are those who look down on the Book Fair and never attend — authors, critics, even publishers and retailers. Perhaps it is the Fair's highly commercial aspect or its circus-like atmosphere that keeps them away … or possibly it is the combination."

The writer went on to discuss the mounting evidence that publishers were less inclined to cultivate authors than they were to pursue the goal of surefire success, and they made every possible attempt to entice the author most likely to produce a bestseller. The quest justified any and all means. Authors, editors, producers, and accountants were all on the "most wanted" list and were stolen at will without so much as a backward glance. The publishing business was beginning to resort to cutthroat tactics.

Observers also bemoaned the fact that many book retailers were no longer interested in promoting works of literary merit. Young poets with their first volume, writers of lyrical poetry, and unknown novelists were no longer cultivated. Instead, the retailer went to great lengths to encourage the sales of bestsellers and promote the bestseller list. He no longer advised or consulted; he simply sold from the warehouse.

On the other hand, beleaguered booksellers were being pressured to accept deep discounts and reductions in profits. It was a case of everybody wanting to benefit at the individual bookstores' expense. And among themselves, it was an acknowledged fact that whatever discounts they offered, there was always someone around the corner who would undercut them and sell their inventory at rock-bottom prices.

These problems were only exacerbated by the fact that publishers and retailers fundamentally distrusted each other. Subsidiary rights interested the publisher far more than the retail sector. To this end, he relentlessly pursued possibilities for further profit through book subscription organizations, paperback publishers, warehouses, radio, and television; his discounts were far too small and he no longer acknowledged the interests of the retailer. There was, however, one issue of mutual concern where the two opposing sides joined forces. It was clearly in the best interests of both publishers and booksellers to do battle with the government policy of introducing a value-added tax and the imposition of fixed retail pricing.

The publishers and retailers were also united in their opinions of book reviews and the people who wrote them. The consensus was that the situation had gone from bad to worse. Critics simply did not read the books they wrote about; they were considered pompous or ignorant, or perhaps even both. In short, they were entirely without any redeeming features. Newspapers were doing all too little for literature, and what they did do left a lot to be desired. On the whole, authors fared little better than the book reviewers. Since many of the reviewers were authors themselves, in the collective minds of both publishers and booksellers all authors were basically ungrateful and egocentric.

The reader, too, should not be forgotten, the article went on to say. Authors, critics, publishers, and retailers all existed for the purpose of attracting readers and, in turn, were totally dependent on the public's desire to read. From the standpoint of the publishers, to be at the mercy of the readers' whims was to be in an unenviable position.

But these were the realities of the world of books and publishing, and because they were recognized as such, certain people with higher standards and expectations distanced themselves from the Book Fair. In general, however, the Book Fair was still a destination of choice — a place where people could mingle, as well as a place where they could find fault at every turn. They complained about the twenty-five thousand new books published in the Federal Republic. Rumours were rife in the stands, in the corridors, in the hotel rooms, in hotel hallways, and in bars. In spite of all this, it was universally acknowledged that there could never be enough books, because the mind's capacity is infinite and every last book — the worst and the best — bears witness to that infinity.

In the final analysis, the raison d'être of the Frankfurt Book Fair was growth, and each year, without fail, the aspirations of the Fair administration were realized. At the official press conferences, new record figures were presented on cue. "Once again bigger, once again a record fair!" Such an announcement was no longer considered particularly newsworthy, since the success of the Fair had become an established fact and, for the most part. Probably for lack of other news, most media reports of the opening day of the Book Fair in 1964 declared that another record had been set. In other words, it was business as usual, but on an even grander scale.

The ensuing commentaries cited the steadily growing numbers of exhibitors, the overabundance of displayed books, the international character of the crowds visiting the fairgrounds, and the inherent superficiality of the contacts that had been made. The reality was that it had become totally impossible to make any kind of valid evaluation of the content of the books on display. The Fair had grown beyond all imagination and the luxury of extended browsing or discussion was virtually non-existent. Instead, the business of the Fair had expanded well beyond its gates into the city's streets, hotel lobbies, city bars, restaurants, taxis, and even its streetcars.

Whether a visitor to the Fair was a publisher, book dealer, librarian, journalist, literary critic, author, or simply an interested reader, each one experienced the Book Fair according to his or her own specific expectations. Year after year attendance figures of more than one hundred thousand visitors were recorded. Although they had all attended the same Book Fair, individual experiences — coloured by the interests and agendas being pursued — were many and varied. Among the professionals, the perceptions and goals of textbook publishers were far removed from those involved in marketing trade books. A similar disparity prevailed between devotees of children's books and art book enthusiasts, and between publishers for the English-speaking market and those producing books in other languages. By the same token, the purveyors of books on religious topics felt worlds apart from those in the political arena. And yet, from the perspective of the organizers, making clear-cut distinctions between categories or divisions was becoming an increasingly difficult problem. The dynamics of the event blurred the dividing lines in spite of vain attempts to bring some sort of order into this organized chaos of colour and movement.

How could anyone report on the Book Fair with any degree of competence? How could the poor benighted reporter sent here to cover its highlights make some kind of sense out of this sea of books and people? What should the unseasoned journalist thrown into this milling mass of humanity so full of opinions and rumours write in his daily report to his editor?

It was hardly an enviable assignment, even for someone with years of experience, but, to their credit, those charged with the task of writing about the Fair threw themselves into the tumult, listened to endless conversations, and spent their nights in bars or at parties and receptions searching for that tantalizing nugget of insider information — usually gleaned well after midnight. In general, the idea was to absorb the feel of the Fair, and, of course, they were always living in the constant hope of hitting on a piece of fresh-breaking news that would make it all worthwhile. For the most part, though, the report issued the next morning seldom amounted to little more than an account of the reporter's personal experiences, a few quotes, and perhaps a smidgen of industry gossip.

A typical case in point is this slightly jaded report published in the *Stuttgart News* on September 22, 1964:

> Book people do not sleep ... at least not during the multi-lingual International Frankfurt Book Fair. Here the 24-hour day is obligatory. The message "We will be available to you starting at 11:30 p.m." is nothing unusual. Those with experience take holidays immediately following the close of the Fair; globe-trotting party-goers count on their past experiences and conditioning; young critics learn — with a wry smile of reminiscence — that the work they do at their desks is the easiest part of their job. "We will be available for you after 11:30 p.m. and perhaps we can take a bite together in the early hours of the morning, but don't forget that Publisher X, Y or Z has invited a few of the book judges for an exclusive breakfast get together."
>
> The agents receive callers anytime between noon and 3 a.m. and meet with them in the lobbies of hotels, or on back stairways where

miniature showcases have been set up so that anyone interested can take the time to examine the books on display and have a closer look at some of the latest hot-off-the-press publications. In the final analysis, the Fair means commerce. And for commerce, the ability to concentrate on detail is a necessity. It is also something that is impossible to accomplish in the melee around the front of the exhibitors' stalls. It can, however, be accommodated in some of Frankfurt's most renowned hotels. It is here that contracts are signed, fees negotiated, royalties discussed; licensing rights acquired and sold. It is also where the small publishers fight for their individuality; the mid-sized fight for their existence; and the ones at the top worry about maintaining their status as a major player.

But the business of marketing books was never of any particular interest to the reading public. What could be more important than the books themselves? Their interests lay in content, ideas, and well-informed writing in a given field, whether it was art or politics, education or religion, travel or entertainment, medicine or technology, nursing or breeding small animals. Eventually, the Fair administration came to recognize this perplexing diversity of subject matter as a reality in need of attention, and in due course it adopted comprehensive themes that catered to the full spectrum of possibilities.

# Chapter 17

## 1968 – A Turning Point

At the 1966 Frankfurt Book Fair, there were already signs of troubling times ahead. One cause for concern was the fact that Yugoslavian exhibitors had expressed fear of reprisals from competing Croatian publishers operating under the name "Nova Hrvatska" out of Stockholm, London, and Buenos Aires. In addition, an organization called "Action for Democracy" announced its intention to take some form of action against eight German publishers because they printed books by certain authors whose names were on the organization's hit list. Although nothing came of either situation, the Fair directors recognized the possibility of problems in the making and issued the following statement:

> In neither case were excesses or difficulties encountered. Nevertheless, the events appear symptomatic. As word of the Frankfurt Book Fair's success continues to spread, its national and international profile will become exponentially greater. And a possible result of this notoriety could well be the temptation to make the Fair a target for political demonstration. In the future, we must dedicate ourselves to remaining aware of this possibility and prepare ourselves to deal with it.

By the following year, however, it was no longer a question of hollow warnings and dire threats. During the last three days of the 1967 Fair, massive protests — mainly involving students — took place in Hall 6 against the giant Springer Publishing Corporation and in Hall 5 against the Greek, Spanish, and South African displays. For some reason, the magnitude of these demonstrations caught the Fair administration completely off-guard. This could only be described as surprising, in the light of the well-publicized manifestations of discontent throughout the previous summer provoked by the death of a student in Berlin during an anti-Shah demonstration. As well, there had already been several incidents of protest targeting the reviled Springer Publications, yet, in spite of these indications of potential trouble, the Fair director expressed his considerable surprise at the inflammatory actions of these young people. Was not the Book Fair a place that, on the face of things, could offer them so many possibilities for exposure to the works of authors from all over the world — authors of every imaginable political and philosophical school of thought?

From the protesters' perspective, the Frankfurt Book Fair was exhibiting books that, in their view, lacked "social relevance." What they espoused was a complete rejection of the "ivory tower" created by intellectuals. Down with literary and cultural elites! The book must be brought back into the realm of social reality along with its inherent contradictions. To many, it seemed crystal clear that the once-upon-a-time book fair of publishers and book dealers was about to lose its long-cherished family atmosphere.

The 1968 Book Fair opened with no apparent indication that it would differ in any substantial way from the nineteen fairs that had preceded it. The opening celebration took place according to established ritual, complete with the usual greetings from the chairman of the Exchange Association, the mayor of Frankfurt, and representatives of international publishers and book dealers. The exhibitors numbered more than 3,000, including 850 from the Federal Republic, close to 50 from East Germany, and an impressively large foreign presence representing more than 58 countries and offering a total of almost 200,000 titles. Encouraged to participate by a program organized through West Germany's Foreign Office, publishers from such far-flung countries as Bolivia, Thailand, Ghana, Kenya, Colombia, South Korea, the Philippines, Singapore, Mexico, Pakistan, and Uganda had all set up displays for the first time.

And once the Fair had been declared officially open, the traditional reception to welcome foreign delegations took place in the Limpurgsaal — the grand salon of the Römer. Later, at the Hotel Frankfurter Hof, a mammoth cocktail party was laid on for all foreign visitors. The event attracted close to a thousand people and was attended for the first time by East German representatives of the GDR's Leipzig Exchange Association, a group whose appearance created something of a sensation among the assembled throng.

The Book Fair opened without incident on a Thursday. In reaction to the previous year's demonstrations against Springer Publishing and the occupation of a stand representing Greece, the Fair administration had introduced strict security measures. No placards. No flyers. Over and above the imposition of these and other stringent controls surrounding access to the Fair, as an additional security measure, riot police in full regalia were posted on the grounds to maintain order in the event of any unwarranted disruption.

The following day, West Germany's finance minister, Franz-Joseph Strauss, insisted on holding a press conference in front of the Seewald Publishing Company stand in Hall 5. As a precaution, Fair Director Sigfred Taubert had insisted that he and Strauss would make their way to the area using an underground passageway. Once there, the controversial author and politician addressed a waiting group of journalists without incident, but, in spite of the strenuous efforts at tight security, another group that included two leaders of the Socialist German Students' Federation, Daniel Cohn-Bendt (better known as Danny the Red) and Hans-Jürgen Krahl, along with a half-dozen or so of their supporters, managed to slip through the net. Although the agitators could be contained within the immediate area around the Seewald exhibit, Strauss was forced to take his leave under police escort.

On the third day of the Fair — a Saturday — in Hall 6 a further incident added to the Fair administration's distress. The Socialist Students' Federation had called for a sit-in in front of the exhibit of Diederich Press, which published the highly acclaimed works of Senegalese president and poet Léopold Senghor. Senghor was scheduled to receive the Fair's 1968 Peace Prize the following day.

A highly inflammatory flyer invoking protesters to demonstrate against Senghor's repressive regime led Taubert to opt for police intervention to close Hall 6 before the demonstration could get underway. When it became clear that the disturbance within the hall would affect only a relatively small area, Taubert decided to rescind the order, but not without incurring a memorable inconvenience to many of the exhibitors and visitors.

To compound the difficulty of mounting tensions, another flyer was circulated calling for demonstrations against the Peace Prize award ceremony that had been scheduled for ten o'clock on Sunday morning at St. Paul's Church. Even before the arrival of the honoured guests, Socialist Students' Federation agitators led by Daniel Cohn-Bendt had begun to demonstrate against Léopold Senghor and Heinrich Lübke, president of the Federal Republic of Germany. By the time the dignitaries arrived, the situation had escalated to riot proportions, and it was only with difficulty that they were safely escorted into the church. Outside, during the course of the presentation, the riot continued unabated, and afterwards many demonstrators began heading for the fairgrounds.

When the news of the approaching onslaught was flashed to the Fair director, he immediately issued an order to close the east gates. It was a sensible precaution, but, in the end, police reinforcements had to be brought in as the demonstration at the gates degenerated into hand-to-hand street fighting. Before order was finally restored, a total of eighteen demonstrators had been arrested on charges ranging from criminal trespassing to breaches of the peace.

Meanwhile, a number of influential publishers had closed their stands or threatened withdrawal from the Fair. There was a marked dissatisfaction among exhibitors over the disturbances and disruptions that had marred the usual atmosphere of commerce and congeniality. As a result, all participants were asked to decide whether or not they supported the strict new measures instituted by the Fair administration to discourage any future possibility of political agitation. In the end, only 5 percent declared themselves in favour of the freedom to demonstrate within the confines of the Book Fair.

Various means of ensuring that order would be maintained were duly discussed and discarded, but eventually the categorical set of "rules" laid down by the 1968 Fair organizers evolved into "suggestions" for visitors to the Fair in 1969. For one thing, the police presence became less visible on the fairgrounds. For another, the recipient of the Peace Prize was subject to proposals from all participants. Meetings held by innumerable committees and workgroups led to the development of the idea of a "Fair Council" to represent the public attending the Book Fair. The speaker of this body was elected to sit on the board of directors of the AUM — the incorporated company charged with the overall responsibility for the general operation of the Frankfurt Book Fair.

In spite of all fears to the contrary, the 1969 Book Fair ran its course peacefully and without incident beyond a few isolated attempts at protest. The disruption of the annual general meeting of the Exchange Association by a splinter group of about a hundred self-designated "producers of literature" was swiftly dealt with. The chairman adjourned the meeting to another time and place, and subsequently this meeting was no longer held during the Book Fair but on specifically designated days in the spring of the following year.

# Chapter 18

~~~

Business as Usual

As a result of the demonstrations and general upheaval that accompanied the 1968 Fair, the choice of a less controversial candidate for the 1969 Peace Prize was foremost in the minds of the Fair administration. In the end, they decided upon Alexander Mitscherlich, a renowned psychoanalyst and the author of two seminal works describing the fundamental causes of the growing unrest in Germany: *The Fatherless Society* and *The Inability to Mourn*. The fact that Mitscherlich immediately donated his prize money to Amnesty International only served to prove that his selection as winner of the award had been an extremely well conceived decision.

Gradually, it seemed, conditions at the Fair were returning to normal and business dealings were generally free of disruption. In spite of the unsettling disturbances of the two preceding years, the Fair's growth had expanded to well over three thousand exhibitors from sixty-one countries. The only perceived setback was in terms of West German publisher participation. Based on the dramatic events of the preceding years, more than one hundred West German publishers had made the decision to observe the 1969 Fair from a distance and take stock of the situation at a later date.

The press, which had strenuously devoted itself to the high drama of the two previous years, craved a little more excitement. Like the majority of other newspapers and magazines, *Die Zeit*, the weekly newspaper of Germany's intelligentsia, had expressed hopes for a continuation of newsworthy discussions and confrontations. The disappointment at the absence of sensational stories was thinly veiled in its report on the Fair in the October 17 edition of 1972. In fact, for the next few years there were frequent complaints in the press about how boring and monotonous the Fair had become. Perhaps, after all, normality was too much of a good thing; as might be expected, its duration was short-lived.

At the insistence of the leaders of the student movement, in 1970 a "Fair charter" had been discussed, drafted, and adopted by the Fair administration and the board of directors, but the movement itself quickly declined in popularity and eventually passed into oblivion. On the other hand, new issues of concern soon supplanted those of the past. Among the increasing numbers of exhibitors, it was noted that certain publishers had begun marketing books that patently espoused national socialist or neo-fascist views. For both the Fair organizers and the fair-going public, this new and unwelcome development gave rise not only to embarrassment but also to a good deal of criticism. Youth groups, always ready for confrontation, immediately seized upon these publications as a made-to-order bone of contention.

On September 25, 1970, a group of thirty agitators moved in to clear away the display of the radical right-wing publisher K. W. Schütz and immediately brought the offending books to the attention of the Fair Council. The protest group then requested that charges be laid under state law; however, seizure of Fair exhibits without permission of the stand holder could not be condoned under any circumstances. On the other hand, the Fair Council did agree to ensure that similar incidents would not be tolerated in future.

On the following day, however, about a hundred demonstrators proceeded to storm the Greek publishers' exhibit in Hall 5, knocked over some of the display cases, manhandled an elderly official, and made off with the entire inventory of books. The action was undoubtedly prompted by the fact that, at the time, Greece was being governed by a harsh military dictatorship, and the display was an obvious and tempting target for those wishing to create adverse publicity against the regime. The next day, the demonstration scene at the Greek stand was repeated, but without any undue aggression. The Fair Council, which had taken great exception to a propaganda brochure being distributed at the Greek exhibit, submitted a polite request from the board of directors stating that the Greek exhibitors should withdraw the offending brochure for the duration of the Fair. An agreement was reached without delay and the matter was amicably settled.

Meanwhile, as if the Greek and Nazi/neo-fascist upheavals had not created more than enough trouble, a similar incident involving demonstrators erupted at the Indonesian stand. To its credit, however, the Fair Authority stood firm once again and made it clear that actions of this sort were contrary to the spirit of the Book Fair and were altogether unacceptable.

On the other hand, the thorny problem of publishers who displayed books with fascist and national socialist content remained unresolved and continued to plague those responsible for the administration of the Fair in the years ahead. In 1971, following demonstrations against the exhibits of the publishing houses of Schütz and Druffel, Schütz closed its display, but not before the Fair Council decided to initiate legal proceedings against them. Druffel, for its part, removed the contested propaganda literature and a modicum of normality was restored, at least temporarily.

The following year, the 1972 Peace Prize was to be awarded posthumously to the eminent Polish author and pediatrician Janusz Korczak (1879–1942), but the choice quickly became a contentious issue when the speaker of the Fair Council, Bernt Engelmann, publicly declared his intention to boycott the Peace Prize presentation. Engelmann's objections were directly related to the rejection of the Fair Council's demands for the closure of offending publishers' exhibits the previous year. In his opinion, it was unconscionable that the publishers in question were once again about to be displaying books that sought to justify, and even glorify, the Nazi cause. How could these publishers be given the freedom to exhibit at the Fair at the same time as the Peace

Prize was to be awarded to a victim of Nazi atrocities? Under these circumstances, he found it morally reprehensible to participate in the award ceremony.

Not surprisingly, Engelmann's views were vigorously endorsed by countless supporters, and true to his convictions, Engelmann submitted his resignation to the Fair Council and recommended its dissolution.

The 1968 federal German law under which charges had been laid against the publisher K.W. Schütz stipulated that both of the provisions of this law had to be violated in order for a prosecution to take place. Like the publications on display at the two previous Fairs, Schütz's 1972 offering, which glorified the actions of a particular battalion of storm troopers in the Warsaw ghetto, clearly constituted a violation of one section of the law in question. It could not, however, be successfully argued that the book was also promoting the resurgence of Naziism — which was the second provision under which a publisher could be considered in contravention of the law. The hands of the court were tied, and

A literary meeting of minds. Dr. Frank Benseler at the microphone with Karl-Dietrich Wolff on his left and Joachim Mansch on his right.

the ruling came down in favour of the publisher. Although K.W. Schütz could not legally be barred from exhibiting at the Fair, in the eyes of many Fair visitors and even a number of administrators, this ruling was seen as a travesty of justice — but it was also one without further judicial recourse at the time.

On other fronts, for more than two years the construction of the Frankfurt subway or U-Bahn system, along with other major building projects, had been making travel to the Fair an extremely difficult and time-consuming ordeal. It had also become the cause of major aggravation to both exhibitors and visitors, who complained bitterly about having to resort to paying exorbitant taxi fares or making an extended hike from the Hauptbahnhof (the main train station) to the entrance of the fairgrounds. Eventually, the city's highly efficient transport system would prove to be an enormous advantage for all concerned, but there is no question that its construction created more than its share of grief and disruption.

A press conference — 1976-style.

Chapter 19
~~~
## Major Book Fair Themes – From Latin America to India

Within the Fair itself, by 1973 the winds of change were in motion. Sigfred Taubert, who had overseen and guided the event as Fair director for eighteen years, made the decision to opt for early retirement at the age of sixty. As Taubert's successor, the board of directors appointed a young man with five years' experience on the Fair's organizational team, where he had been responsible for all foreign exhibits mounted by the Frankfurt Book Fair Company. At thirty-six years of age, Peter Weidhaas (the author of this book) was appointed as the new director of the Frankfurt Book Fair.

In many respects, it could be said that Taubert's departure also marked the end of an era for the Book Fair that had first opened its doors in 1949. By contrast, in 1975 an atmosphere of American-style promotional hype dominated the scene as the publishers of a number of competing biographies, whose subjects included Muhammad Ali, Curt Jürgens, Hildegard Knef, and Gina Lollobrigida, vied shamelessly for public attention. The reaction of the press, which was still subliminally influenced by the 1968 anti-capitalist values of the "protest generation," was less than enthusiastic. Certainly it had no interest whatever in becoming the instrument of ambitious publishers' marketing campaigns, and as a result, most journalists grew increasingly critical of both the book trade and of the Book Fair itself. The industry and the Fair clearly had an image problem.

As one of those responsible for the successful operation of the Fair, the new director had closely monitored this disturbing development during the previous two years. At a prearranged meeting, the Fair's board of directors and selected journalists engaged in frank discussion and presented their concerns as well as constructive suggestions for the future direction of the Fair. The consensus was that there were many commendable aspects to the Book Fair that were totally unrelated to the bestseller list. What about the many publications on art, on religion, on science that were also displayed but that received relatively little attention or publicity in comparison to the high-flying bestsellers? Perhaps the answer lay in the creation of specific leitmotifs, or themes, that could breathe new life into the Fair and act as an alternative to the bestseller mentality that had gradually become a predominant aspect of the event.

The few long-time exhibitors who protested this move were quickly silenced when it was made clear that the business aspect of the Fair would remain entirely unchanged by this innovation. The new concept of themes, however, was a novel approach to dealing with the image problem. In 1976, the Fair opened with "Latin America" as its first major theme, and the general response to this choice indicated that the plan for enhancing the appeal of the Fair had been well-timed.

In France and the U.S., Latin American literature had already been moderately embraced in various quarters. Although a few titles had been translated as early as the 1950s, most had not enjoyed any particular success in Germany or the rest of Europe. In fact, for the most part, they had usually been withdrawn from the market and sold at clearance prices.

The effect of introducing Latin American literature as a major theme was most evident in the case of the Colombian magic-realist author of *One Hundred Years of Solitude*, Gabriel García Márquez. As a result of the 1976 Book Fair, his publishers went on to sell several hundred thousand copies of every new novel he produced. Originally Márquez had first been published in Germany in 1966 by Aufbau Press in Berlin. The licensing rights for the Federal

*Participants at the 1976 "Latin America" Fair. Left to right: Jose Donoso (Chile), Thiago di Mello (Brazil), Moderator Curt Meyer-Clason, Julio Cortazar (Argentina), with Manuel Scorza and Mario Vargas Llosa (Peru).*

Republic were obtained by Sigbert-Mohn Publishing Company, but, at the time, the sales were so infinitesimal that the publishers could not even cover their costs. Subsequent publications of his work in 1968 and 1970 fared no better, and the success of his contemporaries from other Latin American countries was also extremely modest.

In 1976 the Frankfurt publisher Suhrkamp, recognizing the potential of this major theme, decided to aggressively promote the work of several Latin American authors by acquiring the rights from their former publishers and producing first-time translations of others.

The Frankfurt Book Fair issued a number of special invitations to authors from Latin America and thirty of them accepted. A notable exception, however, was none other than Gabriel García Márquez. His refusal was based on a firm conviction that the Fair's interests were primarily aligned with those of major publishers and of capitalism in general. As well, with only six events planned, the program appeared to be doing precious little to further Latin

American culture. As it turned out, reality far outstripped these dire predictions, and the concept of specific themes was about to come into its own.

The special exhibitions and events drew substantial crowds and the reviews in the press were generally favourable. It was obvious that a boom in Latin American literature had been successfully launched in Europe. In fact, this phenomenon also went on to demonstrate that whatever happened in Frankfurt eventually echoed in book circles around the world.

Following the success of the introduction of the Latin American theme, it was almost inevitable that there would still be controversy over the choice of subsequent themes and the programs planned to accompany them, but — in principle — the concept of carefully selected leitmotifs was no longer an issue. It was decided that a new theme would be introduced only every two years and that an appropriate logo would be designed to accompany each theme.

In 1978 the theme "Books and the Child" ruffled a few feathers when, without the knowledge of participating publishers, the Fair direction purchased about nine hundred children's and young adult titles and proceeded to have them evaluated by a panel of experts with an eye to uncovering any whiff of racism or stereotyping. Nor did the results produced by the panel prove to be especially flattering. The publishers concerned, particularly those offering traditional favourites such as *Little Black Sambo* and *Robinson Crusoe*, were also due to come under fire from educators and politicians in subsequent events featuring books for children and young people. The age of political correctness had made its entrance.

The end result, however, was that the theme "Books and the Child" elicited widespread and positive reports. And the quality of the reportage was not only of a higher standard, but — better still — it continued throughout the course of the year. Almost without exception, in the estimation of both the national and international media, the decision to introduce major themes was hailed as a positive move. One clear indication of this was the amount of time allotted for radio and television coverage of the

1978 "Books and the Child" Fair. In comparison with the Latin American theme of two years earlier, the amount of time devoted to coverage had doubled.

In 1980 the theme was "The Literature of Black Africa." Once again, as with the Latin American theme, the purpose of selecting a specific motif was to direct the attention of the fair-going public and assembled publishers to a part of the world where the indigenous literature was virtually unknown. But, as usual, the difference between concept and consensus was another matter entirely.

From the outset, plans for the programming were contentious for a variety of reasons, beginning with South Africa's controversial policy of apartheid. Once the Fair had opened and the protagonists found themselves under the same roof, there were legitimate fears that an incident could erupt at any moment. When the supporters of the opposing factions met face to face — the white apartheid publishing representatives from South Africa and the underground supporters of the African National Congress (ANC) — it appeared almost inevitable. Who could have predicted the profound effect of the words of one man on those who attended the symposium scheduled to take place in the Conference Hall of the Römer on the topic "The Function of Modern African Literature"? The audience sat riveted as South African writer James Matthews spoke from the heart:

> I ask myself what the devil I'm doing here. I am only half-literate, and yet I have been given a room at a super-luxury hotel. I push a button and food is brought to me. Should I be won over? This country, like all other European countries, has exploited my country. And where is the compensation? This is the first time I have even been allowed to leave my country. For twenty years I was refused a passport. How come I have one now? Is your country so powerful that it can exploit us and still negotiate a passport for us at the same time?

> I am no author, I am no poet. I am here to talk about the pain I feel. The pain that my sister and my son feel; prisons are my home.
>
> Do I write poems? No, I write feelings. Once I wanted to write a poem; I wanted to write about a bird, the sky, the sea. But I look at myself, and my people; we are bound in chains; we are held in a prison. I cannot write a poem about beauty; I only know my pain. The pain of my brothers and sisters. I am still totally confused about why I'm here. Shit, shit, shit![47]

From fourteen countries, twenty-six black African authors — some living in exile, others from their countries of origin — came together in Frankfurt-am-Main. Among them was Nigerian writer Chinua Achebe, whose classic novel *Things Fall Apart* is still regarded as one of the greatest literary works to come out of Africa in the twentieth century. Also present was the poet Sipho Sepamla, who, like James Matthews, only obtained an exit visa from South Africa through the intervention of the Fair administration and the German Embassy there. In addition, fifty-four black African publishers from thirty different countries also made their appearance — including the banned South African publisher Peter Randall of Ravan Press, Johannesburg.

Never before had so many important spokespersons for black African identity been assembled together in one place! What better opportunity could be found to highlight so many of Africa's most urgent issues? In order to draw public attention to their mutual concerns, African authors and publishers made the decision to boycott the Fair for a day. The voices of the majority of the authors attending the Fair were being heard outside Africa for the first time and many left for home with promises of translations to come. Among these was a virtually unknown young Senegalese feminist, Mariama Bâ, who signed fourteen licence contracts for her novella *Such a Long Letter.*

*Chancellor Willy Brandt officially opens the "Black Africa" Book Fair in 1980.*

Once again, the Frankfurt Book Fair had become the forum for discussion on a series of wide-ranging problems that also affected the book trade. In 1980, as a direct result of this trail-blazing agenda, a group of dedicated German publishers, book dealers, and academics formed the Association for the Promotion of the Literature of Asia, Africa and Latin America. Within the first year, ten scouts for the association were able to negotiate thirty options on African titles and four licence contracts. Over the two following decades, the association went on to negotiate the highly successful publication of literary works from these continents. The black Africa theme had proved itself not only a resounding success but one with a ripple effect that would be felt for generations to come.

Predictably, criticism and discussion were the usual by-products of the 1982 Book Fair and its major theme, "Religion of Yesterday in the World of Today." In his opening speech, the evangelical theologian Heinz Zahrnt went directly to the heart of the issue: "On the one hand, some people were afraid the theme of 'Religion' sounded too pious and the events planned around the theme could take on the trappings of a literary church seminar; on the other hand, some people felt it was not pious enough." In Zahrnt's view, the theme was one that encompassed the enormous difficulties facing all religious faiths at that particular juncture, and he placed particular emphasis on the serious consequences of ambivalence.

At a press conference, the remarks of Fair Director Peter Weidhaas indicated not only his personal concerns, but those of many of his colleagues in the book industry:

> We have to take care not to become too distracted by the overall growth of the Fair, and to strike a balance between its increased public appeal and the need to maintain standards of quality. This means, among other things, that the requirements of the market and the public's cultural objectives must be balanced and synchronized with great precision. Unquestionably there are areas in which special interests must be allowed to flourish without interference. These interests must remain secure; and competing forces must not be allowed to impede or threaten the identity of smaller groups, regardless of how they may define themselves.

There was, however, a fundamental problem brought to light by the statistics for the display of theological and religious literature. In the previous year — 1981 — this category accounted for only 3,082 titles, representing only 5.2 percent of all book production, although more than two-thirds of these titles were new publications. The question remained, what about the thousands of books on exhibit in other categories that had religious connotations in one form or another? By virtue of this grey area between publications with strictly religious subject matter and those placed in a different category that might be considered relevant, the 1982 Fair was comparatively less remarkable than its forerunners.

Two years later, at first glance, the theme of the 1984 Fair held fascinating possibilities. Entitled "The Idea," it tied in perfectly with an entire spectrum of publications relating to science, ecology, and genetics. The year 1984 also held a special, if unintended, literary significance for generations of students weaned on George Orwell's futuristic predictions for 1984. For some, this was regarded as an aspect that detracted from the breadth of the theme, while for others, such as the science publishers, the concept could be expanded to include the slogan "Orwell 2000."

In his opening speech, Neil Postman, the American media critic and author of *Amusing Ourselves to Death*, took issue with the title of the Fair's theme:

> Without doubt, in certain parts of the world, Orwell's vision has almost been realized. If one reads *1984* and Arthur Koestler's novel *Solar Eclipse*, the result might be considered a fairly accurate picture of the Soviet Union and its use of methods that ensure absolute control…. When it comes to Western democracies, neither Orwell nor Koestler strikes directly at the root of the problem. If a person wants to understand how technology controls the American population, then one must turn to another visionary, Aldous Huxley, and his magnificent book *Brave New World*…. Orwell's tools of tyranny — "Big Brother" and the "Thought Police" — are no longer needed because the population has become totally enthralled by a plethora of technology which they have come to embrace without fear.

Perhaps for the first time, a theme for the Frankfurt Book Fair had been chosen that did not fall directly within the purview of any specific category. One unintended result of this choice was the perception that a deliberately critical approach had been adopted towards the USSR — a fact that greatly angered their representatives and participating publishers. To quell the impending possibility of an incident, Fair authorities attempted to make it absolutely clear that the choice of theme was neither a deliberate slight nor an attempt to discredit Soviet policy.

By 1984, the advance of commercial television had kindled a broad discussion of the future of the printed word in book form and the cultural value it embodied. An installation by the Swiss artist Hans Knecht, mounted on the fairgrounds and entitled "The Kultigator," only served to heighten the debate between the traditionalists and those with an eye to future trends in terms of technology. Knecht's "Kultigator," a thirty-ton printing press disguised as a crocodile devouring television sets and spewing them out as colourful compressed "works of art" acted as an ideal catalyst for heated discussion.

As an event whose primary purpose was to promote books, the Fair had somehow been upstaged by a theme that might be interpreted as an attack on prevailing cultural values. In spite of the deep concerns of book dealers, publishers, and readers faced with the ever-increasing inroads made by the electronic media, the Frankfurt Book Fair was not the place to settle the debate over the loss of these values.

To add fuel to the fire, the Orwell aspect of the theme had suffered from overkill in the literary supplements and electronic media prior to the opening of the Fair. As a result, the Book Fair public had already been inundated with information before even setting foot on the fairgrounds, and — for the most part — instead of enthusiasm, their reaction was one of irritation. Almost a decade later, in 1993 the Book Fair adopted a related theme based on the impact of "The New Media," but by then the future had already overtaken the past in terms of literary or negative criticism, making it possible to explore the theme more dispassionately.

In 1986, in his opening address, the Indian minister for human resources development, Narasimha Rao, expressed deep gratitude for the choice of the theme, "India — Tradition in Transition." On the same occasion, Germany's foreign minister, Hans Dietrich Genscher, welcomed the exhibitors, visitors, poets, writers, artists, and business people who had travelled from India to participate in the city's thirty-eighth Fair since 1949.

*Four of India's prominent women writers are ready to respond to questions from the press as India is featured as the 1986 Country of the Year.*

It was hoped that the selection of India as the Fair's focal point would echo the success of the earlier themes highlighting Latin America and Africa, both of which had first exposed readers from many countries to the vibrant literature of another continent. From the standpoint of visitors to the Book Fair, there was certainly no lack of display material for an interesting variety of presentations: daily readings by the invited authors in their native tongues with simultaneous translation, music and dance presentations, not to mention the added attraction of Indian food specialties. All this and more was intended to bring the literature of India to a broad spectrum of interested publishers and media — and, of course, to German readers, as well. A suitably embellished "Indian Hall" was specifically designated for this purpose and was to be the forum for all activities and events, including a display of seven thousand books from and about India.

Yet, in spite of all its inherent possibilities, the theme failed to live up to the hopeful expectations of those behind the scenes.

Although the tone of initial reports in the media was generally neutral and innocuous, it soon became clear that the coverage was primarily dependent on clichés relating to classical India, instead of addressing the complexities of the present. Yet another stumbling block was the books themselves. Unfamiliar philosophies, complex plot lines, a bewildering delineation of characters, and even the unfamiliar pronunciation of the Indian authors reading their works in English were all perceived as being too foreign for public consumption. The audience remained either puzzled or indifferent. With a prescient sense of foreboding, fully a month before the Fair, the director had already voiced his well-founded concerns that the probability of misguided perceptions and a general misunderstanding of the realities of India and its literature did not bode well for the success of the theme. And, in the end, his worst fears were realized. In essence, as a Fair theme, India had been a flop.

After ten successful years, the concept of major themes had clearly run its course. It was time for new and innovative ideas to come to the fore.

# Chapter 20
~~~
Growing Internationalism

The French weekly *Le Nouvel Observateur* brought the internationalism of the Frankfurt Book Fair to the attention of its readers in 1998. They selected its director, whom it dubbed "Monsieur Bookworld," to be "one of the 101 personalities who are making the Old Continent into the New World," pointing to the fact that "within the past year, 107 countries ranging from Albania to Zimbabwe were represented at the Frankfurt Book Fair with a record total of 9,587 exhibitors." From its earliest days, this internationalism had been vigorously promoted by directors Wilhelm Müller and Sigfred Taubert. During the author's watch as Fair director (1975–2000), Frankfurt became the hub of the international book trade and a strategic planning centre. People all over the world had begun referring to the Frankfurt Book Fair as "the Mecca of the Book Trade."

Sigfred Taubert had tried in 1973 and again in 1974 to entice mainland China back to Frankfurt after it had pulled up stakes in 1957 because of the simultaneous participation of Taiwan. But it was not until 1975, during the first trip to mainland China by a Fair director, that a political solution was successfully negotiated between Taiwan and the People's Republic of China. Down the road, there would be periodic moments of tension, but, at the time, both countries eventually agreed to forego the use of state names, emblems, or flags in their displays. In principle, this compromise remains in place and the publications produced by both mainland China and Taiwan continue to be exhibited in adjacent stands.

After a fifteen-year boycott, Albania also returned to the fold in 1975 and soon became an extraordinarily successful participant. At the time, the reigning dictator, Enver Hodscha, had been in power for decades, but a personal invitation sent to him by the author, Fair Director Peter Weidhaas, produced the desired effect. Fourteen days later, Weidhaas was visited in Frankfurt by official representatives from the Albanian Trade Delegation posted in Vienna, and the stage was set for future participation.

For the Frankfurt Book Fair, the rapid advance of internationalism was serving as a vehicle for the final stages of its metamorphosis. Initially business had been based on the placing of orders and signing of contacts between publishers and retailers. This, in turn, gave way to trade from one publishing house to another. Then, in the 1960s, with a marked increase in international participation, the business of the Fair began to be concentrated on translations, secondary rights, licences, and co-production. At the peak of this

Mexico is celebrated at the 1992 opening of the Frankfurt Book Fair. Left to right: Education Minister Zedillo, Exchange President Hess-Meyer, author Octavio Paz, and External Affairs Minister Kinkel.

period, it is estimated that 80 percent of rights transactions in the book business were negotiated and concluded in Frankfurt. Most importantly, literary transactions and exchange agreements between the Western and socialist countries were almost exclusively conducted at the Frankfurt Fair.

Based on the success of these negotiations, the Fair authorities decided to increase their efforts to bring international publishers to Frankfurt and to start thinking outside the box. They were considering not only homegrown promotional events but also the potential for consulting, conducting workshops and seminars, and participating in such events in foreign countries, as well as holding bilateral book fairs in former guest countries. There was, however, a condition placed on the closing discussions that would finalize any negotiations between participants. The Frankfurt Book Fair, in its capacity as an internationally recognized "book fair territory," would be the site of all further continuation of "the negotiation dialogue."

In 1975, the Fair director undertook visits to publishers in Colombia, Venezuela, Mexico, Peru, Bolivia, Brazil, Uruguay, Argentina, and — for the first time — Havana, where he was able to establish relations with Cuban publishers and also publicize the major South American theme planned for 1976 to all the Latin American countries.

A year later, a cultural agreement was concluded with the USSR in Moscow. This contract was initially intended to facilitate the participation of Berlin publishers in West German book exhibitions. However, it became the basis for all cultural co-operation between the Federal Republic and the USSR. At the same time, consultations took place on the future establishment of the Moscow Book Fair. In turn, these events assured the Fair director of friendly relations with the highest representatives of the state-controlled book trade and the Ministry of Printing and Publishing within the USSR. Consequently, a visit with the minister and an exchange of information on the book trade became a necessary part of every trip to Moscow, and this *entente cordiale* continued until the collapse of the Soviet book trade in the 1990s.

Photograph taken at the Portuguese Pavillion in 1997. Germany's President Herzog is shown in conversation with Portuguese President Sampaio and the region of Hessen's President Eichel.

Workshops

During a five-week promotional and fact-finding tour, African publishers and authors were sought out in Cameroon, Ghana, the Ivory Coast, Senegal, Kenya, Tanzania, and Zambia in order to entice them into becoming participants in the major theme "Black Africa," scheduled to take place at the Frankfurt Book Fair in 1980.

At the same time a series of workshops took place in Ile-Ife, Nigeria, and in Nairobi, Kenya. These "Workshops on Economic Publishing" were modelled after highly successful mini-press operations in Germany in use at that time. Using desktop publishing programs and small offset printers with assembly machines, these operations could print up to fifteen hundred copies on very basic equipment and involved little expense. In both cases, an advisory team of three sent out from Frankfurt worked in tandem with eager employees for eight to ten days, and together they each managed to produce a book. These workshops proved to be particularly popular in Third World countries. In the following years, this same program was activated in Zambia, Tanzania, Nicaragua, and Colombia, as well as in Thailand and the Philippines.

Although the teams could not effectively improve the infrastructure of the book trade in these developing countries, for a number of young publishers interested in book production, the program helped set them on the way to some surprisingly successful initiatives within their own domestic book markets.

Beginning in 1990, workshops were also conducted in eastern European countries where the book trade had been state-controlled. Here the focus was on marketing in the publishing and book business. The content of these workshops, conducted in Russia, the Ukraine, White Russia, Poland, Latvia, Romania, Bulgaria, and Moldavia, as well as in the former East Germany, brought highly useful and practical knowledge to the participants for the creation of new book marketing ventures. Eventually, the most successful participants were brought to Frankfurt at the expense of the Fair Authority, and, not surprisingly, they became among the most loyal and enthusiastic participants at the Fair.

Participation at Other International Book Fairs

In the meantime, the Exhibition Department of the Frankfurt Book Fair Administration was becoming increasingly involved with other book fairs that had been established and were making use of the Frankfurt model. Exhibits for German publishers were set up in Bologna, at the American Booksellers Association travelling book fair in the U.S., in Buenos Aires, in Bogota, Guadalajara, Mexico City, Cairo, New Delhi, Moscow, Calcutta, and Beijing, and later on in Santiago, Havana, Harare, Beirut, Jerusalem, London, Paris, Warsaw, Budapest, Bucharest, Seoul, Taipei, and Tokyo. German books were seeing the world and the world was meeting Germany.

In no sense were these international book fairs regarded as rivals, but rather as venues to be supported and counselled in their significant work for publishing in general. This was true of almost a dozen book fairs where the national associations for the book trade expressed their appreciation by turning to Frankfurt-am-Main for advice. In this way, the Frankfurt Book Fair gradually developed into an information centre for all questions relating to the book trade. In the past thirty years, scarcely a book fair has taken place without the contribution of a Frankfurt expert using the Frankfurt model as the basis for the operation.

German Book Fairs in New York, Madrid, and Paris

In the 1980s those responsible for the operation of the Frankfurt Book Fair concluded that in order to promote contact between book producers and the book industries, it would be in their best interests to attend certain important book fairs being held in other countries. The main advantage was that it would be a useful means of consolidating business connections and strengthening ties between German publishers and their counterparts in the U.S., France, and Spain. The results of these exchanges would then translate into expanded participation and increased possibilities at Frankfurt Book Fairs in the future.

To this end, more than two hundred German publishers travelled to New York in March 1983 to set up their stands as part of a small-scale Frankfurt Book Fair. This experiment — a miniature "Frankfurt on the Hudson," as it was described in the trade paper *Publishers' Weekly* — drew thirty-five thousand visitors, of which perhaps 20 percent were people involved in the book trade. For four days, the participants were offered an extensive program including a series of bilateral speeches on book-related topics, as well as literary readings and discussions. Both the German and American press covered the event in detail, including the influential *Die Zeit*. Rolf Michaelis, one of the paper's top correspondents, began his report by describing the specially designed central symbol created for the German book fair taking place in the city known as the Big Apple:

> The first thing you see is not a book but an apple. A gigantic red apple sliced very fine and projected luminously off the many walls as the turning pages of a book....
>
> The overpowering and familiar aroma of a book fair is in the air — the smell of dust, paper, printer's ink, and throngs of people, who stream through to the surprise and delight of the organizers from Frankfurt. From the first to the last event on the program, people have been stepping on each other's toes to find the best vantage point. The final presentation — a discussion, sponsored by the Goethe Haus and the New School for Social Research, was held in the latter's main lecture hall in Greenwich Village. At this point a serious pushing and shoving match developed between the uniformed security personnel and the hundreds of would-be listeners who had lined up three-deep around the block and wanted to at least gain entry to a neighbouring lecture hall where the anticipated discussion would be broadcast by loud-speaker. Three prominent writers, two American and one German — Joyce Carol Oates, John Irving, and Günter Grass — had been brought together to exchange views on "The Author's Responsibility in a Threatened World."

The event developed into a landmark discussion that was later recorded and featured on hundreds of radio stations throughout the United States and Canada. People were primarily interested in hearing Günter Grass, who had allegedly said in an earlier interview that there were "fascist" or "racist" tendencies among the American people. Little was made of this in the U.S., however in

Umberto Eco officially opens the 1987 Book Fair.

Germany's right-wing press reports of Grass's remarks provoked strong and occasionally unbridled reaction. In Hamburg's daily newspaper, *Die Welt*, the owner of Springer Publishing, Axel Springer, penned an editorial, published on March 16, 1983. In his piece, Springer labelled those attending the book fair in New York as participants in "an orgy of doom and gloom perpetrated by 'progressive' American and German literati and self-styled authorities on culture." Unlike the coverage of the majority of book-related events, in Germany, the "Frankfurt-in-New York" enterprise was given unparalleled attention and publicity.

Showcasing New Themes

By now, the concept of leitmotifs, or themes, had become an established element in the annual program of the Frankfurt Book Fair. As a result, the involvement of the press had expanded considerably. In 1976, with the focus on Latin America, 2,375 journalists attended and reported on the Book Fair. Ten years later, when the spotlight was on India, this number had already increased to 8,100.

The Frankfurt Book Fair had become a widely respected public event, not only in Germany, but internationally. Reports were being widely circulated on what was happening in Frankfurt: the topics of discussion, exhibits, and plans for new regional and cultural themes. Clearly, the concept of these themes, which had had such a significant impact on the Fair's reputation in other countries, needed to be maintained, but as the 1980s drew to a close, the less-than-successful experiences of the two most recent theme years had sent up signals that the public appetite was ready for something new and different. Within the Fair administration, the usual opposition to change was anticipated, but in the end it was agreed that the possibility of introducing specific countries as Fair themes held the most promise. As it turned out, it was a landmark decision that brought Frankfurt worldwide prestige on an even grander scale.

In 1987, which was a theme-free year, Umberto Eco, the celebrated author of the novel *The Name of the Rose*, made a much heralded appearance at the Book Fair's opening. The amount of publicity created by this event inspired the Italian ambassador to Germany, Luigi Vittorio Ferraris, to promote the idea that Italy could be featured within the context of a country-based theme. Ferraris spoke excellent German and was widely read, taking positions on important contemporary issues in the influential weekly *Die Zeit*, as well as in other national papers. He applied himself to promoting this concept with great enthusiasm and won the support of President Francesco Cossiga and Italy's foreign minister, Giulio Andreotti, who approved the DM 29 million budget for the Italian cultural presentation and attended the opening of the Book Fair in person.

The final result of Luigi Ferraris's original inspiration was a magnificent extravaganza, extending far beyond the realm of literature. Most of it was staged in the "Forum," which had been designed by Mario Garbuglia, architect of the Cinecittà. He miraculously transformed the 1950s vintage conference hall into six elaborate Italianate palaces connected by a series of passages constructed out of papier mâché. The first was a reproduction of a fifteenth-century palace, symbolizing the beginnings of the history of the Italian publishing industry; the second was a replica of a sixteenth-century marble palace. Then came a seventeenth-century baroque edifice containing an exhibit of prize-winning Italian literature, and an eighteenth-century palace featuring an exhibition of contemporary works by Italian writers. The fifth structure was a replica of the facade of a nineteenth-century palace, where information was distributed on Italian opera as well as the great figures of romantic literature and music, and finally there was an art nouveau–style kiosk featuring a display devoted to the publishing industry. The end result was a display so colourful and diverse that it almost defied description — a profusion of charm and imagination. The majority of visitors voiced nothing but admiration, but certain Italian exhibitors, whose commercial displays were housed in Hall 4, were critical of what they chose to refer to as the "Palazzo Kitsch." There is no question, however, that there was a powerfully pulsating Italian presence throughout the Fair —among the displays of books, catalogues, and art; in the typical Italian *Café degli Specchi* (Café of Mirrors); in the complete Scriptorium replicated from the film *The Name of the Rose;* and in the small arena set up for a variety of presentations and events.

Seats in the main Forum were always at a premium and the narrow entrances were perpetually blocked with visitors who wanted to hear a few words. Aldo Busi, the author of *The Standard Life of a Temporary Pantyhose Salesman*, was standing outside, ready to take the podium. Busi had been asked to read in German, but he refused and immediately launched into a critical diatribe against the Italian pavilion: "This pavilion has nothing to do with Italy. Do we see the unemployed of the South; the drug addicts? Do we find the real, working Italy? No. We find ourselves here in the midst of mediocrity at its hypocritical best. How can a culture survive under papier mâché?" Eventually Busi did give a reading, but because the German translation was difficult for him, he simply left out the words he did not understand.[48]

In the small arena, every last seat was filled when the Italian under-secretary of state, Susanna Agnelli, whose brother, Giovanni, was the head of Fiat, presented a paper on "The Businessman as Publisher" — a topic that elicited a great deal of interest. When it came to the promotion of culture, Italy's major businesses were the acknowledged pioneers in the field. The larger Italian companies were producing at least two hundred high-end titles annually. At that time, national savings banks alone had published two thousand titles — most of which were art books. The evidence was indisputable. Italian private enterprise had poured huge amounts of capital into book production and the audience was intrigued to learn more about it.

As for the hugely popular Café of Mirrors, the place was perpetually crowded and quickly became the hit of the Italian-style Book Fair, where you could enjoy a cool refreshing Prosecco, a small panini, and real Italian ice cream.

Keynote speaker Umberto Eco deep in discussion with Exchange Chairman Gunther Christiansen and Fair Director Peter Weidhaas, 1987.

Among the high-profile Italian visitors seen pushing their way through the throngs were Frederico Fellini and his wife Giulietta Massini. Fellini had been invited to mount a showcase series of his films at Frankfurt's Film Museum on the Mainquai. It was an obvious tie-in to the theme of the Book Fair and the museum remains a popular venue for film enthusiasts throughout the year.

With the unparalleled success of its appearance at the Book Fair, Italy had become the model for future presentations by other countries. The reason lay — first and foremost — in the lively nature of a multi-faceted festival that far exceeded the limits of a book fair in terms of content, as well as time and space. On the other hand, it had not neglected to emphasize Italy's contemporary cultural identity.

At a later date, vocal critics of the "theme country" concept were at the heart of a certain amount of acrimonious public debate and discussion within the featured country, long before its actual appearance in Frankfurt. In the final analysis, it all came down to how a country decided to present itself and who best represented that particular public face. It was almost inevitable that when it came to making these crucial decisions, there would be wrangling between various homegrown political groups, and it was not always the best or most promising vision that found its way to Frankfurt.

The creative minds behind the scenes in the organization of the Italian theme had been able to make their chosen vision of Italy appealing through a brilliant variety of events and presentations. Their goal — to promote Italian literature outside the country — had been crowned with success. For a second time, the scholar and novelist Umberto Eco was a dominant force in all of the literary discussions — eight years after the debut of the original Italian version of his blockbuster novel *The Name of the Rose* by the Milan publisher Bompiani and the publication of his second novel, *Foucault's Pendulum*. As in the case of the theme of Latin America, the result of exposure to a profusion of promising titles by virtually unknown Italian authors created a remarkable translation boom that continued for several years after the Fair of 1988.

The Frankfurt Book Fair also profited from the continued showcasing of featured countries. France followed Italy in 1989, and the list went on to include Japan in 1990, Spain in 1991, Mexico in 1992, the Netherlands and Flanders in 1993, Brazil in 1994, Austria in 1995, Ireland in 1996, Portugal in 1997, Switzerland in 1998, Hungary in 1999, Poland in 2000, Greece in 2001, and Lithuania in 2002. Russia was featured in 2003, followed by the Arab countries in 2004, South Korea in 2005, and India in 2006. In 2007 the spotlight will be on Catalan culture.

Each year another unique spirit with its own individual folklore permeated the atmosphere of the Book Fair. For a full year, the newspapers and TV channels of the featured country covered the discussions and debates over the details of that country's presence in Frankfurt-am-Main. Frankfurt was the goal and main topic of discussions, talk shows, and disputes. The name "Frankfurt" alone conveyed the entire concept of the annual book fair in that city. Even a publisher who had previously boycotted the Fair had to ask himself whether or not to test the waters should his homeland be selected as the country of the year.

When Italy made its inaugural presentation in 1988 with a total of 386 publishers, there had already been a significant increase in the numbers of exhibitors worldwide. In fact, the total number of exhibitors converging on Frankfurt from ninety-seven different countries was close to 10 percent more than in the preceding year. Clearly, there was no turning back.

Chapter 21
A Changing Infrastructure

ach year statistics relating to the Fair were carefully tabulated, and the figures below give a good indication of the decade-by-decade growth of the Frankfurt Book Fair, beginning in 1970, when roughly 2,500 exhibitors represented 66 different countries. Ten years later, the numbers had increased dramatically to almost 4,000, and 93 countries were registered. By 1990, the number of participating countries had slipped to 90, but the overall total of exhibitors had risen to more than 6,000.

Where the number of exhibitors appears to have diminished in the year 2000, in reality the figure reflects a change in the methods of statistical record-keeping, with the focus being redirected towards individual exhibits. The Millennium Fair featured an additional 79 group exhibits representing about 3,000 publishing companies, whereas the previous system would have recorded a grand total of 7,300 exhibitors from 107 countries — an increase of more than 1,000 exhibitors since 1990.

Within a thirty-year period, the space devoted to the displays had been expanded to almost five times the original area in square metres (from 39,000 to 198,558). A visitor who decided to try to cover every last one of the almost seven thousand booths would have covered a distance of more than thirty kilometres. Guinness World Records might well have an interest in knowing how many people — if any — have actually managed to accomplish this feat.

The same increase applied to the number of visitors. At the beginning of this period, the ordinary visitors, as opposed to the book trade professionals, represented approximately 70 percent of the attendance. Mornings were reserved exclusively for the book trade. But in the last decade of the twentieth century, the staggering increase in professional attendance forced a limitation on public access. In future, this would take place only on the final two days, which always fell on a weekend.

Like a growing city, the Book Fair needed its own infrastructure to facilitate each visitor's ease in finding individual points of contact quickly and efficiently. Groups with specific functions or agendas required rooms in which to meet and work. In the 1960s, the displays had been loosely organized by category such as literature, art, children's and young adult titles, science, religion, and foreign exhibits. With expansion, these categories had to be reorganized into numbered displays that made it easier to locate each individual exhibit and allow the traffic to flow more efficiently.

The beginnings of the restructuring process took place in the mid-1970s. The Fair Catalogue and the organizational system were revised. Alphabetically arranged corridors were furnished with large, easy-to-read identification signs at both ends. In spite of the enormous expanse of the fairgrounds, the new system worked with far greater efficiency. The booth numbers — with even numbers on the right and odd on the left — were clearly marked, and the signage for display hall and group designations made it relatively easy to find the exact location of each exhibitor's display.

The Establishment of Centres

Following the restructuring of the Fair in the 1970s, foreign exhibitors and German exhibitors divided themselves into two distinct entities. Each had its own separate goals and specific target groups. German publishers normally met with German book dealers, librarians, journalists, and only to a limited degree with foreign exhibitors for the buying or selling of rights. Foreign exhibitors, on the other hand, were interested almost exclusively in meeting with exhibitors from other countries.

As a direct result of the 1968 confrontations and ensuing difficulties with the press and media representatives, the Press and Media Centre was created. This, in turn, led to the development of similar centres for special interest groups such as librarians, German book retailers, and literary agents. These centres were organized according to the needs of each group. Every Fair participant had to register on arrival in order to establish his whereabouts for other fairgoers who might want to get in touch. A message board at the entrance of each centre was an ideal means of contacting people, and appointments could be set up as time allowed. Registered members of these centres could make use of the facilities within its defined area: the coffee bar, a restaurant in the Press and Media Centre, and business facilities such as telephone booths, typewriters, and later, fax and computer terminals. In addition, there were cloakrooms and lockers where promotional and other related material could be safely stored.

A Centre for Foreign Book Dealers

A well-known denizen of the Book Fair was a Jewish woman who had fled the Nazis in the 1930s and set up her own German bookshop in New York. Unwittingly she was also the source of inspiration for the concept of special interest centres. Each year, without fail, Mary Rosenberg had lugged her bulging briefcases crammed with publishing catalogues and sample books through the aisles of the Fair. But anyone hoping to actually find the elderly book dealer was faced with the problem of locating her somewhere within the labyrinth. Even Fair officials were at a loss to be of assistance. It was definitely a problem in need of a solution.

The new Centre for Foreign Book Dealers could well have been named the "Mary Rosenberg Centre," since it was so ideally designed to meet the needs of that particular individual. And for countless other book dealers who had been equally hard to track down, it proved to be the answer to this persistent dilemma. It was within the sheltering walls of this new centre that two to three thousand foreign book dealers from roughly sixty different countries were able to find themselves a workplace and a welcome refuge amidst the chaos of the Fair.

A Centre for Librarians

A year later the Book Dealers' Centre was expanded to include a Centre for Librarians. Under the leadership of Andreas Werner, the librarian of Frankfurt's Municipal and University Library, the group hoped to be in a position to develop a specific section for librarians and their clientele. Certainly this was Werner's original motivation. The Fair administration discovered that it had been encouraging librarians to visit the Fair without being aware that those employed in public libraries were unable to claim expense refunds for attendance at commercial book fairs. It only made practical sense for the Fair administration to organize an appropriate program in the form of lectures, discussions, and displays to remedy the situation. About eight hundred librarians, both German and foreign, were present for the opening of the newly established centre. The numbers of those making use of the centre continued to rise. By the 1980s it had swelled to three thousand, a number that remained more or less unchanged until the turn of the twenty-first century.

A Centre for Literary Agents

In the tradition of European publishing, it was generally accepted that an author was involved in a direct partnership with a particular publishing house that, in turn, was represented by the publisher of the firm or its editor-in-chief. For the most part, the publishing house also dealt exclusively with the subsidiary and translation rights to the work that it had published. Only in exceptional cases did it allow the author to participate in this aspect of the transactions.

In the 1980s, however, significant changes in the publishing industry gradually took hold, and these became even more pronounced in the 1990s. With important internal developments emerging within the majority of publishing houses, an opportunity presented itself for literary agents to become the new partner of individual authors. The agents' extensive knowledge of the market and their far-reaching contacts enabled them to advise the author on many aspects of works-in-progress — including their content — and to position themselves to obtain the best possible financial return on the sale of the book on behalf of their client. It goes without saying that this arrangement was also in the agents' best interests in that they received 15 to 20 percent of their authors' royalties.

Literary agents today are unquestionably a highly significant factor in the business of international publishing. With auctions and offers open to several publishers, more than a few agents have been inclined to drive the advances for their clients to dizzying heights. At one point in the 1990s, competition had pushed some advances to the $3 million range for a single title and, at times, this would apply to a non-existent book that was still in its formative stages in the mind of its author. When the Book Fair opened its Centre for Literary Agents in 1978, thirty-six agencies gratefully took advantage of it. By the year 2000, the centre had expanded to occupy a complete hall in order to accommodate its 280 registrants.

A Centre for Book Retailers

Originally the book dealers had played an important role in the Fair, but gradually the orientation shifted towards the publishers and exhibitors who tended to meet almost exclusively with their colleagues to negotiate subsidiary and translation rights. The transition in the role of one group to the other was not, however, entirely seamless. With each passing year, the complaints of the book dealers had been growing more and more strident. The publishers no longer had any time or respect for them. In return, the publishers complained that the number of book dealers was declining steadily. The truth of the matter was that the publishers' fall lists had already been circulated to the book dealers by the publishers' representatives in June and orders for many of the titles had already been placed well before the opening of the Fall Fair. Everyone still arrived on cue, but greater emphasis was placed on collecting information as a basis for later negotiations with various publishers. Perhaps also, in a best case scenario, individual booksellers would make a few additional purchases for the Christmas market. However, in no way was their presence there related to the negotiation of any major purchases. These were deals that were concluded with or without the highly favourable reductions that were available only during the Fair. The need for the creation of a centre at the Fair specifically designed to meet the needs of booksellers was becoming increasingly obvious, and in 1981, the opening of the Centre for Book Retailers was met with great enthusiasm.

Karl Pielsticker, a particularly well-informed retailer, described the centre as "an outstanding and exceptional place to engage in conversation and quietly reflect on important considerations." Or as another retailer, Frau Leuenberger of Lucerne, commented, "The turmoil is reduced by half if one knows that there is a place to return to and rest. There is, as well, the added advantage of being able to conveniently set up meetings." The centre also found favour with Kurt Willy from Lage-Hörste: "We have already met many colleagues and are happy to have found a place to exchange opinions and to make contacts. Naturally business is energetically pursued here."[49]

The centre was also adopted by retailers as a home away from home and, for more than twenty years, it remained their meeting place of choice. A few years later, a special section for book retailers was established within the Fair where consultations by experts in the book trade could be arranged. In the display area, a model book dealership was set up. Remodelling firms mounted various installation possibilities, including do-it-yourself examples. Audiovisual distributors showed programs for the retailers and offered software for inventory management and bookkeeping.

Additional Centres

With the success of the various centres already established, it was not long before other groups of exhibitors began to agitate for designated centres of their own. This led to the creation of centres for publishers of Catholic and Protestant books and for publishers dealing in children's books and young adult publications. The Reading Society of Mainz, established to promote reading, also obtained its own presentation space. An outdoor reading tent was erected and offered publishers the possibility of having their authors read aloud from their works. And, finally, a separate work centre was installed for the use of any and all exhibitors — an oasis where they could rest, use the available conference rooms, eat in the restaurant, meet, and have a drink in the bar.

Even more centres were established in the 1980s and 1990s, such as the Illustrators' Centre, the North and South German Centre, and the East and West German Centre. Each afforded opportunities for publishing companies, book dealers, and authors from these regions to publicize their books. In addition, these centres added a structural dimension to the overall fair and each was in a position to create its own themes featuring authors, panel discussions, and information events.

It is within this context that the amalgamation of these regional centres into the International Centre of the 1990s seemed a logical solution. The newly conceived centre, located in Hall 9, was set up in a small atrium theatre — similar to the one the Italians had built in the 1980s. An almost endless round of events was presented here on a daily basis. Discussions took place on such wide-ranging topics as post-colonial literature in India, market analyses of the Chinese book industry, readings of erotic literature, and women in the literature of the Arab World. And, as an added attraction, international celebrities were often invited to put in an appearance as featured guests.

Earlier Days

In retrospect, it is interesting and instructive to look back to the mid-1970s and the Book Fair's original struggles with restructuring. The Fair had evolved from a sales centre where exhibitors simply placed their products on offer to interested parties into a gigantic international meeting place for anyone and everyone involved in the production of books. It was a huge, colourful, and almost indescribable scene of activity, but, at the same time, it was badly in need of a cohesive infrastructure. There were exhibition halls of all sizes and descriptions, often ranged one behind the other, but where were the much-needed protective walkways to connect them, to say nothing of a totally insufficient number of restaurants, washrooms, snack bars, service facilities, and, more importantly, suitable conference rooms on the premises?

The Book Fair's move in the 1950s from the inner city to the fairgrounds had unleashed enormous enthusiasm for the big, bright display halls that replaced these early contingencies. But the Fair's rapid growth at its new location dictated the need for increasing expansion. The Fair administration repeatedly exhorted the City of Frankfurt and the regional government of Hessen to accept responsibility for covering the walkways between the display halls to protect fairgoers from the worst of the weather. Was this not the least they could do, in view of the huge benefits they had been reaping from the Fair's success?

But, in the end, something completely unforeseen took almost everyone by surprise. The board of directors of the Fair Management Company of Frankfurt scheduled its regular February meeting in 1978 to take place at the site of the newly constructed Düsseldorf Fair. The Frankfurt directors and senior business officials had agreed that it would be interesting and instructive to visit the latest in modern fairgrounds. The press was informed of the visit to Düsseldorf and concluded — without even a shred of evidence — that the Frankfurt Book Fair was moving. Headlines appeared: "Book Fair Moving from Frankfurt to Düsseldorf." As the rumour spread, speculation in other newspapers and media followed, and — to make matters worse — in spite of repeated requests, the Frankfurt Book Fair's administration made no attempt to deny the reports.

Within a very short time, the Metropolitan Frankfurt mayor, Walter Wallmann, who was also the chairman of the Fair Corporation, replaced the entire executive staff of the Fair's business department. The newly appointed officials wasted no time in making long-range plans for the complete modernization of the Frankfurt fairgrounds. The construction of halls 1, 4, and 9; the creation of an efficient system of moving sidewalks and escalators to facilitate movement between buildings; the introduction of the famous "Via Mobile"; and the addition of entrance pavilions, restaurants, snack bars, and parking garages were all part of the plan. Frankfurt would once again be assured of its place in the forefront of book fairs all over the world.

Chapter 22

~~~

Power Struggle:
The U. S. Market Asserts Its Influence

Even in the 1990s, in the general operation of the Frankfurt Book Fair, certain basic principles established by the founding fathers forty years earlier continued to be respected by the Fair administration. From the outset, equality of treatment for all exhibitors — irrespective of rank or market share — had been one of the cornerstones that had remained in place. This was meant to ensure that small publishers would not be overshadowed by the larger companies that dominated the book industry.

Although, admittedly, certain concessions were made to this principle of equality over the ensuing years, the spirit of the tradition's origin was essentially maintained. Exhibition space was available now in five different dimensions. The largest companies took space for each of their imprints in order to retain the names of each of the publishing houses they had absorbed within the parent company. These same companies also subsidized their smaller progeny through the scale of charges for stands. For example, a large concern reserving adjacent space for each of its five subsidiary imprints paid many times more than five individual exhibitors taking the same amount of neighbouring space. And if a large company, in a bid to enhance its image, decided to build its own display facility without using the materials provided by the Fair, the savings were minimal, since the company was charged the same price as if it had booked a fully equipped stand.

Even the ban on company advertising in the Fair Catalogue or outside a firm's own designated space on the fairgrounds was designed to prevent the major players from overpowering their smaller competitors, many of whom were operating on a shoestring.

The same principle of equality was also observed in the allocations of display space — a practice that had always led to heated disputes with the market leaders, who, predictably, expected to be awarded the most favourable positions. For individual publishers in the various exhibitor groups — including country groupings — the equality principle still prevailed. In fact, every attempt was made to mingle publishers from less-prolific Third World countries or those from Middle and Eastern Europe with ten to twelve high-profile mainstream publishers.

In terms of free enterprise, this positioning principle imposed certain limitations on the development of the market. No doubt it also contributed to the amalgamation of many smaller groups of exhibitors, so that eventually the Frankfurt Book Fair evolved into a meeting place that encompassed the entire world.

Yet in the 1990s, all was less than quiet on the Frankfurt front. People were not inclined to accept the strictures imposed by the Fair administration. In 1984, after completion of the new, modern Hall 4, the Book Fair vacated the halls in the eastern section of the grounds behind the railroad lines. The new U-shaped layout of the buildings led to the introduction of the catchphrase "the Fair of the Shortest Distances." This compact area included Hall 3 (two levels totalling 11,129 square metres), Hall 4 (three levels comprising 42,201 square metres), Hall 5 (two levels comprising 21,946 square metres), and Hall 6 (four levels totalling 35,542 square metres).

International exhibitors were situated in the newly constructed Hall 4. The German publishers of belles lettres, specialized books, children's and young adult books, travel books (including maps and guides), religion books, and science and technology books shared Halls 5 and 6. This optimal use of space earned praise for the Fair administration in the second half of the 1980s.

However, a book fair is, by its very nature, in a perpetual state of flux, so it was almost inevitable that this arrangement could not last forever. Some groups grew faster than others. Some sectors declined, but all exhibitors wanted exactly the same amount of space as they'd had in the previous year. And, being creatures of habit, they expected to find their colleagues in the same place as in previous years. Uninterrupted growth, however, was driving the Fair inexorably towards another crisis. Permanently fixed positions and long-standing patterns of movement, themes, and activity centres would all have to undergo a degree of unwelcome change in order for the Fair to remain functional and user-friendly.

From 1984 to 1988, out of a total of almost six thousand international exhibitors, there were more than fourteen hundred new arrivals. And this trend held firm. Hall 4 was bursting at the seams and waiting lists could no longer be accommodated.

Fortunately a new exhibition hall was completed near the main entrance. Hall 1 incorporated two levels and 18,036 square metres, but its main drawback was distance. It was situated nearly one hundred metres from neighbouring Hall 3 and was set apart from the inner circle of the Fair, thus breaking from the "shortest distance" tradition. There was an added dilemma in that the foreign newcomers could not all be located in the new hall, nor could the older halls accommodate everyone. The international sector was linguistically subdivided into Anglo-Saxon, romance, and other languages, but many of the newcomers came from language domains that did not fit any of these categories and had to be classified. In addition, it was imperative that a balance between the weak and the strong be preserved. After the many positioning options were thoroughly discussed, it was decided to situate the international exhibits in Hall 3, with the overflow going into the immediately adjacent Hall 4. Then came the problem of who was to move from the preferred placement in Hall 4 into the less desirable Hall 3 location. Various proposals were put forward and subsequently abandoned because they favoured major publishers in contravention of the Fair's organizational principles.

Finally it was decided to relocate the entire U.S. contingent from Hall 3 into Hall 4, where the number of exhibitors would fill the space perfectly. The implementation of this plan required moving the art book exhibitors into the new Hall 1, which caused yet another upheaval, since the new hall had not yet been used and no one knew whether or not it would suit its assigned purpose.

In the period of more than forty years since the postwar Frankfurt Fair had opened, the Fair management had never made it a practice to inform the affected exhibitors before making a decision. However, times had changed, and it was decided, in this case, to consult them. With appropriate notification, the Fair management felt confident that it would be able to forestall most objections to these latest changes. Accordingly the Fair director and two of his management team went to New York at the end of January 1989 to spend five days visiting various New York publishers and related businesses.

As expected, the reactions from the exhibitors ran the gamut from one extreme to the other, but eventually they did manage to gain a degree of insight into the dilemma facing the Frankfurt Fair administration. They also came to realize that the modifications required for the direction in which the Fair was leaning were not unreasonable. Finally, a consensus was reached that every possible effort should be made to ensure that the establishment of a cohesive and workable English-speaking grouping would be to everyone's advantage.

One thing was made very clear during the course of this trip. A pervasive sense of unease was developing on the other side of the Atlantic with regard to Europe's integration process. This explained, at least in part, the desire of American-based publishers not to be separated from the rest of the English-speaking countries. In general, however, they appeared to accept the plans as they had been laid out.

But not long after the New York meetings, internal consultations followed in Frankfurt preceding the final decision-making meeting of the Frankfurt Fair's board of directors. Alberto Vitale, publisher of Bantam Books, which was now part of the Bertelsmann empire, had made himself spokesman for the opponents of the new arrangement planned for the American exhibitors at the Fair. And, to add fuel to the fire, he had exerted pressure on his Bertelsmann colleague who chaired the Fair's board of directors.

At the February 22 meeting of the board in 1989, a proposal was adopted to keep the American exhibitors in Hall 4. The Americans were delighted, but the decision, which also affected other foreign exhibitors, was the source of confusion on the one hand and irritation on the other. Letters of protest poured in. Several publishers of literary works, now required to move onto the second floor of Hall 1, pressed vigorously for a placement in Hall 5. The protests of the exhibitors continued unabated until the Fair management was eventually forced to postpone the introduction of the restructuring plan by one year.

The 1989 Fair ran smoothly. The American participation increased by 10 percent, and the British — not to be outdone — expanded their already impressive showing by almost 5 percent, but the pressure on Hall 4 continued unabated. There was no question that, at all costs, room for expansion had to be found.

It was clear that neither the U.S. nor other nations with an established and powerful presence would be agreeable to any changes in the positioning of their displays. The only solution was to place all the smaller and less visible exhibitors — who had a known history of acquiescence — into Hall 3. But such a move would be in contravention of Fair policy.

The ultimate solution — among the many possibilities considered — involved the separation of the industry-oriented exhibitors from the primarily German-language exhibitors whose displays were directed towards the general public. These would now be located on the ground floor of all the halls. The book dealers, who essentially dealt with one another, were placed on the second floor of all display buildings, with the possibility of expansion as required into the upper levels. This entirely new plan would also allow the public to move freely in the open spaces between the buildings. This space would then be used in various interesting ways. Tents could be set up to house special displays and events such as readings by authors.

The next stage was to devise practical strategies for moving the two categories of exhibitors to their respective destinations without creating any new problems in terms of access. By 1990 the new horizontal connection routes were in place and the open access policy for the general public was welcomed by most exhibitors.

There were still decisions to be made on the arrangement of the open space that was to be the focal point of the Fair with a view to providing the public with greater access to information. Plans were developed for book displays under canvas on a smorgasbord of themes: electronics, lyrical poetry, religion, and children's books. At one point, a library of new publications was envisioned, as well as an authors' café, a "book mountain," and a theatre that could be reserved by publishers for presentation. The possibility of a promotional tent for the use of future theme countries was also put forward, along with the idea of a "speakers' corner" not only for authors but for visitors and celebrities. Then came the suggestion of a special events tent in co-operation, for example, with municipal theatres, and finally the construction of a "book street" in which the production of a book could be shown from the first sentence to the final cover. Some of the displays already mounted in the halls (e.g., Most Beautiful Books, the Art of Bookbinding, Display of Calendars, and Art Books) could also be viewed there.

To highlight the many featured attractions, information for visitors would be displayed on a huge video wall, as well as at information booths, in leaflets, and via a specially designed direction-finding system for the use of the public.

There was, however, a long road to travel when it came to the implementation of so many ambitious schemes within the space of a single year. In the first place, there was neither the time nor the money for more than a modest nod at future possibilities. If the administration could manage to get through the first year of a restructured Fair, then perhaps slowly but surely they would be able to look forward to the realization of the public programs. To the eternal relief of the organizers of the 1990 Book Fair, in spite of the major changes to the infrastructure, everything ran smoothly. As for the projected plans for the open space, however, very little was accomplished because of the limitations of both time and money. Both were in short supply.

But public acceptance of the restructuring was a legitimate concern, and information was the key. Media coverage was widespread, as was publicity about the new "red carpet treatment" being laid on for the public. No one was disappointed when the usual brown carpet runners were replaced with red. But, in some cases, too much is never enough. As expected, there were protests from some of the exhibitors voicing occasionally vehement objections to the new "horizontal" system, yet, on the whole, it appeared that the first hurdle had been successfully cleared.

The press, of course, had taken an entirely different view. In an unexpectedly negative editorial, the widely read *Exchange News* rekindled the controversy, lending weight to the arguments of the protesting exhibitors and enlisting the support of others. In the face of the ensuing uproar, the Fair management was helpless. They would simply have to revert to the former vertical division of the Fair. With more than a little regret, the board of directors voted for a return to the former structure of the "fair of the shortest distances" for 1991.

This decision also entailed the subdivision of the art book category and the placement of the American publishers in Hall 3. This meant that all the less visible countries would have to vacate Hall 4. There was no alternative, although it contravened the long-standing policy of equal treatment for all exhibitors, and the Fair management was still reluctant to abandon this principle. Yet market forces, over which the board had no control, were difficult to ignore.

There was, as well, an additional and unforeseen argument in favour of this reassignment of locations: the issue of security. The Gulf War was on everyone's mind, and concern about political reaction against the Americans was not without foundation. There was a general consensus that they could be better protected in Hall 3 than in the more open-plan Hall 4. In the meantime, the American publishers had placed all negotiations with the Frankfurt Book Fair officials into the hands of the American Association of Publishers. The agenda of a meeting of the International Division of the AAP, which was held in conjunction with the annual convention and book fair in New York, included the question of whether or not Frankfurt should be boycotted because of the security factor. There was also the matter of a fail-safe strategy for dealing with the Fair management, should they decide to proceed as planned.

A painful recession in the American book market also came into the equation. Many U.S. publishers would have welcomed non-participation, if only because of the expenditure it entailed, but in the end, the full complement of American publishers renewed their participation agreements for the 1991 Frankfurt Book Fair, and only one requested a small reduction in the amount of display space. The U.S. publishers' decision to attend was welcomed by the Fair administration, but post-Fair statistics revealed that only 30 percent of the American participants had been satisfied with their placement as opposed to 75 percent the previous year. As American dissatisfaction grew and consolidated, at its meeting on February 24, 1992, the Frankfurt board of directors decided it would be in everyone's best interests to move the American publishers back into Hall 4.

In spite of all the difficulties, the Fair continued to grow, not only in the mainstream sectors, but also in peripheral ones. This meant that, once again, the problem of expanding the international exhibits had to be confronted. Survival was all about growth. To keep afloat, a publisher had to keep expanding or face the fact that the competition was poised to move in at a moment's notice. But from Frankfurt's perspective, the possibilities for accommodating any further expansion had long since been exhausted. In fact, a master plan was already underway for the Fair in the new millennium.

Once again, the management reverted to a plan involving longer distances and embracing two circular communication routes. The German-speaking market had been concentrated in the central area of the fairgrounds. The international, professional, and rights markets had been situated on the western section of the grounds across the railroad lines, and these incorporated another fifty thousand square metres of rented display space.

There was, however, a walking distance of more than a kilometre between the first building and the last. And to compound the Fair management's never-ending nightmares, 6,500 individual exhibitors had to be relocated to new exhibitors' spaces.

Once again, a dozen plans to meet the needs of participating publishers were studied and re-studied. There was no question that the publishers were going to carefully calculate whether the costs of participation under the new circumstances could still be justified, regardless of which plan was adopted.

The Americans were unarguably the leading market participants and would influence any decision. It was decided to place the Americans and the British in the multi-storeyed Hall 9. All other international exhibitors were to be accommodated in Hall 8. Admittedly, Hall 9 lay on the edge of the grounds, but it was connected by a glassed-in gallery to Hall 8, providing ample space for the rights markets.

The Americans and British were the dominant buyers at the Fair, and as such they were energetically sought out by virtually all other participants no matter where they were placed. The success of a publisher's participation was gauged by the bottom line, but from the standpoint of the Fair's guiding principles, it was also important to ensure that the smaller concerns did not feel marginalized or disadvantaged by the placement of their exhibits.

All the details of the latest Fair plans were published in the international professional press before the 1995 Fair. In a mid-October meeting, delegates from seventy-one countries met with the Fair management, and the ensuing presentation appeared to be surprisingly well received.

In the background, however, Alberto Vitale of Random House had been formulating an alternative plan. His high-powered lobby among influential American publishers and the British Publishers' Association in a bid to place the American and British exhibits together in Hall 8 eventually paid off, and in 1996 this alternative plan was adopted. The U.S. market had asserted itself and made its presence known.

Fair Director Peter Weidhaas in discussion with American exhibitors
concerning new directions for the Frankfurt Book Fair.

Chapter 23
∼∼∼
The Author at the Book Fair:
From Albert Schweitzer to Salman Rushdie

A t the Frankfurt Book Fair, the role of the author or creator was perhaps the least clearly defined of all. Primarily, the author's presence was designed to boost the saleability of his or her book. For certain individuals, this type of promotional activity was little more than an endurance test. But, for the most part, participating authors accepted the inevitable and made the best of their situation.

Although the Frankfurt Book Fair is a publishers' fair and books are its stock in trade, even the creator of a literary work that a publisher has transformed into a book is of only secondary importance in the scheme of things. In the final analysis, the Frankfurt Book Fair is a commercial event, not a festival for writers.

Once a publisher has acquired a manuscript from the author, it goes through the various stages of book production, such as copy editing, graphic design, cover selection, and so forth. Once the book is in print, the publisher's main objective is effective promotion and promising sales figures, in order to be able to recoup the money invested in that particular publication. To produce the book, the publisher has had to pay an advance to the author or translator, edit the text, prepare the layout, and then print and bind the product. Once this has been accomplished, the product needs to be intensively marketed and book dealers have to be convinced to offer it in such a way that the greatest possible number of copies will be sold. It is the publisher, not the author, nor the book dealer, who has assumed all the risks since the onus is on him to take back all the unsold copies. Small wonder that publishers are willing to try anything — including promotional appearances by their authors — in order to make the book a success and bring the balance sheet into the black.

The Author and the Peace Prize

Perhaps unwittingly, those responsible — more than half a century ago — for making the decision to separate the Fair's commercial activities from the Peace Prize ceremonies of the German Book Dealers performed a great service to the future of the book industry. By moving the Fair out of St. Paul's Church and the Römer building onto the fairgrounds, the various branches of the book industry now had a suitable place in which to conduct their business dealings. In St. Paul's Church, on the other hand, invited authors could be in the type of venue where they were given the optimum opportunity to express their personal visions and topical criticisms to their audience.

The world-renowned physician and philosopher Dr. Albert Schweitzer was predestined to be the first to take on this role in 1951. The president of the Federal Republic of Germany, Theodor Heuss, gave Frankfurt's honoured guest a fitting tribute in his presentation speech. Other great men of intellectual stature and oratorical skill followed in the ensuing years. Men like Munich philosopher Romano Guardini, Jewish researcher and philosopher Martin Buber, Swiss diplomat and historian Carl J. Burckhardt, writer Hermann Hesse, historian and poet Reinhold Schneider, American poet and dramatist Thornton Wilder, philosopher Karl Jaspers, and finally, West Germany's President Theodor Heuss himself. And all were presented to the audience by eminent speakers. The legendary mayor of Berlin Ernst Reuter was among them, as were respected authors Albrecht Goes and Werner Bergengruen, along with the former Peace Prize winner Carl J. Burckhardt. This long-standing tradition continues to be honoured today, and each year the award recognizes the achievements of a person of distinction.

Opening Ceremonies at the Book Fair

Another Book Fair ritual was always scheduled to take place on the eve of the opening day. In the early years after the war, authors remained a shadowy presence, without public visibility or recognition. The Fair was considered an occasion that belonged exclusively to the book industry, and the author was left waiting in the wings.

In 1956, for the first time, an author was invited to give the opening address. Peter Bamm chose the topic "Literature and Natural Science" and his presentation was well-received. In 1957, the chairman of the Frankfurt Exchange Association gave the opening address and was followed by Jacques Rodolphe-Rousseau, the chairman of the French association. Rousseau spoke on the role of the book and its potential for uniting people everywhere. The following year, a second author, Rudolf Hagelstange, whose poetry collection *Venezianisches Credo* (1944) was printed secretly during the Second World War, spoke on "The Difficult Business of Producing Books."

A speech by the poet Edzard Schaper, presented in 1959, was preceded by words of welcome by representatives of the German Exchange Association, the foreign exhibitors, and a spokesman from the Frankfurt Cultural Office. In 1962, a third author was featured at the opening ceremonies in the person of the well-loved satirical poet Gerhart Herrmann Mostar.

Author Involvement

With the introduction of major themes at the Book Fair, authors were presented with a new opportunity to express themselves in relation to their work. The Latin American authors, such as the Argentinian Julio Cortázar, the Peruvian Vargas Llosa, and the

Mexican Juan Rulfo, spoke with great fervour about the volatile political situation in Latin American. Similarly in 1980 the majority of African authors devoted their talks to the highly controversial issue of apartheid in South Africa. The authors from the Indian subcontinent, however, had had little to gain from the 1986 Book Fair. Many of those who came felt personally neglected and undervalued as authors, and some expressed a sense of having been treated inhospitably and even unfairly. It was a regrettable outcome, given the worthy intentions of the organizers.

The theme-dictated events at the Fair did, however, offer the visiting authors a unique forum. And so it became customary, in a theme year, to invite an author from the featured country or region to speak at the opening ceremonies. The Fair administration placed no restrictions of any kind on the speakers. The individual who stood on the platform was there as the representative of his region or country, and this fact may have imposed a modicum of discretion. Generally, however, one could rely on an intelligent and stimulating discourse. One has only to think of the speeches by the Congolese writer Tschicaya u'Tamsi, Mexico's Octavio Paz, or Italy's Umberto Eco. More recently, particularly memorable presentations were given by one of Austria's best-known writers, Robert Menasse, and by Hungarian Peter Esterhazy, a leading light in the contemporary literature of his homeland, whose work has been translated into twenty languages.

The Fair's chosen themes also contributed to various cultural events that took place outside the fairgrounds. For example, year after year, Frankfurt's House of Literature hosted an impressive roster of authors from the featured countries and regions to participate in lectures and discussions.

Salman Rushdie

In 1989, the proclamation based on ancient Iranian laws of a death sentence, or fatwa, placed on the life of Anglo-Indian author Salman Rushdie by Iran's revolutionary leader, the Ayatollah

The fatwa against both Salman Rushdie and the publishers of his controversial book
The Satanic Verses *calls for tight security at Frankfurt in 1989.*

Ruhollah Khomeini, made headlines around the world. It also
drew the Frankfurt Book Fair into the vortex of the controversy
surrounding Rushdie and his 1988 bestseller *The Satanic Verses*.
To their huge consternation a number of those involved in the
production of the book also found themselves under the same

fatwa. Many of those involved were among the annual Frankfurt Fair participants, including publishers, book dealers, and translators, to say nothing of the author himself. It was clear that the Book Fair's involvement was entirely unavoidable.

From the outset, one of the Book Fair's guiding principles had been that it should always remain a place for the free, unrestricted exchange of information on topics ranging from culture to the sciences to religion and back again. But the issue of freedom from censorship was now at stake and compromise was not an option. Western culture's central and basic right to the free expression of opinion had been challenged by the invidious charges of blasphemy and injury to religious sensibilities levelled by Iran's most powerful and influential mullah.

The fact that it was not an individual but a book that was at the centre of this historic dispute may well stem from the devout veneration of the Koran — a book that lies at the very heart of the Islamic faith. *Qur'an* is an Arabic word whose literal meaning is "The Recitation." In support of the Christian concept of the Incarnation, the German orientalist Annemarie Schimmel once proposed that for Islam, the equivalent concept would be something known as "Inlibration" or "incorporation into a book." For Moslems, God's Word has become not Man, but the Book. The "people of the Book" (*ahl ul Kitab*) play a very central role in Islamic theology, and even today, in Islamic culture, books have a much different status than in the Christian world.

In the West, a book's value is based primarily on its usefulness as a source of information or entertainment. Its content may well be inconsequential, but in Islamic regions — even those that are relatively free of fundamentalist zealots — a book assumes a singular significance emanating from an innate respect for the written word. This is particularly true when it comes to the inviolability of religious texts. In its earliest manifestation, this same attitude of respect may be compared to that of our ancestors at the time of handwritten Psalters and missals. Both before and after the turn of the first millennium, these beautifully illuminated religious texts were regarded as unique and secret doors to the holy Word of God.

Meanwhile, back in Frankfurt, on February 14, 1989, it was announced that the Iranian head of state and self-proclaimed Imam of the Shiites had exhorted the Moslems of the world to bring death upon the author of *The Satanic Verses* and all those collaborating in the dissemination of his work, "wherever they may be." This declaration constituted an attack, whether intended or not, on the rights and freedoms of the Frankfurt Book Fair. It also threatened the viability of the marketplace, and not for the first time.

Throughout the early to mid-1980s a series of violent incidents had been incited by Iranian militants at the Fair, and in response to the arrest of several Iranian rioters, a retaliatory attack was made on the German embassy in Tehran. It was later revealed that most of the rioters in Frankfurt had been employees of the Iranian embassy, but in any case, prior to the Rushdie imbroglio, relations between Iran and Frankfurt had not been on a friendly footing for quite some time.

It had always been Fair policy not to bar or ban any country, religion, or ideology from participation, no matter what its reputation might be, but circumstances now made it essential to override the patterns of the past. In February 1989, the board of directors made public its decision that "until the death sentence against Salman Rushdie is rescinded, Iran will not be admitted to the Fair." The ensuing months between this weighty decision and the opening of the Fair were filled with dire predictions of terrorist acts, attacks on bookstores, and anonymous threats against publishers. In February 1989 the Berkeley, California, premises of two pro-Rushdie retailers were damaged by explosions set by Moslem radicals, and the offices of a New York daily were also targeted. A month later, in Padua, a branch of a prominent Italian book dealer was destroyed by fire. This was followed by two assassinations in Brussels, two further bookstore bombings in London, and a violent anti-Rushdie demonstration involving thirty thousand fundamentalist Moslems in late May. Yet, in the face of virulent and widespread opposition, Rushdie's now-famous book sold extremely well. In fact, it topped the American bestseller list for weeks, and within a short time Viking-Penguin had to print an additional three hundred thousand copies. There was, however, a definite downside to what initially appeared to have been an unparalleled success, since the proceeds of the total sales of *The Satanic Verses* did not even cover the security costs the publisher had had to assume. It was rumoured to have cost Viking-Penguin at least US$3 million for electronic surveillance, metal detectors, and security services.

In Paris, the Presse-de-la-Cité building was guarded around the clock — even though the publisher, Christian Bourgeois, was already expressing misgivings about publishing the book. The old villa in Cologne at 5 Randolph Street, seat of Kiepenhauer and Witsch Publishing, had assumed the appearance of a fortress with iron bars and gratings on all the doors and windows and surveillance cameras at the entrance.

As for the Frankfurt Book Fair, there were well-founded concerns about the security of the various publishers of *The Satanic Verses*. A police proposal to place them all in a separate hall so obviously contravened one of the basic principles of the Fair that it was rejected immediately. In terms of actual security, it had to be accepted that while the outward appearances of strict security could be guaranteed, the fact remained that the reality was something quite different. How could the entire contents of the hundreds of trucks trying to meet the tight set-up schedule of the Fair possibly be thoroughly searched? Nor could every visitor be so carefully screened as to rule out the possibility of smuggling in a firearm or an explosive device. After considering the practicability of implementing this brand of security, the Fair directors were forced to limit themselves to entrance controls and direct surveillance of all the publishers who had anything to do with the book.

None of these decisions excited as much criticism as the admittance, two years later, of eight Iranian publishers, who had registered as private concerns. The logic behind much of the criticism was based on the facts at hand. The Book Fair's boycott of Iran had done nothing to alter Rushdie's situation. Indeed, the Rushdie affair was fading from public awareness. The long-standing basic principle of freedom to express one's opinion at the Frankfurt Book Fair had been overturned at great cost to its public image. The boycott of Iran had also excluded Iranians who were entirely opposed to the fatwa. And, finally, was it not possible that by easing relations with Iranian publishers, the State might eventually disassociate itself from the fatwa?

The decision to readmit Iranian publishers to the Frankfurt Book Fair launched a storm of controversy in the press initiated by an article in the *Frankfurter Rundschau*. This media campaign finally turned the Rushdie affair into a memorably painful event for the Frankfurt Book Fair and its administration.

The headline of the article that appeared on August 30, 1991, ran, "The Book Fair re-admits Iranian Publishers" with the addition of a subtitle: "Although the Death Sentence against Rushdie is still in Effect." In the course of writing this article, the author, Jürgen Schultheis, had solicited opinions from various celebrities, which he proceeded to quote verbatim. Publishers Klaus Wagenbach and Michael Naumann went on record as being among those who welcomed the decision of the Fair directors. Political commentator Claus Leggewie was adamantly in favour of maintaining the boycott of the Iranians. A good many more opinions were articulately expressed on both sides of the question, all of which served to emphasize the role of the Frankfurt Book Fair as something far more significant than a venue designed for conducting business. Carola Stern of PEN International was quoted to the effect that others had already lost their lives in the name of the Iranian fatwa against Rushdie: "As long as the death sentence against Rushdie fails to be rescinded, doing business with an officially sanctioned Iranian publishing house is tantamount to arms dealing." And she went on to warn that "the Frankfurt Book Fair will be reduced in stature to nothing more than an economically useful event for the book industry."

We are now left with the question of how the Salman Rushdie affair finally came to rest after a decade of turmoil. Once the German and international publishers endorsed the opinions of a number of politically committed authors, the Iranian publishing houses were once again barred from admittance to the Fair.

Finally, in 1999, the newly elected Iranian head of state, Mohammad Khatami, disavowed continuation of the fatwa against Salman Rushdie. This announcement also renewed the prospect of possible participation by Iranian publishers at the Frankfurt Book Fair. The previous year, Salman Rushdie had not registered for the Fair, although comprehensive security measures were still undertaken. However, on the occasion of the fiftieth anniversary of the Frankfurt Book Fair in 1999, Rushdie turned up at the opening ceremonies and personally expressed his appreciation of Khatami's gesture.

The events surrounding the persecution of Salman Rushdie and the eventual participation of Iranian publishers added a new and important element to the intrinsic worth of the Frankfurt Book Fair. From now on the Fair would be known worldwide for its stand in support of the free expression of opinion as well as its stand against censorship and against the persecution of authors and journalists anywhere in the world. Once again the purely commercial aspect of the Fair was relegated to the sidelines.

Chapter 24
The Era of the Agent

"Book production has always been a microcosm of the society of which it is a part and whose developmental tendencies it reflects. Yet, to a certain degree it also shapes that society's way of thinking and expands its ideas...." These are the words of André Schiffin, a leading American publisher and, for many years, director of New York's renowned but now defunct Pantheon Publishing. He was looking back with regret at an era when almost all the major publishers of his time, including Michel Gallimard, Giulio Einaudi, Samuel Fischer, and Ernst Rowohlt, espoused a similar philosophy. From his perspective, it was an ideal whose time had come and gone.[50] His German colleague, the business operations director of the Heyne Publishing Company in Munich, expressed similar sentiments in his own very direct style and with even greater precision: "What was once Grandpa's publishing company is long dead, and newspaper articles about the book trade now belong in the business pages rather than in the literary section. The only survivors will be those publishers who can economically calculate attractive offers that are well-packaged and cleverly marketed."[51]

The developing commercialization of the publishing world had its beginnings in the United States, and one of the results of this was the extensive loss of what Schiffin saw as the inherent values of book production. The role that fell to the American publishing establishment in the 1980s was described in 1995 by the well-known British publisher Lord George Weidenfeld in his autobiography:

> Until the war [Second World War] British publishers played a dominant role.... This era lasted until the late 1940s; however in the Fifties, a closer balance was re-established and the British publishers, compared to the Americans, took on a position similar to that of the Greeks relative to the Romans. Obviously the American domestic market already overshadowed that of the United Kingdom, however the Americans had not yet discovered their enormous export potential and tended to leave the rest of the world to their British counterparts.
>
> By the end of the Fifties, as the Americans gradually became aware of their progressively powerful position, they exercised considerable influence. In the meantime, Frankfurt had established itself as a major marketplace and took on an increasingly international atmosphere. Publishers, wholesalers, and agents attending the Frankfurt Fair far outstripped their colleagues at home and abroad as a result of their first-hand knowledge of the machinations of the book trade. All over the world, publishing houses began competing with one another in the buying and selling of rights. The era of co-production had dawned.[52]

Although Lord Weidenfeld viewed the Anglo-American publishing scene as remaining relatively calm, his estimation fell distinctly short of the mark. In 1966 Random House, the pre-eminent American publisher of authors such as James Joyce, William Faulkner, W.H. Auden, and other such luminaries of the literary world, was bought out by the Radio Corporation of America and this, in turn, generated huge excitement on Wall Street. As a result of this change of ownership, a development took shape that saw books, not as the independent medium they had been for centuries, but rather as a component of the communications industry — that vast entertainment behemoth that included radio, television, film, music, reviews, and illustrated magazines, and eventually the entire spectrum of electronically generated media.

Two decades of spectacular takeover battles proceeded to rock the United States, but in the end, the high-profile Paramount Pictures Corporation emerged as one of the top players in the country. In the course of its acquisitions, it assumed ownership of Simon & Schuster, the second most important publisher in the American book industry, as well as absorbing Pocket Books as part of the deal.

Neither was the takeover fever launched by these events confined only to the United States. Publishing houses the world over became the objects of speculation for possible acquisition to balance market portfolios, to make strategic alliances, to consolidate rights potential, or in reaction to competitive manoeuvres.

Mark Woessner of Bertelsmann AG welcomes Foreign Affairs Minister Joschka Fischer and his wife to the 1995 company reception at Frankfurt's Inter-Continental Hotel.

The British market experienced the spectacular takeover by Pearson of the renowned family firm of Longmans, which traced its origins to 1724, and also the buyout in 1970 by McGraw-Hill of Penguin Books, which had been in the business of producing books since 1935. In France, one of the major publicly owned publishers, Librairie Hachette, was bought out by Matra, a large industrial and military equipment corporation. On the other hand, foreign takeovers initiated by American companies were not always successful. Time Magazine's investments in the French publisher Laffont and England's André Deutsch ended in ignominy. And Crowell, Collier & MacMillan's buyout of Cassell and other British concerns eventually led to the downfall of most of these newly acquired publishing houses.

On the other side of the Atlantic, a few of the takeovers on the American front that were instigated by off-shore concerns enjoyed appreciably greater success. In rapid succession, Germany's Bertelsmann acquired Bantam, Doubleday, and Dell and topped it off with the spectacular takeover of Random House in 1999 to become the largest American publishing enterprise for the production of fiction and specialized books. Matra Hachette took over Grolier, and Australia's News Corporation acquired Harper's — to name only a handful of striking examples.

In the 1990s the usual rumours and snippets of hot-off-the griddle gossip about a certain book or a particular author took a back seat to talk of who was negotiating a deal with whom and for how much. The Book Fair became the launching pad for countless deals as an army of movers and shakers — company analysts and agents whose stock in trade was facilitating sellouts and takeovers — made their entrance. A whole new facet of the book business had evolved. Company representatives on their quest for inside information haunted the corridors and halls of Frankfurt and made appearances at any number of the countless receptions given by various competing publishers. The inevitable outcome of this development was that in order to outdo the competition, the dominant players invested more and more heavily in their corporate image, set up larger and more extravagant booths, and threw even more lavish receptions in Frankfurt's finest hotels.

The process of consolidation — negotiating takeovers, buyouts, and mergers — continued right through the 1990s, until 90 percent of the entire U.S. book market was controlled by no more than twenty companies. In France, twenty-six publishing houses cleared a cumulative total of close to 100 million francs a year and effectively controlled 75 percent of the French book trade. The two largest, Hachette and Havas, accounted for about half of this, but these two concerns were merely subsidiaries of even vaster enterprises that were primarily concerned not with books but with logistics services, finances, and the bottom line. Havas, which had previously bought out highly traditional publishing companies such as Robert Laffont and Larousse in the interests of acquiring "names," belonged to a French water supply consortium, Générale des Eaux, which did business under the trade name Vivendi. Hachette, like its industrial equipment parent company, Matra, was part of another major holding company, Lagardère.

Inevitably, the battle among the band of increasingly powerful international competitors, each jockeying for position to attain their share of the market, finally extended into the realm of title purchases. New York's Random House, once again seizing the initiative, set the trend for a future development that involved the introduction of horrendously inflated advances to authors — the kind of money that would have driven most smaller publishers into the poorhouse. In 1980, the multi-millionaire media magnate S.I. Newhouse had already taken over Random House for "only" $60 million, and then went on to acquire both Pantheon and Knopf, two of America's most respected publishing houses. An integral part of the Newhouse strategy was his insistence on paying out exorbitant advances to authors from whom future bestsellers were expected without any perceivable risk.

The autobiography of Donald Trump, referred to by André Schiffrin as "that ridiculous real estate tycoon from New York City," drew the first of these outrageously inflated advances. By the same token, $3 million was put on the table for the memoirs of Nancy

Reagan, the U.S. president's wife. Not to be outdone, the Australian newspaper and publishing mogul Rupert Murdoch instructed his directors at Harper Collins to offer even more absurd advances. Author Jeffrey Archer, then chairman of England's Conservative Party, received $35 million for three crime novels. Increasingly, in order to compensate for these extravagant outlays, necessity dictated that publishers could produce only highly saleable titles. It soon became unmistakeably obvious that the so-called niche products, such as lyric poetry, were completely out of the running. All resources had to be concentrated on the number one priority — the acquisition and promotion of the bestseller.

The newly acquired power of the leading authors also applied to their literary agents, and they, in turn, considered it their mandate to protect their authors from the threat of profit-mongering publishers. In reality, however, their demands served only to inflate the advances to astronomical heights and undermined the independent publishers, who were still producing quality books but were faced with a financially untenable situation. In the article that appeared in *Die Woche* in 1998, cited at the beginning of this chapter, Lothar Menne describes the emerging conflict of interest between the independent publishers and the literary agents:

> When a publisher has successfully sold the works of an author, he may make an exclusive offer on that author's latest book. If the proffered advance, which is deducted from the author's percentage of sales and income from subsidiary rights (book clubs and paperback distribution), measures up to expectations, the deal is considered satisfactory to all concerned. If, however, the agent is unhappy with the conditions, he or she usually opts for an auction whereby competitors can also get into the act. With new and perhaps potentially promising authors not bound by established connections to any given publisher, agents frequently choose the auction route from Day One.

Then it becomes a question of nerve, high hopes, and a huge amount of wheeling and dealing. You make your bid and a half an hour later, the response comes back that four other interested parties have made offers, the highest of which is combined with an unsatisfactory advance. Won't they consider going any higher? To at least 10 percent, perhaps?

In this arena, the route to success is finding a key title to spearhead the Fall line-up that the book dealers can use as a door-opener to the rest of the list. So you go one step further. And this process continues until the number of competitors bidding against each other is pared down to only two or three. Then it is time for the final ultimatum: the best offer submitted by Friday at twelve o'clock! One last push and it's over. The deal is signed and the competing publishers retreat to lick their wounds or make for the nearest bar. Thanks to the American propensity for invention, this contest of overblown egos, of authors and agents hoping to pull off a coup, and of publishers being pushed to compromise their balance sheets for the next two seasons, soon became known as "a pissing contest."

When all is said and done, the book business is scarcely less speculative than investing on the commodities exchange over the fluctuations in the price of cocoa beans. You convince yourself repeatedly that you can second-guess future trends, but then, without warning, everything changes. Competitors have dashed madly off in opposite directions; some misjudging the commercial viability of a new author and others learning to live with the success of a rival. Yet, in spite of this — or perhaps because of it — each year we allow ourselves to be enticed by the prospect of the next Book Fair and the next auction in the hope of coming up with a future John Grisham.[53]

Throughout the course of the 1990s, there is no question that the Book Fair belonged to the literary agents. Their influence and self-assurance was unparalleled. It was also a time when murder once again came into its own as a number of TV crime dramas and novels appeared on the scene: Hamburg author Regula Venske, for example, with her *Double for a Corpse* (1997), and Canada's Anna Porter, herself an active participant in international publishing for more than twenty years, with her popular novel *The Bookfair Murders* (1997).

Canadian author and publisher Anna Porter,
a frequent visitor to the Frankfurt Book Fair.

In Porter's book, bestselling author Margaret Drury Carter is about to be recognized as the star of that season's Frankfurt Book Fair. Or at least this is the objective of her ambitious editor-publisher, Marsha Hillier, who has just paid $20 million for the world rights to Margaret's next three novels — without having yet seen a single word. She also wants to sell the licensing rights for a bundle. At the lavish Bertelsmann reception held at the Intercontinental Hotel, Marsha's latest deal is the hot topic of discussion. Marsha, on the other hand, has set her sights on wheedling the first chapter of Margaret's new novel out of her agent, Andrew Myles. As it turns out, things don't quite evolve according to plan. The party is in full swing when Marsha finds Andrew dead in his armchair. Frankfurt Police Inspector Hübsch then questions Marsha about her activities and wants to become more fully informed about the lucrative life of a literary agent.

> Inspector Hübsch: "Advance?"
>
> Marsha: "We tend to give authors some minimum guarantees against their future income from the sales of their books after they're published. It's become an incentive for them to choose one publisher over another. A higher advance suggests to the author that the publisher putting up the money will do its best to sell a lot of the author's books."
>
> Inspector Hübsch: "Why?"
>
> Marsha: "It's the only way the publisher has of earning back the money it has just given the author. It's a guarantee. It's not refundable."
>
> Inspector Hübsch: "How much would an advance be?"
>
> Marsha: "Depends on the author … Or the book … Sometimes both."
>
> Inspector Hübsch: "Average?"
>
> Marsha: "There are no averages."
>
> Inspector Hübsch: "What's a large one, then?"
>
> Marsha: "Barbara Taylor Bradford got thirty

million dollars for three novels a while back."

Hübsch whistled appreciatively. "That is a lot of money," he said. "What's the agent's portion?"

Marsha: "At fifteen percent … around $4 million."

Clearly the publishing houses had to protect themselves against this partially self-inflicted bloodletting by concentrating more and more on highly saleable titles and by avoiding — as far as possible — those that might prove harder to sell. In the end, the answer for the publishers lay primarily in expansion, combined with the forces of economic and technological change. Increasingly the individual product — the book itself — lost significance. "It is not a question of books, but of rights!" These rights — sometimes including the digital version of a book — could be freely converted, transferred worldwide, and exchanged through the use of various media.

The alliances and amalgamations of these years, reinforced by the annual reports of the leaders of the pack, confirmed, for the first time, the direction of the course on which they had already embarked. "After all, we have over 44 million subscribers worldwide," Bertelsmann chief Thomas Middelhoff proclaimed as evidence of his firm's leading advantage in "the battle for the last customer." Under the Bertelsmann umbrella, a network was generated that encompassed not only publishers such as Random House and bookselling chains like Barnes & Noble but also partnerships with online services and computer companies such as AOL, which was, in turn, affiliated with Netscape. In effect, Bertelsmann's involvement in online business went far beyond the sale of books. The components of the empire Bertelsmann was building, according to Middelhoff, tapped into complex transfer arrangements within its own worldwide company network: "A positive example [was]: our music company BMG mounted a production of Puccini's opera *Turandot* in the Forbidden City in Beijing. A CD was made of it; our TV subsidiary CLT-Ufa produced a film; our illustrated magazine *Stern* also featured an article. And now we can market the CD through our clubs and over the Internet." To acquire a share in the bounty of this type of co-operative venture — to get a piece of the action, as it were — international concerns were obviously prepared to invest substantial sums of money.

Such developments had gone far beyond the point where the Frankfurt Book Fair could still make a contribution in its own right. Without mincing words, *Die Woche*'s Lothar Menne concludes his article on a pessimistic note: "Nobody needs book fairs. Without a viable commercial component, book fairs may be relegated to fulfilling the universal purpose of social rituals." Menne even went so far as to compare book fairs to "family celebrations, company parties, and doctors' conventions," where participants may experience "a feeling of well-being — a sense of belonging to a bigger, more meaningful entity, where it becomes possible to realize one's desire for security, envy, or gossip, as well as to lick one's wounds."

Many surviving publishers, generally those with established reputations, tried to ensure their continuing existence either by publishing titles that could potentially be more marketable or by assuming the role of a subsidiary company representing the trademark of a multi-national with deep pockets and high expectations. On the other hand, there still remained a few dedicated publishers — primarily smaller houses — that concentrated on serving the established niche markets.

The events of the past decade have defined even more distinctly the book trade's trend towards industrialization, whereby the book as an entity is subordinate to a reassessment of its cultural significance. Throughout the ever-advancing commercialization of publishing in the context of globalization, certain kinds of books lost the essential components of their identity. Books became increasingly an exchangeable mass-produced commodity that could sustain itself only by its ability to maintain its position in the marketplace.

On the other hand, books had the intrinsic advantage of being the source of a broad spectrum of cultural inspiration by virtue of the intellectual independence of their creators. For centuries, the essence of the social recognition accorded to books has been the values that have determined the sense of confidence and pride shared by all branches of the book trade. It cannot be concluded — and for good reason — that books will become superfluous as a medium just because, in a particular area, a book is limited by its contents alone to those popular and saleable topics that can be profitably mass-produced. There are still instances in the publishing field of a series of combined calculations whereby — financially — the successful titles are used to offset the important but less profitable ones. Certain publishers have, in fact, maintained a sense of responsibility and openness towards the concept of fostering culturally diverse titles. Despite the fact that we are experiencing the gradual abdication of an entire generation of publishers, a new generation of committed publishers will take on projects dealing with the bright, the extraordinary, the secondary, the difficult, the beautiful, and the necessary themes, without, of course, ever quite losing sight of the interests of economic viability.

Regardless of their considerable power in terms of available capital, those companies that effectively determine the way the book business is conducted are also impeded by a distinct handicap: they are not the creators of their mainstream products. They can buy manuscripts, but they cannot create them. Of course, if the profit margin were to be pared down still further, it would reduce the marketing of books even more, perhaps to the point that, eventually, it could totally cease to exist. In the interim, they can continue to satisfy their voracious appetite for the acquisition of rights by buying up still more publishing houses.

In this climate of consolidation and diversification, the book fair almost inevitably becomes a microcosm of the greater world of publishing and its many machinations. It is at once a sort of workshop for the creation and realization of book projects, a pool of rights available worldwide, an exchange, an orientation centre in market comparisons, and a weathervane for recognizing new trends. The true "book people" are always in search of like-minded contacts and the thrill of an unexpected discovery, an interesting title, or an innovative project. The possibilities for this — and for much more — all contribute to the enormous attraction of the Frankfurt Book Fair.

In any case, despite the massive changes in the book industry in the last decade of the twentieth century, interest in the Frankfurt Book Fair does not appear to have diminished in the least. In fact, statistics indicate quite the contrary. Between 1990 and 2000, participation in terms of bookings for individual booths increased from 6,035 to 6,887 (about 15 percent). In the same period, the number of visitors grew about 25 percent, from 245,000 to 302,857, and the area covered by exhibitors' booths expanded by 66 percent, from 131,171 square metres to 198,558 square metres. In short, there was absolutely no evidence of "fair fatigue" in Frankfurt.

Chapter 25
~~~
Frankfurt Goes Electronic

In 1984, the Frankfurt Book Fair was caught up in the ever-widening sphere of the pervasive new media — a theme emphasized by George Orwell in his futuristic view of society in the year 1984. Discussion that had been raging for years about the decline of the book as a medium for communication could not be quelled, and through the inroads made by the increasing use of computers, it received new impetus.

This recent trend was perceived by many critics as a distinctly alarming threat, and their fears were fuelled not only by economic concerns but by future implications for cultural and political developments.

A few far-sighted publishing firms — primarily those in the business of producing scientific and specialized books — had already moved into the electronic age. Meanwhile, more and more subsidiary companies — such as software producers — crowded into the burgeoning electronic information marketplace. For the most part, however, people in the book business still had their heads stuck in the sand. At the time, for many book dealers, technical expertise was in very short supply. Others felt overwhelmed by the expenditure involved in purchasing the necessary electronic equipment or were wary of the computer's potential to produce major change at an alarming rate.

Initially, it was only specialty book publishers who showed any particular interest in electronic products. They saw themselves being pressured into a position where they would have to create a market for their products before other competitors, especially software producers, could effectively make their move into the electronic information niche. In this area, the CD-ROM technology offered substantial advantages; besides its impressive storage capacity, it also possessed copyright protection for the stored data. As a multi-functional and versatile product of the new technology, it could combine picture, sound, text, and animation with mind-boggling efficiency.

An electronic version of the Bible is presented on 1980s-style floppy disks

The introduction of this new medium had created an atmosphere where alternating hopes and fears were competing within the branches of the book trade. Then, in 1992, out of the blue, the management of the Frankfurt Book Fair made a landmark announcement. The electronic media had expressed the desire to create their own forum. The Book Fair director addressed the official meeting of the "Electronic Publishing Concerns" on October 28, 1992:

> For some time, the product lines of publishers and booksellers and the varied nature of the book trade have not been limited to the production of books and magazines, or even just to printed information. In the last five years, the technological reality of digitalized information — in the form of text, picture and video — has begun to alter worldwide book dealing in a radical way. By many book trade participants, this is perceived as a departure from the customary practices of book dealing that have been primarily concerned with content and familiar modes of operation....
>
> As a service provider to the world's book trade we have reached the point where we must give reality its due. The quantity of rapidly advancing changes in the various branches of the international book trade must find expression in a new quality, in a new dimension within our Fair.

Certain elements of nervous anticipation and concern over the challenge of this venture into uncharted waters were in evidence at the opening press conference for the 1993 Book Fair theme, "Frankfurt Goes Electronic," but this was only to be expected. The Frankfurt Book Fair was growing exponentially and creating its own future. It was carving out a place for itself as a leader in the vast and ever-changing world of communications as it applied to publishing and the production of books.

For the first time, all the latest accoutrements of the new technology were on display at the Book Fair: 160 exhibitors from 14 countries, including a number of technology-related companies that did not belong to any specific branch of the book industry. A multi-faceted presentation package was set up to make the trade visitors more aware of important aspects of electronic publishing. Lectures on applications and practices dominated the program. A critical evaluation of technology as it had existed in 1984 was assiduously avoided.

Through participation in this series of lectures, it was hoped that book trade dealers would be encouraged to become converts to the wonders of new technology; however, in spite of a certain amount of initial enthusiasm, the attempt failed to produce any significant results. For the most part, the expense of acquiring expertise was not an option for the book dealers. Neither did the potential profit margins from the production of electronic products justify forcing the issue any further. The time was not yet at hand.

In the following year, 1994, there was talk of the role of Frankfurt as a possible trendsetter in the field of the electronic media. Could the Fair not provide a meaningful forum for the marketing of all forms of publishing and information technology?

A major point was made to the effect that the Fair should make every attempt to act as a bridge between traditional publishing houses and those offering emerging opportunities related to the new technology. The Frankfurt Fair's accommodation of the new media in conjunction with its long-standing publishing traditions was, in fact, the distinguishing feature that set it apart from other multimedia fairs being held in Europe at the time. At Frankfurt, the book remained, as always, the centre of attention — now supported by the CD-ROM as a tool for rapid access to information.

Among the electronic products on display, the wonders of "Edutainment" — educational products for schools and private consumption — formed a thematic focal point that attracted keen interest. In addition to these off-line products, the field of online Internet communications and its enormous potential captured the attention of the Fair management in particular.

At this point, Hall 1, which accommodated Electronic Publishing, housed 227 exhibitors from 26 countries and an exhibition space that had already more than doubled. This alone underscored the growing interest in the Fair's newest attraction. At the 1994 Fair, the possibilities of electronic publishing also created enormous interest. A total of 115,000 visitors was recorded — 18,000 more than in 1993. In Hall 1, 420 exhibitors displayed their wares, and another 820 did so within their traditional book publishing displays. The integration of the new media was progressing at an impressive pace.

There was no question that CD-ROM technology had overtaken and replaced the original floppy disk as well as its smaller and more recent substitute. At the same time, the online domain generated a huge amount of interest, but a degree of uncertainty prevailed. Was the use of the Internet economically feasible within a foreseeable timeframe, especially in the light of the emerging problems over copyright? It had also quickly become apparent that the trade in rights and licences played only a secondary role in the multimedia industry.

Finding marketing partners and sales outlets for their products was a matter of primary importance for exhibitors in the electronic field. Not all exhibitors were successful in this endeavour, with the result that the German dealers were rarely considered as potential marketing partners. In the retail book trade, off-line electronic media comprised an average of just 1 percent of the gross turnover. Still, the exhibitors valued the Fair as a point of contact and exchange of information and were delighted by the opportunity to present their electronic products to a largely receptive marketplace.

The demand for increased space was so great that the exhibitors' area had to be expanded yet again in 1996. Close to five hundred suppliers and marketing enterprises of the electronic media were set up in Hall 4.1 and 4.2. Over and above these, a further one thousand suppliers were represented among the exhibits of the traditional publishers' groups participating in the Book Fair.

For the moment, the CD-ROM remained in the forefront of off-line use. Yet the centre of attention was shifting more and more towards the Internet and online publishing. These multi-faceted media and multiple-access possibilities through various service providers excited the interest of those who have since become known as the "media users." Spectacular online offers commanded the attention of passersby, but at this point the companies involved were barely able to cover their production costs.

Eventually, the euphoria of the previous few years of experimentation gave way to a certain disillusionment that neither two-figure sales nor even the hint of profits could dispel. By 1997 commercial availability and the use of information-oriented content on the Internet had increased dramatically, but in spite of these positive signs of progress, the market share remained relatively insignificant. And there were still financial considerations and ongoing questions of copyright to be resolved.

Publishers and dealers were further disquieted by the appearance of libraries on the scene with their independent offers of access to information. For book dealers there was an implicit danger that the transformation of libraries into content providers would mean a reduction in the purchase of their former stock-in-trade. As a result, certain publishers had already begun flogging their electronic products aggressively to various potential buyers within this newly emerging market.

In 1998, for the first time, there was a decrease in the total number of exhibitors in the electronic media group. Almost all publisher-produced offerings in the domain of electronic media were exhibited in the book display areas of the Fair, with the result that Media Hall 4.1 was increasingly occupied by technology-oriented products. The growth in the total number of those offering media products advanced to 1,782 exhibitors.

Two new developments relating to the electronic book provoked discussion at the 1998 Book Fair: the Softbook and the Rocket eBook. The simple downloading of texts, along with a substantially improved viewing screen and the expanded memory capacity of notebook or laptop computers, could place the electronic book in a position to enter into serious competition with its printed and bound counterpart. In order to attract marketable material, partnerships would have to be established with publishers. Bertelsmann was the first to enter this new galaxy with the introduction of its Rocket eBook.

In both 1999 and 2000, however, there was a slight decrease in the presence of the electronic media. True, the software giant Microsoft had offered a prize of US$100,000 for the best eBook at the Frankfurt Fair, to be administered through a specially created foundation with New York's Alberto Vitale at the helm, but the promise of the prize accomplished little in terms of exhibitor numbers. According to predictions made by Jason Epstein, an editor with Random House in New York, it would not be long before books would only be purchased electronically and printed at will by print automats that would resemble automatic cash dispensers. Perhaps he was disinclined to consider that in spite of improved on-screen reading capacity or new booklike, easy-to-handle formats and impressive storage capacity, the fact remained that electronic books had not yet been embraced by readers as an appealing alternative to the real thing.

From an economic standpoint eBooks hold little appeal for publishers. The reasons for this are twofold. First, there is the ongoing and unresolved problem of authors' rights, and second, the issue of payment by people with the capability to download books from the Internet is still a concern. The payment factor played a large part in the decision of one of America's most successful authors, Stephen King, to stop work on his Internet serial novel *The Plant*. The harsh reality was that "if you pay the story rolls, if you don't the story folds," because fewer and fewer readers were paying their subscription fees.

As Fair organizers, the Frankfurt administrators had taken what they considered a logical step when they became involved in moving forward on the media front. Initially, this took the form of offering additional services to "real" exhibitors to the Frankfurt Fair, as opposed to those engaged in a newly emerging extension of the Book Fair known as the "Virtual Fair." Behind the scenes, a brisk Internet market had been growing by leaps and bounds, fuelled by competing Internet providers aggressively involved in the rights business — dot-com companies such as Rightscenter.com, Rightsworld.com, and Subrights.com.

The Fair organizers also took a boldly innovative step in 1994 when they produced a CD-ROM version of the Frankfurt Rights Catalogue. The CD also featured an exhibitors' catalogue complete with a full complement of 8,826 addresses, as well as an electronic "Who's who at the Frankfurt Book Fair," which had been appearing since 1970 in book form. This included the names of affiliated exhibitors for a total of close to 17,000. In 1994 and 1995 this novel piece of technology, generally referred to as the "Frankfurt CD-ROM," had to win the acceptance of the participating publishers, but it also had to contend with a number of technical glitches. Because of this, the CD-ROM compiled for 1996 was supplemented by an online version of the Frankfurt Rights Catalogue. This proved to be a bonus for all visitors, exhibitors, and the press, as they were able to access information online as well as the detailed directory of all services and presentations through the website www.buchmesse.de/www.frankfurt-book-fair.com. In 1997, all the information in the catalogue was made available through the Fair website, not just in October at the time of the Fair but throughout the entire year. Additionally, each year an off-line CD-ROM version was available. In 1998, the capability of the Frankfurt Rights Catalogue was extended so that it was now possible for publishers to update and edit their own lists of titles. Prior to this breakthrough, changes and additions to publishers' listings could only be made through communication with the Fair's editorial office.

In the year 2000, the introduction of "eStands" became an integral part of both the "real" and the "Virtual" Fair. These eStands featured the stand-holder's company presentation on the Internet under the umbrella of the Frankfurt Book Fair's microsites. Using these Internet facilities, exhibitors were presented with the opportunity to design their own virtual Fair stand within specified parameters. An eStand could also provide information about a particular publishing company, the titles it carried, and further specifics on its affiliate companies. Using their client number and individual password, stand-holders could design the layout of their own eStand, insert updated content on demand, as well as provide promotional material and the dates and itineraries of authors' tours. Information using text and visual images could also be made available for downloading. Even the number of visitors to an eStand could be monitored through a tracking function. In addition, each eStand possessed its own Internet address, which could be of particular interest to firms without a company website. In the case of the higher-priced "eStand modules," feedback and newsletter functions were designed to enhance client contact.

Registration for the "real" Frankfurt Book Fair, which it has been possible to complete online since the year 2000, includes entries in the Exhibitors' Catalogue and the "Who's Who." Relevant data such as the company name and address is included and automatically replicated when an eStand is created. Exhibitors could choose among three different eStand modules. When the concept was first introduced, the cost of the basic version was approximately US$75.

In contrast to the real but short-lived activity of the Frankfurt marketplace each October, the idea of an Internet offspring offered the possibility of year-round information about the participating publishers and their products, as well providing a platform for their affiliates. But the concept of a cyberspace fair was not well received by many exhibitors and the idea was eventually put to rest. The book trade in general and the rights business in particular are both contact-intensive and communications-oriented operations of relative complexity. Any possibility that the real Frankfurt Book Fair could ever be replaced by an Internet clone is purely and simply a figment of some futuristic visionary's fertile imagination.

Visible evidence of Information Overload.

Author's Note

The history of the Frankfurt Book Fair that I wanted to present ends here. The various branches of the world's book trade need a place like Frankfurt to meet, to garner information from all sides, to lay themselves open to whatever it has to offer, to enjoy chance encounters with themes, books, colleagues, and competitors. As always, book projects are born and formulated through close personal contact with other people. Book fairs like the one held each October in Frankfurt have, for more than six hundred years, channelled the flow of ideas from the writer to the producer and finally to the reader. A book needs the spoken word and convincing discourse to bridge the gap from one to another. Although it plays a part in the equation, the acquisition of information — titles, content, and price, in addition to certain technical details transmitted by the tools of the new media — will never be able to compete with the rewards of personal contact.

Meetings between book producers and distributors — publishers, authors, book dealers, librarians, and publicity people — are all a part of a unifying experience. It is also important that the book industry be prepared for the power of collective action. It is good for a personal feeling of self-worth; it is good for the influence and public recognition of the book industry. Book fairs all over the world must continue to provide meaningful forums for book publishers, book dealers, and readers as far as the future will take them.

Peter Weidhaas
2007

Endnotes

1. Albert Kapr, *Johannes Gutenberg: Persönlichkeit und Leistung* (Leipzig, 1986).
2. Fried Lübbecke, *Fünfhundert Jahre Buch und Druck in Frankfurt am Main* (Frankfurt am Main, 1948).
3. Carl Wehmer, *Deutsche Buchdrucker des Fünfzehnten Jahrhunderts* (Wiesbaden, 1971).
4. Peter Burke, *Die Renaissance* (Berlin, 1990).
5. Mathias Tank, *Die Buchhändlermessen in Frankfurt und Leipzig. Ein Rückblick auf die lebendig-dramatische Messegeschichte,* Steinheimer Jahrbuch für Geschichte und Kultur, Bd. I (Hanau-Steinheim, 1990).
6. Oskar Hase, *Die Koberger: Eine Darstellung des buchhändlerischen Geschäftsbetriebes in der Zeit des Übergangs von Mittelalter zur Neuzeit* (Leipzig, 1885).
7. Walter Fischer, *Die Abwanderung des Buchhandels von der Frankfurter Messe nach Leipzig,* Inaugural-Dissertation zur Erlangung der Doktorwürde der Wirtschafts — und Sozial wissenschafttlichen Fakultät der Johann Wolfgang Goethe Universität (Frankfurt am Main: Bottropp, 1934).
8. Albrecht Kirchhoff, *Beiträge zur Geschichte der Pressmassregelungen und des Vekehrs auf den Buchmessen im 16 und 17 Jahrhunderte: Archiv für Geschichte des Deutschen Buchhandels, Bd. 4* (Leipzig, 1879).
9. M.J. Elsas, *Umriss einer Geschichte der Preise und Löhne in Deutschland vom ausgehenden Mittelalter bis zum Beginn des 19 Jahrhunderts* (1940).

10. Gottfried Glocke, *Kleine Chronik der Buchhandelsbeziehungen zwischen Lyon und Frankfurt im 16. Jahrhundert* (Frankfurt am Main: Verlag Waldemar Kramer, 1962).

11. Hase, *Die Koberger.*

12. Egon Friedell, *Kulturgeschichte der Neuzeit* (Munich, 1931).

13. Glocke, *Kleine Chronik der Buchhandelsbeziehungen zwischen Lyon und Frankfurt im 16. Jahrhundert.*

14. Alexander Dietz, *Zur Geschichte der Frankfurter Buchmesse 1462–1792* (Frankfurt am Main, 1921).

15. Friedell, *Kulturgeschichte der Neuzeit.*

16. Heinrich Estienne (Henricus Stephanus), *Lob der Frankfurter Buchmesse 1574.* In Frankfurter Lesebuch (Frankfurt am Main, 1985).

17. Bernhard Wendt, *Die Frankfurter Buchmesse als Gesprächsthema in einer theologischen Kontroversschrift des Jahres 1570.* In Archiv für Geschichte des Buchwesens. Bd. 8 (Frankfurt am Main, 1967).

18. Thomas Coryate, *Coryates Crudities hastily gobbled up in five months travels in France, Savoy, Rhetia, commonly called the grisons country, Helvetia alias Switzerland, some parts of high Germany and the Netherlands; Newly digested in the hungry air of Odcombe in the County of Somerset and now dispersed to the nourishment of the travelling Members of the Kingdom* (London, 1611).

19. Elizabeth L. Eisenstein, *Die Druckerpresse: Kulturrevolutionen im frühen modernen Europa* (Vienna, 1997).

20. Dietz, *Zur Geschichte der Frankfurter Buchmesse.*

21. Lübbecke, *Fünfhundert Jahre Buch und Druck in Frankfurt am Main.*

22. Dietz, *Zur Geschichte der Frankfurter Buchmesse.*

23. Peter Orth, *Ausführliche Abhandlung von den berühmten Zwoen Reichsmessen so in der Reichsstadt Frankfurt a. Main jährlich abgehalten werden* (Frankfurt,1765).

24. Berthold von Henneberg, *Edict* (Mainz, 1486).

25. Lutz, 1986.

26. Fischer, *Die Abwanderung des Buchhandels von der Frankfurter Messe nach Leipzig.*

27. Sigrid Jahns, *Frankfurt am Main im Zeitalter der Reformation (um 1500–1555)*. Frankfurt am Main — die Geschichte der Stadt in neun Beiträgen (Sigmaringen,1991).

28. Wolfgang Brüchner, *Die Gegenreformation im politischen Kampf um die Buchmessen.* Die Kaiserliche Zensur zwischen 1567 und 1619. Archiv für Frankfurts Geschichte und Kunst. Heft 48 (Frankfurt, 1962).

29. Aldalbert Brauer, *Die kaiserliche Bücherkommission und der Niedergang Frankfurts als Buchandelsmetropole Deutschlands.* Genealogisches Jahrbuch, Bd. 19 (Neustadt an der Aisch, 1979).

30. Brückner, *Eine Messbuchhändlerliste von 1579 und Beiträge zur Geschichte der Bücherkommission.* Archiv für Geschichte des Buchwesens, Bd. 3, 1961.

31. Brauer, *Die kaiserliche Bücherkommission und der Niedergang Frankfurts als Buchandelsmetropole Deutschlands.*

32. Friedrich Kapp, *Geschichte des Deutschen Buchhandels.* Band 1: bis ins siebzehnte Jahrhundert (Leipzig, 1886).

33. Kirchhoff, *Die Anfänge des Leipziger Messkatalogs.* Archiv für Geschichte des Deutschen Buchhandels, Bd. 13 (Leipzig, 1879).

34. Dietz, *Die zwei Reichsmessen zu Frankfurt am Main* (Frankfurt am Main, 1910).

35. W. Fischer, *Die Abwanderung des Buchhandels von der Frankfurter Messe nach Leipzig.*

36. Wolfgang J. Hundt, *Die Wandlung im deutschen Messe-und Ausstellungswesen im 19. Jahrhundert und seine Weiterentwicklung bis zum Jahre 1933 unter besonderer Berüchsichtigung der Messen in Frankfurt am Main und Leipzig. Von der Warenmesse zur Mustermesse,* Inaugural-Dissertation zur Erlangung der Doktorwürde der Wirtschafts -und Sozialwissenschaftlichen Fakultät der Johann Wolfgang Goethe Universität (Frankfurt am Main, 1957).

37. Dietrich Kerlen, *Messe-Präsenz als Politikum in der deutschen Buchwirtschaft des 19. Jahrhunderts.* Leipzigs Messen 1497–1997, Teilband I . (Cologne, 1999).

38. Monika Estermann, *der Buchhandel in der Weimarer Republik.* Buchhandelsgeschichte 1995, B.169B.171; Beilage zum Börsenblatt 100/1995.

39. Buchhandelsgeschichte 1995, B.169B.171; Beilage zum B39. Memorandum No. 2 of the Association for Foreign Book Trade E.V. [registered association], Leipzig, November 1919.

40. Excerpts from the Minutes of the 15th Executive Meeting of the Exchange Association in Stuttgart on September 23, 1949.

41. Cobet, *500 Jahre Buch und Druck in Frankfurt am Main.* Unveröffentlichter Vortrag, 1988.

42. Cobet, *Die erste Messe war 1949.* Unveröffentlichter Ansprache beim Mittagessen am 6. Oktober 1988 aus Anlass des Jubiläums der 40. Frankfurter Buchmesse im Hessischen Hof.

43. Hannelore Bernhart-Haag, *Die Wiederbegründung der Frankfurter Buchmesse.* Beilage zum Börsenblatt für den Deutschen-Buchhandel-Nr. 24, 1990 und Nr. 95, 1990.

44. Bernhart-Haag, *Die Wiederbegründung der Frankfurter Buchmesse.* Beilage zum Börsenblatt für den DeutschenBuchandel-Nr. 24, 1990 und Nr. 95, 1990.

45. Leipzig *Exchange News*, No. 40, October 7, 1950.

46. Wickes, 1974: 170–192.

47. Karsten Garscha/ Dieter Riemenschneider (Hrsg.) *Afrikanische Schriftsteller im Gespräch* (Wuppertal, 1983).

48. *The Exchange News*, No. 82, October 14, 1988.

49. *The Exchange News*, October 23, 1981.

50. André Schiffrin, *Verläge ohne Verleger*, Berlin 2000.

51. Lothar Menne, "Börse der Gockel," *Die Woche* vom 9.10. 1998.

52. George Weidenfeld, *Von Menschen und Zeiten* (Munich, 1995).

53. Menne, "Börse der Gockel," *Die Woche.*

Index of Names